Militant Methodism

The Story of the First National Convention of Methodist Men

HELD AT INDIANAPOLIS, INDIANA, OCTOBER TWENTY-EIGHT
TO THIRTY-ONE, NINETEEN HUNDRED AND THIRTEEN

EDITED BY

DAVID G. DOWNEY   E. W. HALFORD
RALPH WELLES KEELER

THE METHODIST BOOK CONCERN
CINCINNATI - NEW YORK

The Purpose of the National Convention of Methodist Men

1

TO increase missionary intelligence and to deepen the spiritual life.

2

TO present the definite responsibility of Methodism, both at home and abroad, in relation to other denominations and Christian agencies.

3

TO adopt a practicable denominational program and policy of advance.

4

TO place more definitely before the Church the New Financial Plan as adopted by the General Conference for the Church as a whole and for the local Church.

5

TO emphasize the principles and practice of Christian Stewardship as adopted by the General Conference.

6

TO discover and enlist more men for missionary and evangelistic service.

Editorial Foreword.

THE story of this first Convention of Methodist Men might be told in either one of three different ways. The editors might have summarized the addresses, gathered up the general impression, and given the conclusions and results of this unique gathering. That method, however, would inevitably make the record a transcript, for the most part, of the editorial viewpoint and would deprive the Church of the collective wisdom of the many speakers who out of their wide observation and experience contributed to the total result. It was also open to the editors to tell the story of the Convention in terms of days. A careful examination of the program, however, showed that while it was logically and cumulatively arranged, certain subjects could not be treated in their entirety in any one day. Any attempt, therefore, to follow the Convention day by day would necessarily mean a breaking up of subjects or themes, treating them in part on one day and returning to the same or similar topics on a second day. Inasmuch as the makers of the program planned for the presentation of certain outstanding themes, it was seen that the story could be told in terms of the various subjects considered. This last method is the one adopted. By this method it is believed that every reader can easily follow and find the main deliverances on all the subjects discussed. This method is further to be commended because it reduces the editorial note and comment to a minimum and makes it possible to give to the Church a

5

fairly complete report of the papers read and addresses delivered.

Obviously, some things had to be omitted. To include everything said and done it would be necessary to produce a volume that would be unwieldy in bulk and prohibitive in price. It would have been an editorial pleasure to feature each special session with fitting characterization of presiding officers and full reports of the always interesting and frequently inspiring opening and closing exercises, but it was deemed best, for the most part, to omit this feature of the Convention. There is included, however, the full Convention program, with the names of the presiding officers and those who so reverently and helpfully conducted the several sessions of intercession and praise.

In this brief foreword the editors wish especially to emphasize two features of the Convention: First, its high seriousness, and second, its intense religious spirit. It was evident from the very first moment of the Convention that the delegates had come together not for pleasure, but for high and serious business. There was a quietness, a purposefulness that manifested itself at the start and maintained itself to the very end. To see from two thousand to three thousand men sitting together for three sessions a day (each session approximately three hours long) for four days, considering the things that tend to hinder or to advance the Kingdom of God in the earth, was a sight to thrill the soul and fill the mind with radiant hope for the days to come. But the seriousness of the Convention was no whit more evident than its religiousness. This religiousness did not expend itself in emotion or in shouting or in any merely external manifestation. There was emotion, deep and timely,

6

EDITORIAL FOREWORD.

and there was the proper expression of the deep inner feeling. But the religiousness of this Convention of Methodist Men was something apart. It was an inner fire, a quiet contagion, something that one felt and experienced rather than talked about. This deep religious purpose was evident in the prayers and in the addresses and in the giving and in the spirit that pervaded every gathering—even the social and business gatherings—during the entire four days. If the spirit of high seriousness and of earnest, genuine piety that characterized the Convention can be carried down to the local Church, the long-waited-for revival will be well on the way.

We send this record forth with the sincere and earnest prayer that God will make it a fountain of blessing and a source of inspiration to all who read it and to the Church of Jesus Christ in all the lands.

DAVID G. DOWNEY,

E. W. HALFORD,

RALPH WELLES KEELER.

7

Table of Contents.

I.

OPPORTUNITY AND TASK.

II.

THE FORCES AND THE FIELD—A SURVEY.

I. OUR DENOMINATIONAL SITUATION.

TABLE OF CONTENTS.

TABLE OF CONTENTS.

III.

FORWARD, MARCH! A CALL TO ADVANCE.

TABLE OF CONTENTS.

IV.
ACTUALIZING THE PROGRAM.

I. A WORKING PROGRAM OUTLINED.

II. METHODS FOR ACTUALIZING THE PROGRAM.

III. THE NEW DAY AND THE PROGRAM.

IV. THE LAYMEN AND THE PROGRAM.

TABLE OF CONTENTS.

V.

THE LARGER OUTLOOK.

TABLE OF CONTENTS.

VI.
SPECIAL FEATURES.

14

Introduction.

IF there should go forth a call for three thousand Methodist men to serve the Church for an entire month as legislators and electors in General Conference, with all expenses paid, the ready response of fifty thousand volunteers would not be nearly so remarkable and hopeful a fact as was the coming together at Indianapolis of two thousand five hundred busy Methodist men from all sections of the country, and at their own expense, to consider the living problems now confronting the Church, to pray for a clearer vision of duty, and plan for the larger sacrifices demanded by the vision. Besides Bishop Moore, all the effective bishops in the country were present—the largest number ever in attendance at any gathering except at General Conference or at their own semi-annual meetings. District Superintendents were there from almost every Conference from the Atlantic to the Pacific. Pastors and laymen counted into the thousands—men who see and read and feel and act—not seeking more burdens, but larger results through more effective methods. These leaders of the Church, ranging in age from twenty-five to seventy-five, remained four days in sessions aggregating over eight hours daily. In compact masses they sat, filling the floor and platform and galleries of the large hall, listening with intense religious concern to the messages which followed each other in rapid succession. Nearly every speaker was a specialist in the part assigned him. Leaders of other Churches, men known the world over,

15

were heard with generous appreciation, and our own men were at their best. Systematically, consecutively, cumulatively, the affairs of the Kingdom at home and abroad were canvassed, problems measured, needs arrayed, and resources marshaled. Again and again conviction found voice in prayer and faith broke forth in song. Vision succeeded vision, fact was piled upon fact, appeal added to appeal, yet there was neither surfeit of speech nor loss of inspiring effect. God's power was upon the assembly. There these men sat and sang and prayed until they at last exulted in the very vastness of the task that challenged their faith in the leadership of Christ and the almightiness of God. No general interest was neglected.

When it came to the discussion of methods and means, the Financial Plan adopted by the last General Conference was heartily approved. The unifying of the appeal for the several great Boards, a persistent informational and inspirational campaign, both by literature and co-operative field work, the every-member canvass, the use of the duplex envelope for weekly or monthly payments to insure regular and systematic giving, the standard, "as much for others as for ourselves," as the common measure of our stewardship as Christians; the protection of our congregations against indiscriminate and unauthorized appeals—these were the great features of the plan commended.

To aid the benevolent Boards to put this plan before all our Churches in an effective way, the sum of sixty thousand dollars was pledged by those present. This fund should be at once increased to $300,000 for the next two years.

China and India are ready for our Lord *now*. The planting and watering of many years have made ready such a harvest time as the Church has never seen and can never see again. The conditions in our own country are perilous in their portent unless we multiply our evangelistic agencies everywhere. Every one of our benevolent Boards has its place among the forces that must be active if the Republic is to live and fulfill its mission.

THIS BOOK IS THE GREAT CONVENTION IN PRINT. It is therefore awakening, arousing, energizing, informing, persuading, convincing, inspiring. For every live pastor and layman its facts and visions will flame into quick action. For the listless and inert, who prefer ease to service, we must trust to the fuses lighted by the Spirit of God at Indianapolis. May they burn until they reach all the stored and latent dynamite of Methodism!

District Superintendents, pastors, and lay speakers will here find just the material for effective team-work in their own district and local areas.

May the spirit of the great Indianapolis meeting of Methodist men spread throughout the entire Church!

EARL CRANSTON.

PART I.

Opportunity and Task.

The World Brotherhood.

THERE was ever a wistfulness in Jesus' voice. The sense of the unrealized often fairly ached through His words. A wistful look was in His eyes, a wistful mood was in His tears, a wistful cadence gave His words the rainy sweetness of tears and laughter intermingled. The how things were to be was on Him, not in a lowering way, like a threatening storm. Nothing Carlyleian was with Him. He did not practice high invective as an end. His swish of cords upon the vulgar shoulders of the sellers in the temple was not His custom and never His delight. His custom was compassion. He was not ominous, despairing, for His prophecy swung golden bells in a blue sky and rung them as a holy, hymnic chime.

Christ was wistful; for a world He dwelt among races of provincials. The Jew, the Greek, the Roman were all provincials. Their provinces differed in girth a little, only a little. Christ whispered, trumpeted, wept, sung, preached, lived, died—all framing a wide, unprovincial word—The World. "Unto the uttermost parts of the earth," was the summons and the direction. We have been learning AT it a long time, yet have we not learned it. The size has bulked too vast. It has taken the breath clean out of us. The lash of a storm-wave of the sea which leaves the swimmer drenched, breathless, bleeding, and prone like seaweed on the shore is not more fierce in its effects than this majestic word of Jesus—"The WORLD!"

Yet breathless as we have been, we shall soon stumble to our feet. In a brief hundred years earth has learned earth, world has perceived world beyond what it had known in all its lifetime. That is provocative of hope. We are coming on. "Who is my neighbor?" "Nobody much," was the contemporaneous reply. "Everybody mostly," is OUR contemporaneous reply. We are learning, blessed be God! We are provincials, but are slowly acquiring the world-speech. The vocabulary of a planet shall by and by express the thought that blazes within the soul.

A World Brotherhood! How majestical and tidal! It rises like the beat of drums that challenge to a fray. We fought men long, too long. We shall now answer the summons of the drums to fight for men.

These Methodist men from many wheres have prayed together, laughed together, wept together, dreamed together, challenged together, learned the world-mood together. We have been conscious of the whirling, tremendous planet. We have felt it swim beneath our feet like the rush of flying angels. The World Brotherhood! The black, the yellow, the brown, the red, the white, equal the world—equal what Christ died for. Hallelujah and amen.

"God hath made of one blood all kindreds of the earth," was a proclamation of incalculable breadth and wonder, but could not get on. The consanguinity of blood seems to lack dynamic. That doctrine made no specific headway. It stood inert, or nearly so. But the world brotherhood, by the shedding of the blood of Christ, has made headway, and will make headway. Christ, God-Man, blood of our blood, and the mingled blood of man and God, and that blood spilled for THE WORLD, has produced world brotherhood. "This is My Blood of the New Testament, shed for you and for many"—that many being all, has availed. The prevailing blood was what the Christ sacrifice proved to be.

And thus has the World Brotherhood passed from an aerial phantasy to a terrestrial actuality, permanency, beneficence. Brothers, let us clasp hands. Brother men, let us exalt the name of the Lord Christ together. Brother Men, let us unite in prayer.

WILLIAM A. QUAYLE.

20

Opportunity and Task.

THE larger vision of the life in Christ was experienced in the opening minutes of the National Convention of Methodist Men, for the home of the Hon. Charles Warren Fairbanks, who as general chairman of the Local Committee was to have opened the Convention, was a house of bereavement. Almost on the eve of this great gathering of men, whose coming he had anticipated with earnest desire, the beloved comrade through the years of his labors as citizen, statesman, and Churchman, passed to the commendation of Him in whose service she had spent her life. Dr. Joshua Stansfield, the pastor of Mr. and Mrs. Fairbanks, speaking a word of welcome to the Convention in place of Mr. Fairbanks, said: "In the decease of Sister Fairbanks the home, the Church, the State, the Nation, aye, the Methodism of the round world, mourns the departure of one of the noblest daughters of the Church and one of the most loyal, gracious, and serviceful of women, a truly elect lady. But while we sorrow, we sorrow not as those who have no hope, for we have laid away her precious body in sure and certain hope that the dead in Christ shall live again, and we are confident that so noble, strong and good a soul has gone forward and upward to a yet larger life and service."

Bishop David H. Moore, who as co-chairman with Mr. Fairbanks of the Local Committee, opened the Convention, declared in announcing the death of Mrs. Fairbanks, that she was to her husband "the companion of his life, the sharer of all his joys and sorrows, his steadfast friend and counselor, a woman who illustrated all the beauties of the domestic relations, of social and public life, and particularly of the Christian life." He was also compelled to announce the death of Dr. Robert Forbes, corresponding secretary of the Board of Home Missions and Church Extension—"a man who has been in the forefront of the battle to bring this country under the dominion of our Lord Jesus Christ."

It was, therefore, with a new and sharpened sense that the King's business demanded efficiency and haste, that the

21

delegates, their hearts tender and warm with Christian sympathy and love, listened and watched as the foundations for the work of the Convention were laid by such master builders as Speer, McDowell, and Nuelsen. For no mean study was to be made. Methodism early took the world for her parish, albeit, scarcely realizing what its content would be in the many-sided life of the nations of to-day. It was both essential and fitting that the central task of the Church of Christ be faced squarely at the start in order that it might be discovered whether Methodism's mission and message are attune to the heart-cry of the world-folk. With a full appreciation of the central task and an interpretation of Methodism's mission and message into its universal demand, the achievements of our Church take on new meaning, and the larger opportunities set before her become privileges of service for all her children.

The Central Task of the Church of Christ.

ROBERT E. SPEER.

WHEN the future student of the history of the Christian Church and of the higher life of man looks back upon our time, it is interesting to conjecture what his judgment will be as to what was its really greatest movement on life. Will he select popular education, with its emancipation of the mind of man from superstition, its new sense of human values and possibilities? Will he select the great scientific advancement of our day and its influence upon our common life, or its bearing upon our thoughts of God and of the world? Will he select the changing emphasis which our day has seen from the individual to society as a whole? Will he pick out some one of the theological movements of the time involving changed emphasis in men's thinking? I do not believe he will select any one of these, but a movement greater than any one of these, affecting and including all of these. I believe he will select the courage and the success of the rediscovery and the reaffirmation of the missionary principle; that, looking back over the century and a quarter that lie behind us, and the seventy-five years, perhaps, that lie just in advance of us, he will select as the deepest and most characteristic movement of this time Christianity's readjustment of its mission and the reassertion by Christian men of their obligation to carry the sovereignty of the gospel over all the world and into all the life of men. It may be that some will answer that in no small measure, at least, this is not a movement peculiarly of our day; that this is only the central characteristic of what we speak of as the Protestant Reformation. But the Reformation was really a geographically provincial movement. It influenced the people of only one continent, and of only part of that continent. It never faced the great issues of comparative religion. It knew nothing of great areas of human life that lay beyond the territories in which the influence of the Reformation was felt. And even within those territories it did not deal with all the life of men. Even the dawn of the nineteenth century had left the common man outside the real, penetrating purposes of the Christian gospel. It is clear, with no exaggeration of the movement in which our own lives are cast, that the future student, looking back upon our day, will pick out that great movement illustrated in the Church, that great movement of the rediscovery and reconstruction of Christianity in missionary times as the great movement of the world's life in the nineteenth and twentieth centuries.

I spoke of the courage of that rediscovery and reaffirmation. It is an easy thing for us gathered here to-day to take a world vision and dare to front all the life of our own time with the name of Christ and say, "Over you Christ shall be Sovereign, King." Looking back a century and a quarter, we realize what a bold and daring thing it was for the men of that time, who for the first time saw the glorious missionary character of our Christian faith, that, with resources or without them, in the name of their new vision they came out of the old to help the world into the new. I speak not alone of the courage of the rediscovery of the missionary prin-

23

ciples, but its success as well. A success that has now eaten itself into the whole moral conscience of the world, so that everywhere men and nations are doing their thinking to-day because they do their breathing in the atmosphere of Christian faith. And, looking ahead in imagination, that student whom we have in mind will judge all the activities of men by the relationship which they bore to this movement, by the clearness and the daring in which they dealt with the great problems confronting the Church of our time. Those problems are shifting under our eyes. When we speak of the central task of the Christian Church we say what John Wesley and Charles Wesley and John Rollins and William Sutcliffe said a century and a quarter ago, but in another sense we must say an entirely different thing. I have been working for a quarter of a century in connection with this missionary enterprise, and I have seen the problems shift at least five times in that period, so that men to-day who are to grapple with the Church's central task must look out on the world with different eyes from what men looked out with twenty-five years ago.

For one thing, we have had driven in upon us, as no other decade ever had, the problem of putting a new spirit in the whole relationship of the world, of turning this world neighborhood that has been created into a great relationship of brotherly men. Now, that the neighborhood has been created, there is no gainsaying. We might as well come out of our insular provincialism and face our problems. God has given us one compacted life to live in. Three years ago I rode up the west coast of South America with a Peruvian gentleman who had just then been appointed prefect of the city of Equitos, far up the head-waters of the Amazon. It was only a few miles from the capital city of Lima. The route he was taking took him two weeks' journey, from Callao to Panama. Another week's journey from Panama to New York City; another week's journey from New York City to Liverpool, and four weeks' journey from Liverpool back across the Atlantic

24

OPPORTUNITY AND TASK.

and up the Amazon. That was the shortest route. We used to say that the whole world was larger than any of its parts, but when you have to travel to Europe, going twice across the Atlantic Ocean, to reach a point that would be but a short journey across land in Peru, it would seem that the whole world is smaller than most of its parts to-day. We are facing a geographically contracted world which compels every man to touch elbows with every other man, and we are beginning to realize that there is but a single industrial community in which we have to do our work. Four years ago I spent the winter in Scotland, a great part of it in Aberdeen, which is the center of the greatest meat market in Great Britain; they said it would always be their own, but, walking along the main street, I saw a new shop and in glittering letters "The River Platte Meat Company." I went down to the city of Dundee, where the jute mills were lying idle, and when I asked the reason they gave me the answer in the terms of the crops in the Philippine Islands. A friend of mine came from China a few months since, and in one of the Eastern cities told about a cargo of iron that had been made in the blast furnaces of the city of Hankow, and they brought that iron around the world and sold it in the harbor of New York. When he got through, a gentleman came up and said, "I bought that iron, and I paid all the duty that was levied in New York upon it, and took it to Buffalo and paid the duty charged by Canada, and I sold it at a profit in Toronto." Whether we like it or not, the fingers of God are closing in upon us and making us one industrial community and making out of us one common family with a single intellectual life. I was in South America during the Arctic episode of a few years ago, and I found that the chief topic of conversation in South America, even away on the top of the Andes Mountains, was that same subject current all over the world. There died this last month in the city of Tokio the nestor of Congregational missions in Japan, Daniel Crosby Green, one of the really great men of our

25

day, because he saw that there is not any longer an insulated people; that all that is stirring in the local life are the things that are stirring through all the life of mankind. We have to face the fact and construct the work of the Christian Church in the light of a single compacted world. It is a terrible thing to deal with conditions like these unless all your neighbors are your brothers. If a man is not to be the friend of another man, the wider the distance separating them, the better; if he and the other man are to live with no fence or a low fence between them, woe be to them if they can not live there like brother-men! We face a new world, a world in which Christianity has not to deal with any isolated people, but with all mankind at once, and we have to penetrate that human neighborhood with the spirit of brotherly good-will.

In the second place, we have to face to-day the new problem of directing and controlling the great tides of life which are astir for the first time across the world. There is no gentleman here who can not remember when the standard books on the life of the great East were the books of Mr. George Curzon and Mr. Meredith Townsend, every one of whom was preaching twenty-five years ago the doctrine of the perpetual isolation of Asia, that one half of humanity was isolated from the other half by a chasm that could never be bridged, that a fiat of arrest had fallen upon the yellow races so that they were inaccessible to any new principles of life from without, and that we had to accept the situation that the world was split in twain; but we have lived to see the utter stupidity of such views, and we are called upon now to direct a great, swelling tide of educational interest such as was never in the world before. You know the problem that we have in the United States of keeping our secular education from destroying us; here you have to toil to undergird it with morals and religious sanctions; but how are you to do where the Christian tradition does not permeate the whole life of the land? I ask you to think what that problem is among the eight hundred millions of Asia, where that Christian atmosphere is not to be found, where the old religious sanctions have decayed, where our modern secular education is operating upon the lives of eight hundred million people who can not supplement it in their own homes with the saving principles of sound ethics. We face to-day the great problem of moralizing the education of one-half of humanity. We have to deal with the great industrial current that is beginning to sweep across the world. The Argentine Republic to-day exports every year about twenty times as much as China exports, leaving out of account their relative population. China exports to-day about one hundred and eighty-eight million dollars' worth of goods; if she exported as much per capita as the Argentine Republic to-day, and she is far richer—she has mineral resources of which Argentina can not dream—she would not be exporting one hundred and eighty-eight millions, but twenty-seven thousand millions of dollars every year! We stand to confront the most tremendous industrial avalanche that ever broke loose upon mankind, and we have to fraternalize that great human power. Then, there is the great tide of nationalistic feeling that is making a new world out of our world, differing radically from that in which our fathers lived. Great Britain subdued India with not more than two hundred thousand white soldiers, and has kept India in a species of serfdom, and the question is asked, How were they able to hold two hundred and ninety-eight millions of people? And the answer is, Because there was no such thing as an Indian nation, but only a great chaos of diverse races. Why was it that people after people, whom China in the day of her power would shake off as a strong man, were able to humiliate China in the days gone by? Because there was no Chinese nation. But now a spirit of nationalism is arising in those Eastern lands. How are you going to humanize this nationalism? We must bring to bear upon it a universal religion with universal brotherhood, with a spirit of universal relation; and every one of the non-Christian religions has denied that brotherhood. We have seen

2.

3.

27

turned loose in the world to-day great energies that make a
man stand still and gasp unless there is somewhere in the
world a hand that can be laid upon them and say to them,
"I am your Lord."

III   In the next place, we face the problem of reinforcing and
re-empowering our home Christianity so it will not be a refu-
tation of our whole-world proclamation of the gospel, so that
it will penetrate human life and all human relations, and one
looking behind him to the land from which he came will not
see a denial of his doctrine.   I have talked with groups of
students on this subject, who have raised the argument of our
failure to have our Christianity regnant in the social and
moral life of our land.   Among our problems that we have
to solve is that of the organization of the Christian Church
so that we can go to the people on the other side of the world
and say, "This is the Christian Church; it will apply anywhere."   How do you explain the turned keys in the doors
of the country churches?   How do you explain the numbers
of Churches at home that stand impotent before their tasks
as though they were planted across the sea?   How do we
know that we have the Christianity and the terms and forms
that really fit the lives of the Asiatic peoples until we have
found how they fit perfectly the lives of our own Western
peoples?   Here are the problems, industrial, ethical, educational, social, moral—the great questions of our own day.
One of the great problems of our day is the problem of so
releasing in our own land those energies of the Christian faith
in which we believe that they will make out of the very character of our Nation an unanswerable proclamation of Christ
to all the world of men.

IV   In the next place, we are facing the problem of how to put
God to a greater test than we have ever put Him to before,
how to prove what we have never dared to prove Him to do in
the days gone by.   We believe in His sufficiency.   We stand
confronting the great unsolved problems of our own modern
world: why are they unsolved in view of the sufficiency of

God? Because the men have not been found yet who are
ready to venture out far enough upon the divine sufficiency.
We stand in the presence of the great problem of trying God
out, of putting Him to the tests to which He has challenged
us against the intricate problems of our own land, against
the mass of world problems rolling in upon us from the non-
Christian world. I dare to say again that the unbiased student
of the future, whom we have been imagining looking back upon
our day, will judge of movements and men by the clearness
with which they discerned and the courage with which they
dealt with these great problems that constitute to-day the
central task of the Christian Church. There is no evading
these tasks. Long enough the Church has sought to evade
them, and what has been the consequence? She has tried to
make out of the gospel a solace to the soul of the individual
man (which, God knows, it was meant to be) and tried to
make out of it a sort of a separate institution planted in the
world, holding itself aloof from all the great things of the
world for which the Savior laid down His life. And what
has been the consequence? Why, the Lord has multiplied our
problems: He has said, "You will evade your obligations to
the rest of the world, will you? Well, here are the Negroes;
take them." He has said: "You will sit down within your
own gates, will you? Well, here are the Philippine Islands;
take them." He has said: "You are content with what your
fathers had, are you? Well, I will open the Eastern gates
wide and pour in the uncounted hordes from Europe; take
them." There is no escaping these modern central tasks of
the Christian Church: Every year's negligence of any one
of these tasks provokes the righteous God to multiply our
burdens and to confront us with larger problems to be dealt
with.

Great as the problems are, and loud as the challenge of
God may be, we know that in this very missionary reconstruction of Christianity, which has defined for us our new
tasks, lie also powers adequate to cope with those problems.

29

The missionary reconstruction of Christianity has shown us that the gospel is the great educational power of the world. We are beginning to discover that the Church has back in her hands once more those great agencies which for a little time it seemed she would let slip into the hands of the enemy. I spoke of those great tides that had begun to stir; who started them? The Christian missionaries who planted the first real school in each one of those non-Christian lands. They were the ones who laid the foundations of real education for the people in those non-Christian lands. There is in our new reconstruction of Christianity the educational force that can drive home to the world's need. We have found the great vitalizing power. Never can you solve those problems by any mechanistic methods, such as inhere in commerce: life has never been transmitted except by life; life can not be communicated to the great world except by life. I think that is what Sir William McWorth Young had in mind when he came home the other day from the lieutenant-governorship of the Punjab, and spoke to a great gathering of men like this in London; he spoke as a business man to business men, and he said: "I am prepared to say that what has been done by the life of Christ through missions in India is greater than all that has been done by the British Government in India from the beginning; I do not underrate the influence of British justice and enlightenment, but I am prepared to say that the work that has been done by Christian missions in the Punjab is vastly greater; the Punjab bears on its roll the names of some great Christian statesmen—John and Henry Lawrence, and Herbert Edwards—but I am prepared to say that if they could speak to us there is not one of them but what would say that the work that had been done by missionaries like French and Newton and Clark and Foreman was a greater and nobler work and more far-reaching in its consequences." We possess in this missionary reconstruction of our faith the final power that can penetrate beneath the crust of the world's death and plant the germs of life and power there.

OPPORTUNITY AND TASK.

Last of all, we possess in this new construction in our modern conceptions of Christian faith what always was there, but what for long centuries men have lost the consciousness of as a great conciliating and unifying power. You know how prominent that was in Saint Paul's mind when he spoke of the power of Christ to break down partitions built across the world and to preach to them that were near and far and bring them all into one great peace. That is the greatest problem of our own modern day; surely every man must see that that is the deepest and most unsolvable problem in the face of the facts that confront us, the problem of race. How long does God intend it to continue? How much does He mean that each race must guard its own separate racial personality? Who knows what He means by race? We stand dumb before the problem that faced us in California last year, and the problem that faces us in the whole woman movement of our day, and the problem fronting us now in the Negro situation of our own land, the problem of the relation of race to race. Who holds the solution of that problem, the problem that is going to fill our children's world after us with hate and hell unless we begin the solution now? Who holds the solution of that problem but those who know that in Jesus Christ there is neither Greek nor barbarian, bond nor free? A great ethnologist has told us that the profoundest word that St. Paul ever said was that word that in Christ the chasm of sex, the chasm of slavery, and the chasm of citizenship had all been wiped away and all mankind made one. Do we believe that? Has the missionary reconstruction so woven itself into our lives that we believe that? I conceive this to be the great central task of Christ's Church in this present hour—that you and I like men, clear-eyed, unfearing, with a new and living confidence in God that has no limits to it, who dare cope with any problem on earth, shall face the world in which we live and claim that world, this world that we face to-day, as a world over which Jesus Christ is to be King. He asks us to try Him as to whether He can

31

carry a scepter. "Prove Me now." That is His old word. Prove Me now, prove Me now herewith, by bringing your tithes—all the tithes, the whole of them—which are Mine, bringing these to Me, and trying Me now. O, that in the days of this gathering there may come down such a new spirit of simple and living faith as shall make us bold to try to the limit the limitless God!

Methodism: Its Mission and Message.

WILLIAM FRASER McDOWELL.

I DO not quite like this topic. Methodism has no message of its own, and no mission except as a servant of Jesus Christ. We speak of the Christian message, and if we are true, we perform Jesus Christ's task. For our world's plans were not made either at Fetter-Lane or at Oxford. They have been made in the heart of the eternal God. And that ancient Methodist who in a moment of pious rapture thanked God for John Wesley's plan of salvation was just a litle bit wide of the mark. Now, if there were time, I should want to amplify three propositions, which three propositions, I frankly state at the beginning of what I have to say, conscious that the exposing of the whole outline in advance is not always good homiletics.

Proposition number one: Christianity has a message so unique, so necessary to the world, so rich and fruitful in its contents so superior to any other message known to the world as to constitute it not only a real gospel, but the only gospel for mankind. Proposition number two: The world is lost and will continue to be lost unless in some real fashion the world gets this message, which is the glorious gospel of the blessed God. Proposition number three: The message of Christianity is this message, and the mission of Christianity is the carrying this message in Christlike fashion to the world which dies for the lack of it. Now, these are the three points I wish to make. I am not quite sure but that, having stated them, they are sufficiently made. And yet perhaps it may be fair to emphasize them a bit for the purpose of their simple statement.

What, then, is Christianity's message which constitutes it

a gospel? As significant books as have appeared in recent theology have been those books which in one form or another have sought to answer the question, "What is Christianity?" And I am bound to say that, recognizing fully our large debt to these very able discussions, it seems to me that they are rather needlessly elaborated and complicated. I think they would bother a Chinaman or a low-caste Indian or a native of the interior of Africa just a bit. They would not quite meet that test of the gospel which is the practical test, namely, Can the gospel be immediately preached on the streets? So if you ask what is Christianity's message, I should try to answer, thinking of the Indian man that stands here making his first inquiry about Christianity, of the Chinese man standing here asking, "What is this message?" And I should answer in terms that were perfectly simple, This Christian message is this, "God was in Christ reconciling the world unto Himself." This is Christianity's message, "The Son of man is come to seek and to save that which was lost." This is Christianity's message, "God so loved the world that He gave His only begotten Son, that whosoever believeth in Him should not perish but have everlasting life." We have lost something of the sharpness and acuteness of this wonderful message by our long familiarity with it. But we ought to thank God with our whole hearts that we have a message that can be stated in a dozen words.

Now I will rest Christianity's case upon one word, "Redemption," and I will risk Christianity's case upon one Person, the Redeemer. In any land at any hour I will face the sin, the sorrow, the strife, the hate, the shame, and the death of that world with that Person, the Redeemer, and that message, His redemption. The Redeemer is Christianity's Gift to mankind. The redemption of all life is Christianity's purpose for mankind. I would not cross the street to give India a new theology; India has more theology than it can understand. I would not cross the street to give China a new code of ethics; China has a vastly better ethical code than ethical life. I would not cross the street to give Japan a new religious literature, for Japan has a better religious literature than religious life. But I would go around the world again, and yet again, if it pleased God, to tell India and China and Africa and the rest of the world:

> "There is a fountain filled with blood,
>   Drawn from Immanuel's veins,
> And sinners plunged beneath that flood
>   Lose all their guilty stains."

Some of us were brought up on certain familiar lines. I do not doubt that I could set this great assembly singing, if I had time to do so, by the simple repetition of these lines, which were true in our infancy, which are true this morning as we face manhood's tasks:

> "There is no name so sweet on earth,
>   No name so sweet in heaven:
> The name, before His wondrous birth,
>   To Christ the Savior given."

"Thou shalt call His name Jesus, for He shall save His people from their sins." This constitutes the message of Christianity; this makes it unique; this makes it essential; this separates it from all others. Dr. Speer has just spoken of the new adjustments that have come in consequence of the study of comparative religions. I myself am old enough to remember when we were almost afraid that we would discover some excellence outside of Christianity. It seemed to us then that if we discovered anything good in any other religion, it some way would disparage Christianity as the absolute religion. And honestly, I myself shared that fright and was not a little bit disturbed when it was pointed out in my youth that in negative form the Chinese did have the Golden Rule. The time was when some of us were almost afraid to discover any virtue in the lives of those whom we called broadly "Heathen." Long since, bless God! we have got past that. We are no longer disturbed by the discovery of virtues outside of Christianity, or excellencies in other religions than the Christian religion. The one heart-breaking thing as you face the non-Christian world and its religions on the ground, is not the virtues that you can discover, but the virtues that you can not discover. And if you find a shining character standing up in the midst of them, you have it for a point of contact between Christianity and that land in which he has arisen. And if there be a truth that arises out of the non-Christian religion, instead of being disturbed by that shining truth, you thank God and go forward, knowing this, that in spite of it all the great tragedy of it hangs like a pall over the non-Christian world. You go, for instance, into India and China with as large an assortment of liberal views as any man ought to carry around the world with him. You go determined to be generous to the non-Christian world, and you receive with gratitude the courtesies of the elegant gentlemen who show you courtesies. But you come out saying, with an emphasis that you never dreamed it would be possible to you, ''There is no other name given under heaven or among men whereby men must be saved but the name of Jesus Christ, neither is there salvation in any other.''

So this is Christianity's message. We do not offer a Western Christ to the Eastern world. We do not offer an Eastern Christ to the Western world. A universal Christ, adequate for the salvation of the whole world, constitutes our proclamation, and I venture to say that one of the imperative needs of Christendom in this hour is a re-creation of full faith in the adequacy of Jesus Christ for the world's salvation. There are a good many kinds of skepticism in the world, some of them distressing, some of them amusing; but the one skepticism that cuts the nerve of faith and lets it die is that skepticism that questions the necessity of Christ to the world and the adequacy of Christ to the world; so we need to stand straight at this point. Gentlemen of this great Convention, in some parts of the world it is a plain, straight issue between Jesus Christ and Mohammed. In other parts of the world, a plain, straight issue between Jesus Christ and Buddha. In other parts of the world a plain, straight issue between Jesus Christ and Confucius. We confuse and befog the whole matter when we make it a vague and a general comparison between one ism and another ism. I will take my stand in New York or Chicago or Calcutta or Bombay or Foochow or Shanghai or Pekin or Tokio or anywhere in the world beside Jesus Christ, not simply that He is better than anybody else, but that He alone is adequate to world redemption. There is no salvation apart from Him.

Now, my second proposition, which I shall discuss with a good deal more brevity, is this, that this world is lost and will keep on being lost unless we bring to that world that message of Christianity in some fashion like unto the fashion in which it was brought to us. I suppose the very finest thing in the world is humanity unaided trying to build its tower up to the heavens. Humanity awakens a shout or a song. The Christian message in the beginning was conditioned by two factors: first, what God in Jesus Christ brought to mankind; secondly, what man out of Christ needed from God. No man could go into the Eastern world to-day without being tremendously stirred with the similarity between the conditions in the Far East and those conditions into which Jesus came. Now do not misunderstand. What God had on one hand, what man needed on the other hand—you can begin either way, but you come out at the same point. Dearly beloved brethren, there is a widespread error in the world, a widespread and fatal error in Christendom; that error is a twofold one. First, that the world without Christ is upon the whole a pretty good world without a very good religion. Secondly, that the world without Christ is a fairly happy world without a very adequate religion. One wishes that this were true—and it is not. Many terms have been used to characterize the age and many to characterize the race. The time in which we live has been called an age of doubt and an age of faith and an age of materialism and a skeptical age and a

37

socialistic age, or a junction of the two, by those that want to be wise and strike a balance. And the nations have been characterized as the supple Hindus and sturdy Chinese and alert Japanese, etc. O, brethren beloved, with all these shifting, passing terms we are perfectly familiar. But the one outstanding fact with reference to the ages and the nations is this, that the ages have been ages of sin and the nations are nations of sin, and that the pall of sin falls across the centuries and across all continents. It is, in other words, not simply the necessity of a changed religion or of missionary propaganda. If it were possible for us to induce the people of Africa to forsake Mohammedanism, to change their religion without changing their character, all the great struggle would be utterly useless. It is not simply a changed religion, but a changed *life* that the world needs, in Christendom and out of Christendom. The world is not being destroyed by its poverty, and the world is not being destroyed by its diseases. The heart of the world is not breaking because of its poverty, or because of its sickness. The heart of the world is breaking for life. The heart of the world is broken by sin. Shall I tell you, shall I confess to you how many times I have been asked, how many pitiful times I have been asked, whether the non-Christian world is not getting along pretty well with the religions it has? Frugal men, economical men, men with their benevolent emotions under perfect control, have asked me over and over again if the non-Christian world is not getting along pretty well with the religions it has—as though Christianity might be a convenience! I make this answer to-day as though it were the only word I should ever speak to you, as though it might be the last word I should speak to you. This is my answer, "Nobody on the planet is getting along pretty well without Jesus Christ." Now, I am not thinking chiefly about the escape of the heathen from hell hereafter. God is good. I am thinking of their escape from the hell of this life. And I am praying that we shall not easily use these figures out of which we take the meaning and which we keep for homiletic purposes exclusively. We have a homiletic acquaintance with water, a homiletic acquaintance with bread, a homiletic acquaintance with sheep. We, who have never been athirst, who have never been hungry, have never been sheep without a shepherd, have a homiletic acquaintance with these great terms. But the non-Christian world is dying of thirst and of hunger, and is scattered and torn as sheep having no shepherd anywhere within its fold. Jesus Christ to them and to us is something more than a convenience. As Forsythe puts it, ''We owe him not simply our thanks, we owe Him our lives.''

My third proposition is, that we must identify ourselves with Jesus Christ for the carrying of this necessary and adequate message to the world that is dying without it. We must identify ourselves with Jesus Christ, I said. More and more, I think, we are to hear certain supreme and thrilling words in our religious speech. More and more, I think, we are to hear such terms as ''the practice of the incarnation'' and ''the practice of the atonement.'' A tolerably interested God, complacent and comfortable, might have sent word that He had angels enough to scatter around over the whole race of men—to tell them that He was tolerably interested. But a divinely interested God had to come—I speak it reverently. He could not see the world in sin and keep out of it, and He could not see the world in sorrow and keep out of it. I would not say an irreverent word, but God could not be the kind of God He is and keep out of the conditions that He saw. I do not see how an angel of God can deliver the message of God, can fulfill Christianity's message, unless in the spirit and practice of the incarnation strength puts itself at the service of weakness the world around; light puts itself into and at the service of the world's darkness the world around; goodness puts itself into the world's evil the world around; until all that is high and blessed becomes all that is earnest and self-sacrificing, I do not see how we can keep out of the gracious reconciliation that gives the Lord of life His life.

39

At Cornell University a young Dutch student from South Africa came to see me. He said, ''I want to talk with you, sir, about the nations of the earth.'' That is a pretty large topic for a young Dutch student. He said, ''I am thinking of a topic for my graduating thesis, and I am preparing to write a thesis upon the 'Synthesis of the Nations.' '' That recalls the old story of the boy who wrote his first essay and wanted to take a subject that would be big enough so that he would not run out of things to say, and proposed as the subject for his first essay, ''The World and What It Contains.'' ''The Synthesis of the Nations!'' Well, we talked it over, and the boy left me. Brethren, he left me with a word— the nations may become one or the nations may remain separate, but they will not become one in any body except Jesus Christ. The races may become one, or remain separate, if God's plans are thwarted, but the races are not going to become one in any body but Jesus Christ. Humanity may be saved, saved in its personal life, saved in its social life, saved in its political life, saved in its industrial life, saved in its international life; or it may go down to doom. But it is not going to be saved, as far as anybody can see, except by Jesus Christ.

This, then, is the message. Christianity has a message so unique, so necessary to mankind, so rich and fruitful for all life, as to constitute it a gospel and the only gospel for mankind. The world is lost and will keep on being lost, unless the world vitally gets this divine message. It is our mission in the world, in the fashion in which Christ brought that message to us, to take that message to the world in His name and in His spirit.

Methodism's Achievements and Opportunities.

John L. Nuelsen.

"What has God wrought!" From this text John Wesley preached a sermon in which he traces the history and spread of Methodism. "What has God wrought!" we may fitly exclaim when at this juncture we pause to review some of the outstanding achievements of Methodism since the days of Wesley. We have no desire to boast. Self-glorification is worse than useless. All honor and glory belongs to God. He has called Methodism into existence. He has given her her commission. All that the Methodists can do is to be faithful to the divine voice, to trust in the divine power, to be led by the divine presence. Has Methodism by her history up to the present hour demonstrated her divine calling? Has she shown herself to be a part of that Church which St. Paul calls the body of Christ? Is the function of the body to make real the plans of the head? Has Christ used Methodism to carry out in a measure His world-embracing plan of salvation? It is in this spirit that I desire to rapidly sketch this survey.

Under the summary designation of achievements of organization I may be permitted to point to the numerical growth of Methodism. The youngest of the great denominations, the Methodist Church, is now the largest Protestant denomination, the membership of which is purely voluntary. It is true, the statistics would show that the Lutherans are the most numerous Protestant Church. Over against the thirty-two millions of Methodist population are forty million Lutherans. But while the great bulk of the Lutherans are found in countries where their Church is established by law and supported by taxes, there is among all the millions of

Methodists not one who is a Methodist because the laws of the land where he was born made him such; nor is there anywhere a Methodist Church the support of which is borne by an appropriation of public funds. Every last Methodist is a Methodist because he personally has chosen to be a Methodist, and he knows that all expenses of the organization have to be met by free-will offerings. Considering that one hundred and fifty years ago the most brilliant of the leaders of thought on the European continent predicted the total extinction of the Church of Christ within a generation, and that again and again modern prophets have proclaimed the impending end of Christianity, it is a distinct achievement that there are to-day thirty-two millions of men, women, and children who willingly and thankfully place themselves under the influence of the message of life as preached from Methodist pulpits.

In the next place, the territorial expansion of Methodism may be pointed out as an achievement worthy of notice. One hundred and fifty years ago Methodism was hardly known in any country outside of England; to-day there is hardly any country where Methodism is not known. This world-wide expansion derives its deeper significance from the fact that Methodism has thereby given to the Protestant Church the world view. There were foreign missionary efforts before the rise of Methodism. But they were desultory; they met with opposition in the Churches. The Churches of the Reformation were not missionary Churches. It is true, the Moravians had caught the vision of the world-embracing love of the Savior. Many of them went to foreign countries. Beautiful examples they are of missionary heroism and martyrdom. But they did not succeed in arousing the Churches out of their lethargy. The impulse to the modern missionary movement was given by the Methodist revival. Wesley's famous saying, "The world is my parish," proved to be the sledge-hammer that battered down the stone walls of national narrowness by which the Churches were hemmed in. It was Methodism that led the Church of Christ out of the valley of provincialism upon

OPPORTUNITY AND TASK.

the mountain heights where can be seen the countries beyond. The conception of Christian imperialism, the vision of the Kingdom without frontiers, the compulsion of the Savior's love to all mankind, the dynamic of the wideness of God's mercy like the wideness of the sea, the longing for a thousand tongues to sing the great Redeemer's praise—truths that burned in the hearts of the Wesleys and Whitefields, the Cokes and Asburys, that found expression in sermons and songs and were realized in the blessed experience of thousands of men and women—these were the forces that have transformed the Churches from petty sects, disputing about metaphysical distinctions and wrangling about ecclesiastical millinery, into a vigorous, aggressive army, eager for the conquest of the world, ready to plan great things, to undertake great things, to suffer great things in order to crown Him their great Captain, Lord of all.

And while Methodism was growing in numbers and expanding her world parish, she built up an ecclesiastical organism combining firmness with elasticity, democracy with strong central power, unity of aim and purpose with adaptability to local needs and conditions, allowing for the greatest measure of individual liberty without running into religious anarchy; providing for strong leadership without opening the doors to hierarchical absolutism. The dominant principle has been tersely expressed by Wesley in the slogan, "Everybody at work and always at work." The Methodist Church is not a clergy Church; it is a people's Church. The aim of its organization does not look towards prelatical or hierarchical aggrandizement, nor towards the conservation of time-honored formularies or modes of worship. It is the crowning achievement of Methodism, as far as organization is concerned, that it put into operation the higher ideal of the Church of Christ, which conceives the Church, not as a haven of rest for weary souls, not as merely a place of preparation of the soul for heavenly bliss, not as an ascetic institution for luring pious souls away from the interests of life, not as

43

sacerdotal pretension holding men's minds in bondage to dogmatic demands, but as a great training school for the people, where the men and women who are doing the world's work and are bearing the world's burdens are trained and inspired and vitalized and energized to stoop down still lower and take upon their own shoulders more of the burden of the weaker brother, to stretch out the hand still farther and lift up him who has stumbled and fallen. Thus the highest ideal of Christian character may be attained, namely, perfect fellowship of and fellowship with Him who came not to be ministered unto but to minister, yea, to give His life for the salvation of others.

Turning now from the achievements of organization to the *impact upon the Church at large* of the message of Methodism, I shall, of course, not attempt to speak of the message itself. This has been done so beautifully by Bishop McDowell. I merely desire to remind you that Methodism has ever been more than an organization; it has been and is now a great spiritual movement making itself felt far beyond the confines of its own household. The Methodists themselves have ever been the least result of the Methodist movement. The direct results are vastly outnumbered by the indirect results. It requires a tremendous vitality to remain both an organization and a movement. Great movements have lost their vital impulse when crystallized into organized forms; great organizations have weakened and have disintegrated in the endeavor to exert wider influence. The Methodist message has retained and strengthened its constructive power while not diminishing its dynamic force. It has quickened the spiritual life of all Churches. By its insistence upon the great fundamental facts of Christian experience it has changed the character of Protestant preaching. Its jubilant proclamation of a salvation that is free to all and possible for all, a salvation that can be known and felt, that strangely warms the heart and tunes the life to joyous praise, a salvation that reaches the innermost recesses of the soul and touches all the issues of life, a salvation that can be interpreted and lived in terms of holiness and perfect love—this proclamation has been like the warm spring sunshine, melting the icy crusts of lifeless formalism and fruitless dogmatism which enshrined the Churches and bringing forth the sweet flowers and fruits of the life of the Spirit.

Methodism has been to all Protestant Churches the teacher of aggressive evangelism. The evangelistic note in modern preaching is the echo of the Methodist revival shouts. Nearly a generation ago a German Lutheran university professor said that the great dominant force in modern Protestantism is the spirit of Methodism, and only about a year ago a French Romanist summed up his observation on the Church of the future by voicing his expectation that in its characteristic features and its spirit the Church of the future will be Methodistic. To record these statements, coming as they do from representatives of the Catholic and the Lutheran Churches, may suffice to show Methodism's achievement in impressing her message upon the Church universal.

Any religious movement or organization is to be judged also by its influence upon the community and the nation. Religion is not a department of life isolated from the other interests. It is not a peaceful island in the turbulent river, but a force giving direction to the currents of life. From its very beginning Methodism was closely connected with the great national and world movements. They shaped to a great extent the outward course of Methodist history, and by directing its message to the needs of the hour, Methodism became a determining factor in influencing and molding the National and social life of the times. This is true in England. It is likewise the case in America. The first Episcopal Church in the new American Republic, the first Church to officially recognize the new Federal Constitution and the Chief Magistrate, George Washington, its history parallels the history of the Union. The great problems of the Nation have been the problems with which Methodism undertook to wrestle. Take, for instance, the problem of population in its threefold form as a problem of territorial expansion, of immigration, of races. It has confronted the Nation with the gravest tasks, and never was the Methodist Episcopal Church found shrinking from its duties and responsibilities.

The task of building the greater American Nation in that fertile area between the Alleghenies and the Rockies, and later beyond the Rockies, was stupendous, both on account of the vastness of the territory and of the mighty inrush of population. The greatest empire in all history—Rome, with her population of one hundred and twenty millions, her genius for government, her long and compact civilization—perished utterly under the pressure of a less copious flood of incursion than rushed into the young American Republic with its scanty population and its new and untried institutions. Rome declined and fell, not by force of arms, but by the disintegrating influences exerted by the masses of foreigners who were made Roman citizens without becoming true Romans, and this was and is the danger of America. Even under the most favorable conditions, emigrations on a large scale are fraught with dangers. Torn away from his accustomed surroundings, no longer hemmed in by the restraints of Church or Society, engaged in a fierce struggle against poverty and deprivations, the immigrant must be backed by a tremendous moral or religious motive if he is not to fall off from the standards of a civilized community. While the organization of the American Churches was well adapted to the normal conditions in a settled country, it was utterly inadequate to the needs of the hour. No other system than that represented by the Methodist circuit-rider, the Methodist class-meeting, could save the West. And as the Westward movement rushed on till it reached the breakers of the Pacific Ocean, the Methodist circuit-rider was ever in the van of the unending procession, building into the foundations of the coming Commonwealths the solid, precious marble blocks of faith in God, of moral responsibility, of self-respect, of altruistic service.

Need I speak of Methodist service in helping to solve our problems of immigration? When towards the middle of the last century the old homeland of the Angles and the Saxons began to send her sons and daughters by the tens of thousands, and when from Scandinavia the blue-eyed, flaxen-haired children of the Vikings and Norsemen came to people the newly-formed Western States, Methodists welcomed them with the gospel message in their own tongues. And in our day, when the doors are wide open, and when from all parts of the world the immigrants pour into this country at the rate of over one million a year, the Methodist Church can point to mission halls and chapels and churches and schoolhouses where in many languages the gospel of Christian principles, of American civilization, are promulgated. The achievements of Methodist home mission work in foreign languages take a high place when we enumerate the forces that make for the Americanization of the heterogeneous elements and for the unification of the Nation.

Shall I speak of Methodism's achievement in helping to solve our perplexed race problem? The noble words uttered by President Lincoln, well nigh fifty years ago, still ring in the ears of Methodists. May I quote them? "Nobly sustained as this Government has been by all the Churches, I would utter nothing which might in the least appear invidious against any. Yet without this it may fairly be said that the Methodist Episcopal Church, not less devoted than the best, is, by its greater number, the most important of all. It is no fault in others that the Methodist Episcopal Church sends more soldiers to the field, more nurses to the hospitals, and more prayers to Heaven than any." I am not going to give you any statistics as to our work among our colored people nor among those of foreign speech. I shall not tell you how much money we have invested in our hospitals, orphanages, old people's homes, deaconess institutions, and other forms of mercy and help work. I shall not speak of our colleges and universities; all these details will be presented to you by the speakers who will follow. But this one thought I am desirous of impressing upon your minds: wherever you touch American life to-day, you will find the Methodist influence. You speak of the nation-wide fight against the drink evil? Need I tell you that the Methodist Church is leading the hosts? You are thinking of the great social struggle, so complex and comprehensive. Let me point you to the fact that the declaration of the General Conference of the Methodist Episcopal Church on the relation of the Church to the social problems have been adopted almost literatim by the Federated Churches of America. All Americans love to think of the spread of education and culture among the broad masses of the people. While in no wise detracting from the splendid work done in our public schools—and, by the way, the Methodists stand by the public school system—I remember reading in the foremost French Review that the American Chautauqua system presents the greatest system of popular education that the world has ever seen, and I further remember that the Chautauqua system was founded by a bishop of the Methodist Episcopal Church.

Men of Methodism, lift up your eyes and behold what God has wrought. It is marvelous. Truly a great heritage the fathers have left to us. It does not behoove us to boast. We did not make Methodism. It behooves us to bow our heads in gratitude for what God has wrought through our fathers; but more than that, to lift up hearts and heads in exceedingly great thankfulness that He has given to us still larger opportunities than our fathers ever dreamt of. Larger opportunities? Yea, verily.

A larger opportunity I see in the modern quest of the soul, in the desire for individual life. Our age is no longer satisfied with blatant materialism, nor with perverted socialism. In the terrific rush of modern life, amid the tremendous strain of business pressure, in the wild dash for the dollar, the insatiate hunger for pleasure in the restlessness of the age, there is seen the wistful longing for a soul life, for strong, independent personal life. In art and literature and philosophy can be discerned the plea for recognition of the soul, the insistence upon a life higher than and independent of the physical life, a life independent of its material surroundings, stronger than its environment, a life that is not the result of evolution but of regeneration. I am here to say to you that the men and women of our day, the world over, in spite of apparent materialism, have a greater longing for a higher life than the people had when Methodism was called into being. And furthermore, modern scientific thought has a greater appreciation of the facts of religious experience, especially of the fact of regeneration, than philosophy ever had. I am not disturbed by the mass of incidental things that appear on the surface. Go down to the hidden currents that determine the direction of the river, and doing so, I would say our age is an age of the quest of the soul. If there ever was a time when the distinctive message of Methodist theology met the needs of the hour, the time is now. The message of the soul life attained through the new birth by the power of the Spirit of God, who makes old things pass away and makes everything new, is distinctively the message of the hour. God help us faithfully to preach it, loyally to live it! To save souls may have a somewhat different meaning for us than it had for our fathers; our opportunities for saving souls are vastly greater.

I see a larger opportunity in the present emphasis upon social service. Let us not be misled by the apparent selfishness, greed, injustice, corruption, and graft. All of these evils and many more are obvious. But, again, we discern in modern society not only a vague, inarticulate desire for social betterment, for service, but a real passion for it. It is within the Church, it is outside the Church, it is even in many instances

4   49

hostile to the Church, but its presence is one of the most significant and hopeful signs of the times. Methodism's summons to social service was uttered clearly and compellingly at the beginning of its history. In our age of social reconstruction, of great impending changes, of unrest, of yearning for social justice; in our day when we begin to estimate a man's success in accordance with his service to the community; in our times when we begin to learn that privilege spells obligation and that obligation is a synonym of service,—Methodism has the larger opportunity to connect the currents of humanitarianism with the life-springs of vital religion. Socialism, estranged from religion or hostile to religion, will never lift society. The passion for social service will burn out and die unless it is constantly quickened and energized by the love of Christ that constraineth us also. The history of Methodism, her genius and achievements, are a challenge to us to furnish the larger world of to-day with social leadership that leads from the reborn individual to the reconstructed society.

The larger world furnishes to Methodists the larger opportunities. Wesley's word, "The world is my parish," means vastly more to us than it could possibly mean to him. To-day we can, yea, we must, speak of world influence, of world power, of world obligation. What is done in one country affects life in every other country. Especially is this true of America. America, the threshhold between the two large oceans around which modern life pulsates; America, with her immense material resources; America, with her mixed population, from which you can trace lines of influence to nearly every hamlet in every country of the world,—America has to-day opportunities for world influence as no other country ever possessed. Men of Methodism, the Methodist Church is the strongest Protestant Church in America. Draw your own conclusions. Get the vision. Hear the summons. Face the larger opportunities.

PART II.

The Forces and the Field—A Survey.

Prayer by Bishop Wilson.

O GOD, our Father, we have been sitting together thinking of Thee and Thy Kingdom, and Thou hast been with us. We have been thinking of the King, and our King has been in our midst, and our hearts burned within us as our faith discerns Thee, and the sense of responsibility comes upon us as we look upon the scarred face of our King, and as His pierced hands beckon us to the opportunity of to-day and point to us the way of service. Our loving hearts would answer to Him and we would give ourselves as never before in sacrifice and in service in the name of Him who loved us. O, Master Divine, Thou who hast, by the sober words of this convention, shown us the possibilities; Thou who hast breathed upon us Thy Spirit, so that our love for Thee has been quickened; O, Master Divine, save us! so that we shall not leave here the influence of this Convention; that we shall not turn and go down again to those low levels where we have lived; that we shall not henceforth be satisfied with narrow thoughts concerning Thy great grace; that we shall not willingly interpret the Divine purpose in terms of our own personality. O, Master Divine, help us that we may save Thy world, the world for whose redemption Jesus Christ died, the world that Thou hast sought to place upon the heart of Thy militant Church. O help us, that our eyes may never fail to recognize the measure of Thy love; that our hearts may never fail to answer to Thy call, but that Thou mayest by Thy Spirit put Thine own life into our hearts and lead us ever henceforth. O, Master Divine, here we are, a little company of Thy workers, a little group of Thy disciples, but the land is here, the world is here, and millions of Methodists are here! They are to be influenced by this great Convention. They will either tarry where they are upon the lower reaches of life or they shall rise and see the vision that Thou art seeking to set before them. We are going down again, or we are to rise. Master, come and help us to rise!

There is a vision of the home life, and we are face to face with the great question of our sons and daughters—some of them in Thy Kingdom, but some of them wandering afar. O breathe on us, Master, that in wisdom and in love it shall be at once our high responsibility and our exalted privilege to bring the sons and the daughters of Methodist homes into the family of our God. The cities are wailing, they are wailing in their ignorance; they are sobbing in their wretchedness; they are wandering on in their sin, down from darkness into a deeper darkness; O, Master Divine, quicken us in all the energies of our spiritual life, breathe on us by Thy Spirit, so that the Church of Jesus Christ may lay hold on the great cities of America, may lay hold upon the country places of America, may recognize in America God's great redemptive purpose, and may devote itself utterly to that purpose. O, Master Divine, a world-crisis is before us. Africa cries unto us; China reaches out its hands imploring to us; India and Japan are asking our aid; Mexico, in confusion and in turmoil, utters its imploring cries. O, Master Divine, where shall be the sufficiency that shall satisfy these hungry multitudes? Where is the light that is to illuminate these darkened lands? Thou must be the bread for the satisfying of the world's hunger, and Thou must be the Light of the world. O may Thy Church, represented here, receive the bread from heaven and distribute it to the hungry of the world. O, Light of Life, shine in upon

52

our hearts, that so our quickened faith, our life intensified shall enable us to go out and strive and pray and serve, until the shadow shall lift from all lands, and until the world shall be lifted up into the light and the love and the life of God! Hear us in this prayer! We are not sufficient in ourselves, but Thou hast taught us to believe that the things that are not may bring to naught the things that are, if only there be the dedication of purpose and of profession to Thee, and here this morning we would pledge ourselves to our King; our sacrifice we would place on the altar until the great task be wrought, or until Thou shall call us from the field to the City of the King. Amen.

The Forces and the Field—A Survey.

WISDOM calls for a careful study of every task and a consideration of the resources available for service. When it comes to the work of the Church, this is even more necessary, for the Church membership is vastly different in range of opportunity and ability. Her leadership also is so varied that no one viewpoint gives the entire problem or its solution. The helpful feature in these discussions is that it is possible to compare the many viewpoints, so that secretaries, editors, district superintendents, pastors, bishops, and laymen may see their own estimates and solutions side by side with those of men who reach their conclusions from a different angle. A survey of the condition of the Church, revealing the variety of its departments and activities, proposing remedies, and showing how a proposed remedy has worked in a given situation, will provide material against which may be projected with profit both the experience and the theories of men from widely separated fields of toil.

The story of how other denominations have faced their situations and solved or partly solved their problems furnishes still more data for comparative study.

Into every Episcopal Area Conference and into the Sectional Conferences held for District Superintendents, Pastors, Brotherhood Men, and Sunday School Superintendents, this material was taken to see if it would fit the field and could be actually applied to the particular local needs.

The special purpose of this section of MILITANT METHODISM is to give a comprehensive survey of the field, the forces, and the problems, and to show how the forces have been mobilized and used and the problems met in various parts of the wide territory under our care.

I. OUR DENOMINATIONAL SITUATION.

The addresses at this session were illustrated by many maps and charts specially prepared for the Convention. It was found impracticable to reproduce these maps in this volume.—EDS.

The Drift of the Church.

W. B. HOLLINGSHEAD.

I REALIZE that I must hasten the message of the morning. My. first question is, Why this map? First, that it may portray to the eye in colors the places where our bishops reside and the fields over which they preside. Second, that the per capita standing as to the ministry and the benevolent enterprises of the Church may be set before your eye that you may see the whole field at a glance. Third, that we may by graphic illustration try to portray to you something of the distance and the measurements, the miles over which these chief leaders and general superintendents of ours must preside in order to do the work of the Church of God. May we ask, Did the General Conference make a mistake in creating new episcopal fields? Did it impose upon the Church a financial burden which it is unable to pay for its leadership? Have our bishops not sufficient territory over which to travel or sufficient interests to develop? Then, to be brief with this statement, I desire to illustrate first one area in the Church. You will note the field to the northwest and the west in the green on the map, the field over which one bishop presides, and take its development. It would reach from New York City to New Orleans if we could change the form of it. I have not told its magnitude in miles from east to west. Did the General Conference give to Bishop Luccock a full

54

man's job? This is a new area; some of you have traveled it from east to west, and when the fast express starts from the East toward Bishop Luccock's field and travels to the West, you are traveling some, to use a common expression. I sat a few weeks ago in the station at Denver. I had an hour and a quarter to spare. A man with a familiar face entered the door. I greeted him, and he called me by name. We sat down and for more than an hour we talked together. It was Bishop Luccock, who led our devotions this morning. He began to tell me about Montana and Idaho and the Dakotas, and his very soul was on fire with enthusiasm for the bigness of his job and for the opportunities which the Church had put into his hands, and when he went on with his earnest story, I said to him, "But, bishop, who is to tell your story to the great East?" And then, as he hastened in graphic terms to portray conditions which made my heart's blood thrill within me, I said again, "Who is to tell your story to the great East?" And as he went on with that earnest enthusiasm, telling me of opportunities too great for the average man to comprehend, I said again, "But who is to tell your story to the great East?" I have not yet received an answer to my question. Men of Methodism, if some man could stand before our people in this American land and tell them what is transpiring on this American continent, and the opportunities Almighty God has opened to our Church, there would be such an awakening in benevolent activities as the world has never known. But who can tell it? When you see it you can not comprehend it. I used to travel over the district out yonder in the northwest corner of the State of Oregon. I came in every quarter and said, "It is all new, opportunities everywhere, a field white unto the harvest." If I should stand here this morning and try to portray to you conditions in our great cities and rural districts, every man would go back to his field with a deeper interest in the extension of the Kingdom of God. Men of Methodism, our people lack conscience concerning the great connectional claims of the Methodist Episcopal Church. Our people lack vision of world problems. They have not gone down into the heart of the great city to develop or understand the conditions of city life. They know but little about the great frontier in that Western land. They know but little about conditions across the sea or in the islands of the sea. And this great Church of ours is doing comparatively little in the great work of extending the Kingdom of God throughout the world. You challenge the statement, and you tell me the Church is doing great things. We have not yet touched our opportunity. We have not touched the hem of the garment. We have not yet caught a glimpse of the world's needs. If we had we would measure up to our standards, we would not offer to God the meager sums we are now offering; we would not offer a man here, and another there, and another yonder.

The question of leadership is vital to the benevolent problem. Some of our bishops have too much work to handle. Any man acquainted with the records knows that no man can work things out successfully when he has too great a task. There are distances which no man can travel and do efficient work as a leader. The question of leadership is the question which has to do primarily with the question of developing a benevolent spirit in the Church of God. If we are short here, we fail. My business is to deal with the records of the Church. In order to do the work to which we are assigned we must work out some system. Every Church in Methodism stands upon the records. It is a record for last year and the year before and the year before that, as to its membership, its property, its ministerial support, its benevolent collection, and every Church that is running down, the story is told. Every Church that is making good, the story is told. And who makes that down-hill record? It is the same man. Who makes that up-hill record? It is the same man; wherever you send him, he uplifts it; wherever you send the other man, he drags it down. And this whole business of taking care of the benevolent interests of the whole

Church depends primarily upon leadership. If our men will put themselves to the business of the Church in a business-like manner to take care of the needs of God's Kingdom as expressed in the great connectional Boards, and if they have the right leadership, we can reverse the figures in a single year. Personal sacrifice has something to do with it, but do you mean to tell me that there is any degree of personal sacrifice represented in our Church when the average annual contribution from the Church for the eight great connectional Boards is fifty-three cents per capita? Can you preach sacrifice in the face of that record? In the Sunday schools we have twenty-three cents, making seventy-six cents in all; that is the total per capita from the Methodist Episcopal Church in the United States for the extension of God's Kingdom at home and abroad. Who can stand before a congregation and say that our people are a sacrificing people? We have lost the spirit of sacrifice in regard to world movements.

Now, turning to this big map; there is a black block there; there is a red line at the top of 53, which is the per capita contribution from the Church; there is a second red line at the top of 23, which is the per capita contribution from the Sunday school; if the area falls short, there is a white spot indicating that the per capita offerings from that area were not equal to the average from the Church. You will observe under the point of this rod, which I am using to point out things that the Methodist Episcopal Church must know if she is to save the world. All this territory (pointing to large sections of the United States) falls short of the Church's average. Where civilization is settled—between Philadelphia, Baltimore, and Chicago—over one million three hundred thousand Methodists reside; and yet, in this section each of the Episcopal Areas shows a white space in each of the black blocks upon this map. In that great Western country you will notice that the black block in that San Francisco area stands fourteen and a half inches high. On this great American continent of ours no section shows that record for our

57

eight great Boards except in the San Francisco area, and why? Not because they are richer than other places. I have traveled in every State and Territory of the United States from my boyhood to this day; I have gone over this continent, up and down, with my eyes open, and it is not because they are richer. There is not to be found on this American continent a single area where the idea of the Scriptural tithe has been so persistently and so carefully taught as in that San Francisco area. I say in plain words that the Church of God has drifted away from her obligation of the tithe for the extension of the Kingdom of God, and until she comes back to it or comes back to more than the tithe, she can not take this world for our God.

The red figures represent the average of ministerial support. Perhaps after this service is over you can look over the red figures and the black and make some study of them.

We are asleep on our job when it comes to the business of saving this sin-cursed world; we are alseep on our job when it comes to the business of redeeming America. Pardon the homely language, but you will understand it better; we are asleep on our job when it comes to discharging our responsibility to the various benevolent Boards of the Church. We are not doing for the extension of God's Kingdom that which is right in these days of financial prosperity.

Why the wheel? I can not explain it at length. Twelve dollars and four cents is the amount every member contributed for all our Church purposes in the year 1912; $5.32 of that $12.04 goes to ministerial support; $3.36 is spent in property matters, repairs, church buildings, payment of debts—mainly spent in increasing values. Two dollars and twenty-one cents is spent for current expenses—electric light, janitor, fuel, etc. Brethren of Methodism, that figure represents more than seven million dollars in a single year; but I must not tarry. The Church benevolent offering, the average in the Church represents fifty-three cents. The average from the Sunday school, twenty-three cents. The average from the woman's missionary societies, thirty-nine cents. Add your five dollars and thirty-two cents, your three thirty-six, your two twenty-one, your fifty-three cents, twenty-three cents, and thirty-nine cents—a complete circle—and you have twelve dollars and four cents within the center.

Now, brethren, the relation of the benevolent segment to the center of that circle is so small that every man of Methodism has occasion to fall before God in earnest prayer and ask for a larger vision of the world's need. As much for others as for ourselves! This part of the segment for us, and this part for others. I wish you would study that chart.

Now, when you study these charts and hand them down to Conferences and to districts and to charges, you begin to locate the responsibility of failure and success. An earnest young preacher, a graduate of a great university and a theological school, said to me, "What can I do to increase my support?" I said, "Let us see." I drew a wheel and he looked at his Minutes, and he gave me figures, and the rate in here was $17.52, of which he was receiving forty-six per cent for his salary, a little segment for property, a little segment for current expenses, and then just enough to be seen for benevolences. He said, "I will give it up." Now, brethren, if our preachers are in the business of preaching to get money for themselves and forget the claims of Calvary, we had better change preachers. It is a question of leadership, and until the men who lead realize that their business is to lead toward the cross they fail, and the business of waking this great Church of ours from her sleep is a tremendous task.

Why this Convention? This Convention is to map out a program, to mark out a line of procedure, and then upon our bended knees before God pray that His seal of approval may be upon the Convention program and its recommendations. The business of this Convention is to send every man home aflame with new enthusiasm, a determined enthusiasm that will keep up the struggle until the last man in the congregation shall have contributed something for the extension of the

Kingdom. How many of your people are paying? Answer me quickly, answer it in your mind. How many are contributing? How many are in line, how many of your people gave something in 1912? You say we have heroic, self-sacrificing people; yes, we have; but listen. Forty thousand dollars reported as the annual receipts for benevolent collections. "Good." Forty thousand dollars from sixty thousand well-to-do Methodists. Applause on the Conference floor for that is not right before God. We deal with totals. That is our trouble. We say: "O, we are doing gloriously! We are climbing up by tens and hundreds of thousands and millions." No, we are not! We are dealing in totals. Yes. But when you count totals, count also the members and the wealth and the increase of prosperity that comes with the passing days. We are moving—hear me. We are moving backwards in reference to the total budget that we spend for Church purposes.

What is our record? Forty-two per cent increase in property in eight years, but the increase in benevolent offerings only five per cent. Brethren, across the sea we have almost doubled our probationers' list in eight years, while in the homeland we have fifty-two thousand less probationers than at the beginning of that time. In those foreign fields they stand and knock at the door of the Church, and no man opens to let them in. We can not take care of the people who are offering themselves to the Church of God across the sea? Why? No money! Those of you who have attended the General Committee of the Church will understand when I say this. In China and India and the islands of the sea our missionaries to-day are anxiously waiting for the returns of 1913, to know whether it is retreat or advance for them. There are ten thousand men (9,943) on this American continent who are preaching to-day with less salary than $1,000 cash, including house rent, Conference Claimants, District Superintendents' and Bishops' Fund. There are 4,155 men no one of whom receives as much as $500 cash, house rent,

Conference Claimants, District Superintendents' and Bishops' Fund. They are waiting anxiously to know whether the great Church is coming to their rescue or not. The whole world is waiting to know. We have been playing with the job. Seventy-six cents per member from Church and Sunday school does not represent personal sacrifice on the part of our people.

I came from Philadelphia, through the charming farming district east of the Alleghenies, across the Alleghenies, through that prosperous, thrifty section of the country to Pittsburgh, where I was born; then across the farm lands and valleys to Ohio, where I was reared, to this spot in which Indianapolis is located, and, brethren, when I stop to think of the contrast between the civilization of these favored places with the civilization of our West land, on the coast, in the mountains and the plains, in the new and sparsely settled district, where they have everything to build— churches, schoolhouses, mills, factories, homes, everything— it seems to me so great—O! if God could only move the hearts of the people in this East land to give a tithe unto God, we would be able to save this world.

The Size and Complexity of the Organization to Be Moved.

S. Earl Taylor.

Last night a delegate of this Convention said to me, knowing that I had been on the Program Committee, "Taylor, what is it you men have up your sleeve?" If there is any inside plan for this Convention, I suspect that I know it, because from its beginning I have been with the Laymen's Missionary Movement as its general secretary or a member of the Executive Committee, and from the beginning I have been on this Program Committee, and I told him what we had up our sleeve, and I will tell you. I said: We shall not have a collection, and I suppose it will be the first time in Methodist history when a great Convention like this came together and was permitted to go away without a collection. In the second place, we do not have any cut-and-dried program, as we are in very great doubt as to what ought to be done; we have absolutely nothing up our sleeve, but we have deep down in our hearts, so that we feel it clear from the crown of our heads to the tip of our toes, that the time has come for the Methodist Episcopal Church to face her whole task and face it whole. This is in view of the facts presented to you by Dr. Hollingshead, that the whole Methodist Episcopal Church during the last four years decreased her offerings to all the benevolences. If you take the congregational collection alone, that great body of our people who met week by week decreased the offerings to these great benevolences $84,066. I am not speaking of the foreign missionary work alone, but to give you an illustration, because I have these facts more at my fingers' end, in the face of what Bishop Stuntz told you last night and what Dr. Oldham told you in the afternoon, in 1910, of the Spring Conferences nineteen decreased their offerings to Foreign Missions; the next year twenty-eight decreased their offerings to Foreign Missions; the next year, thirty-three Spring Conferences decreased their offerings to Foreign Missions. Of the Fall Conferences in 1910, twenty-nine decreased; in 1911, sixty; in 1912, but for the extraordinary efforts led by Bishop Lewis, we hardly know what would have happened, but twenty-eight decreased. We are now facing a condition like that, and we ought to bow before Almighty God and ask Him what we ought to do.

Now, a great general is never a pessimist. He knows the weakness of his own army, he knows the obstacles to be faced, the strength and weakness of the enemy, better than any pessimist does. It is my task here this morning to review with you some of the difficulties that are in the way of the Church, and if I have any right at all to speak upon this subject, it is simply because of the fact that for fourteen years you have set me to the task, first, of organizing an educational campaign, then a financial campaign under the Commission on Finance and the Board of Foreign Missions, and an inspirational campaign to give the Church higher standards, and if we have not learned how to do it, we have at least learned some of the difficulties in the way of doing it, and it is well to face them for a little while.

First of all, the size of the organization to be moved. A bright, clear-eyed minister of a Northern Minnesota Conference came to me and said: "Mr. Taylor, the trouble with this whole benevolent enterprise is that you do not keep our membership definitely in mind; you do not keep the gift-givers definitely informed. A large number of the members of my Church receive from the companies with which they are connected an annual statement, and the benevolent enterprises of the Church ought to see that an annual statement, giving definite information concerning receipts and expenditures, is sent with a personal letter to every giver to its causes." I said, "That will be a very fine thing to do," and then I took my pencil. I knew something about the cost of stenographic work and how long it takes an expert stenographer to do his work. He said, by the way, "Don't send circulars, but write a personal letter." I found it would take an expert stenographer fifty-nine years to write the letters, and that for envelopes, stationery, postage, and the rest, it would cost $131,-000 to do it. Another man said to me—many have said to me, "Why do you not send statements concerning these financial plans to all the official members?" Hundreds of pastors have sent in their lists. They have said, "Write to each one of our official members." By calculation I found it would take nine stenographers one year to write the briefest letters. It would cost more than $30,000 to do it. One of the great Boards of our Church has stood aghast at the proposal of the Commission on Finance to spend $15,000 for all the Boards for field work, printed matter, publicity, and all the rest. How, then, are you going to do your job? How will you move the Church? Even to address a letter to the pastors, Sunday school superintendents, Epworth League officers on our lists (and we do not have more than one-half of the Sunday school officers) would make a list of more than fifty-nine thousand names; and it would cost more than $5,000 to send out a personal letter.

We have another problem—the amount of money to raise, the size of the budget. I have a letter here, a sample rather of the letters we get, but only occasionally—perhaps they do not all tell us what is in the heart; this man did. He addressed it, "Gentlemen!" "Gentlemen: It is enough to take the grit and heart out of a fellow. Here you men are on fat salaries and spending large sums of money on office expenses, conducting everything in the most affluent manner. You would not touch with your little finger the burdens laid upon us. Just one turn of the hand and you demand more than we can beg and scrape and collect from our people in all the year. Your Brother in Christ." No, he is not a bad man. Some of these men do not understand the situation. You take a man in a small rural parish, the money comes hard and in small amounts, and tell him that we have to get $4,000,000, and it is a staggering amount. Now, how will you lift the Church up? Is it a staggering amount? It is the merest bagatelle compared with what we are doing as a Church. I have here the statement concerning the gifts of all Protestant Churches in the United States to all colleges, as estimated by the Church News Association—$260,000,000 a year. I have here a statement of the amount spent by the Methodist Episcopal Church for all colleges in the last twenty-four years, as far back as we have an accurate account on these lines. Since 1888 the Methodist Episcopal Church has spent for all colleges $188,144,242. Last year we spent for ministerial support, in round numbers, $16,000,000; for property, $10,000,000; for current expenses, $17,000,000. Huge sums of money, if you take the totals. The point I am making is, that if you deal with Methodism and take the totals you have to deal in millions. Our people must be trained to think in larger terms than ever before.

Turn from Church affairs to larger statistics, and sums are blindly staggering. We do not understand them. For army and navy the United States spends annually $217,-000,000, and Great Britain $334,000,000, and Germany a correspondingly large sum. If you come to education, New York City alone spends $85,000,000 annually, and on her educational plant she has spent $524,000,000. If you take the farm products of the Nation you pass out of all human understanding—$9,000,000,000 and more in farm products a year. You can take twenty-dollar gold pieces and pile them up a half-mile high, two miles high, seven miles high, one on top of another, to show the value of our farm products annually. Our increase in real estate alone in the last ten years is of almost incomprehensible proportions. In Minnesota alone, the Southern half of the State, a banker told us that the increase in real estate and farm products for two years had turned into the pockets of the people of that State a billion dollars in cash. In the face of these larger totals, $4,000,000 is pitiably small. And this Church, instead of thinking four millions, must think in terms of twenty and thirty millions if we are to do our job. The city mission enterprise alone ought to have the entire four million dollars. You can not handle city missions in New York City or Chicago on a budget of fifty or eighty thousand dollars. The West Side Branch of the Young Men's Christian Association in New York City spends $300,000 annually on its budget, and so wisely that they are commanding increased support of business men. We Methodists in New York City spend something like $89,000 for the entire work of our City Missionary Society.

In addition to all these facts, we have the complexity of organization to deal with. Somebody has said that the Methodist Episcopal Church is the greatest organization on earth; it is, and it is becoming one of the most complex organizations on earth. Take the local Church; the General Conference made the plan of having a Committee on Foreign Missions, Home Missions, Freedmen's Aid, and so on. These Committees have brought in independent reports, and when a new society was created the founders have had put in the Discipline certain little jokers to carry forward their institution; and if you will put on a chart the things to be done by the average preacher for the average Church, if they are faithful to the Discipline, you will find it is an utterly unworkable program. If you go to an Annual Conference, possibly there will be seventeen men to speak on the platform, representing great enterprises, but if you will sit down with the Conference Board of earnest men, who say that they ought to do something and begin to plan definitely to have an inspirational program; and then, if you sit down with the Home Missions and the Conference Board on Freedmen's Aid, you will find that if these Boards become efficient there will be a head-on collision in six weeks. The only thing that is feasible is to have them federate and have a campaign. Otherwise your district superintendents and pastors are facing the request we sent to Dr. Fisher in Baltimore; we requested him to have a campaign for a certain cause, and the district superintendent said that the representative of another cause had arranged for a campaign and they could not have two campaigns at the same time or in immediate succession. We are actually staggering our district superintendents and our preachers and the Church by multiplied appeals unrelated to each other, until our people don't know what to do. I was at a District Conference, where a fine district superintendent said, "Let us face the whole task, let us have the representatives of the great Boards come and present the task to us;" and being down nearer the Church—to the collection, I mean—they had the practical side of it. This is what happened: a representative of the Conference Claimants, one of the finest of their preachers, had been chosen to carry on a campaign, and he made a superb statement about that great cause, and he said, "We raised $50,000 last year in this Conference, and this year we want to raise a dollar a member, and we want, the first Sunday in November, to have a thorough campaign; and we will send you the literature, and the responsibility is on you pastors;" and it was, and they walked up to it as earnest men and they said, "We will do it." The college representative came along, and he said: "We raised a half million dollars for buildings; we must have a gymnasium, and we have got to have a great endowment fund, but I will not talk about it; but we must have a sustentation fund, and I want fifty cents per member, and we will send you the literature as soon as you get the Conference Claimants out of the way, and the responsibility is on you," and they voted it. And that was followed by the rural question, and it was shown how the rural ministers change—ninety out of a hundred—because they could not live under the conditions; and he said, "We must put into the hands of our district superintendent $8,000 and I move we raise so much per capita, and the responsibility is upon you." When that had been done, they came from the hospitals and the Brotherhood and they said, "The responsibility is upon the pastor to organize the Brotherhood;" and I was there prepared to represent the Freedmen's Aid and the Bible Society, and I didn't have the nerve to do it. An old college chum came to me and said: "This puts me out of business; I am going back and do what I did last year, and you fellows can write until you get black in the face." I said, "I want to take lunch with you." He was a fine fellow, but he was discouraged. I said, "The only way you will do this thing is to go to the Church with a whole program which the people can understand, and put it up to the people and have everybody give and give systematically, and you can do the whole business."

I want to deal with my final point, and do it frankly and with absolutely nothing in my heart but the interest of the Kingdom of Christ. If there was a vote taken here concerning the number of secretaries, I have no doubt that the vote would be for reducing the present number. Let us face the facts. I want to say in behalf of my brethren in secretarial relationship that if the Church will demonstrate that our offices are not needed, our resignations are in your hands immediately. We are not trying to save machinery nor ecclesiastical prestige, as Bishop McDowell phrased it, but we are trying to save men, and the machinery can go on the scrap-heap. But I notice in this hand-book the pictures of the General Conference officers, two pages here in number, and if you will open it you will see the official list of the secretaries—not all of them official, but taking in other things. In other words, just a handful of men to take charge of this great program of the Church. Now, what are the facts? There is a sensitiveness in the Church about secretaries, and justly so. Yet I undertake to say that, aside from the corresponding secretaries, we have not too many secretaries to handle this great enterprise. Why? I was examining the facts. I got the facts from the editor of the Year-book, and this is what he said: "There are in the Methodist Church three hundred and thirty-four ministers of the gospel set aside to handle the denominational charities and the outside organizations like the Anti-Saloon League. There are for all these enterprises three hundred and thirty-four men." And if the cost of these men—counting postage, stenographer, traveling expenses, house rent, and salary—if the total should be $2,000 a year, which I consider a modest amount, do you know it would cost us in a quadrennium $2,672,000 for this alone? And I want to say to you that the reason why we are giving more to non-connectional than to connectional causes is because there are three hundred and thirty-four men out after this, and in the great connectional enterprises you try to put in a common budget and have two or three or four men, and the Church says we are having too many secretaries. There was an editorial in one of our semi-official papers, presumably under the approval of a bishop, and this editorial says in substance, "We have too many secretaries in the Church, especially foreign missionary secretaries.'' Now, I went back over the records for a period of years and I found during the past quadrennium if you draw a line from the Mississippi River to the Coast, where other Boards have one or two men we had one man for Iowa, Illinois, Wisconsin, Kansas, Nebraska, Minnesota, and all the Pacific Coast, and one other man for the central area; and for the whole Atlantic seaboard, New York, Pennsylvania, and New England, all of that rich territory, we did not have a man. We have not that many now. We threw out a drag-net in an effort to get all the secretaries together, and what did we find? Four men, one of whom was a recording secretary. We found four men, plus some men among the colored people of the South. We have not that many now. If you threw out a drag-net to-day, you would get two white men in the North, and some of the men among the colored workers in the South. I undertake to say, gentlemen, that you can not lift this Church of ours up with that sort of a staff.

And now I come to what is in the back of your minds. You are saying: ''But you are not taking into account our connectionalism. You are not taking into consideration the fact of our pastors and our district superintendents.'' I am taking that into account, and I recognize that these men are our leaders, divinely appointed. We follow them as our leaders, and what happens? We are now trying to bring our Methodist Episcopal Church over from an old, antiquated financial system fully outgrown, to a new plan that takes organization methods, and the average pastor will tell you, if you go to him and say, ''You need forty men to conduct this campaign in your Church,'' he will say: ''My men are not ready for it, for they have not done this kind of thing. Can you help me lift them up? Come to my Church and we will try it.'' And when we have gone to a Church where the pastor had that help, the work has been done. We have in New York City, in one of the largest Churches, a condition where they came to us and said, ''If we could get forty of our big men in this Church, if we could get these men to set aside a day or two to work for this movement, we would succeed." They had Dr. Fisher up there twice, and myself two or three times, and finally they got lifted out. At first they met us with every objection. Finally they did it. The pastor said, when the achievement was reached: "We have done certain types of social work in this Church. We have had sewing circles, and put out a patronizing hand. But the biggest piece of social service ever done to this Church was when forty of our men went down on the East Side, among the poor people, and met them face to face and counseled with them." What was the result? Five thousand dollars increase over all they had ever given before, and two hundred new givers added to the list.

A cry comes up from the pastors and district superintendents, of whom there may be three hundred here, perhaps the largest number ever gathered togther. They are coming around and saying, "Can't you help us have a campaign over all our district, as in North Indiana? We want to do it, but must have help." If this great Church of ours is to swing from that old basis of an annual collection to the basis of correlation of forces, it will only be done by efficient business methods which business men know so well how to introduce. I am not pleading for a large increase in the number of field secretaries. But let us not be turned aside by any petty criticism. Let us face the facts squarely. Let us lay out a plan here that is adequate, and then go ahead and do the things in the name of Almighty God. The Methodist Episcopal Church is face to face with a supreme opportunity. It is not yet determined whether or not we will enter into the door. I talked with old Dr. Reed, over here in Michigan, who has been in the Methodist ministry longer than most of us have lived. I said, "As a result of your long life and ministry, what is the result to a Christian if he disobeys God deliberately, with full knowledge of the facts?" He said, "The man will die spiritually." I said, "Do you believe it?"

He said, "I know it." I said, "What will happen to a denomination if it sees that it is called of God to do a great task and deliberately refuses to do what God calls it to do?" He said, "It will die spiritually." Then he quoted that striking sentence of Bishop Fowler, at California Avenue, some years ago: "It is a solemn thing for an individual or a Church or a Nation to stand before the door opened in the providence of God and not enter that door. The shores of time are strewed with the wreckage of nations and of ecclesiastical organizations and individuals that have deliberately disobeyed Almighty God." And if ever God wanted a Church to go forward, He calls us now.

The Proposed Remedy.

J. B. TRIMBLE.

THIS screen with the views thrown upon it will give us variety. Holding in our thought the drift so startlingly presented by the first speaker this morning, and the size and complexity of the constituency to be moved, the task assigned to me seems to be rather difficult. I think that the wording of the topic is in my favor: Note, it is not a remedy, but *the* remedy proposed. Before answering the question, what the remedy is, may I say this? That in the light of what we have heard this morning, whatever the remedy be, if effective it must do two or three things: it must make clear the existing conditions referred to by Mr. Taylor by means of a great educational campaign. I take it that Secretary Taylor's remarks were based upon the conviction that if our people know, they will do. I wonder if that is debatable? Hardly, if we intelligently and persistently emphasize the *know*. You can not do that with the annual missionary sermon preached semi-quadrennially, and the monthly missionary concert of choir never observed, and the Sunday schools of our great Church organized into missionary societies in part. If we find it difficult to instruct our young people

71

in mathematics, spending ten minutes a month or two hours a year, then how can we expect to have a benevolent Church in the history of to-morrow in the way we have been conducting an educational campaign? There is a better way of doing it than that. How succeed? "By the impartation of facts," said the second vice-president of a district Epworth League in the West some time ago, who was succeeding marvelously. She was a doctor. She said, "By the impartation of facts, and if you will allow me to express it medically, I first apply them externally and then apply them internally, and keep at it eternally." Now, let us look at this chart a moment. The General Conference action of 1912 provided that a full month be given to educational preparation before the every-member canvass, and it assigned intervals during the year at which the various causes should be presented. I said to a pastor some time ago that under the rule he ought to preach on missions once in three months. He said, "When would I preach the gospel if I did that?" It also provided that "Provision be made in every Church for special sermons and inspirational addresses and systematic instruction and stewardship."

Second, the remedy if effective ought to be comprehensive enough to cover all Church finance. Any Board that forgets the interests of other Boards cuts the nerve of its success, and ought to. The Boards that forget the base of supplies and get all the money they can regardless of how you take care of the local budget, are on the wrong tack and ought to fail. Any remedy to be effective ought to cover all Church finance. Look at this chart. When each Church provides for subscriptions for benevolences and current expenses—that is the result of the General Conference covering the whole field. Third, the remedy must deal with the many—not only with all Church finances, but with the people who contribute. I think it ought to deal very effectively with the people mentioned by a speaker yesterday, who have unusual capacity for controlling their benevolent emotions and never contribute anything at all. What are the real facts about that? Two-thirds of the people in the Methodist Church are not in benevolent activity at all. I sat at dinner yesterday with a prominent layman of Indiana, and he said, "In our Church under the old plan we only had one hundred and sixty-seven out of a membership of six hundred." Ninety-six in a Kansas Church out of a membership of six hundred. I talked to a group of men in Iowa, pressing them to adopt a business system in Church finance. A leading layman said: "Why, we are in debt here; all our people now are giving all they can. What would you do in a case of that kind?" I said, "You have this argument—are they all giving?" The secretary read how many were giving, and found they had a hundred and fifty-six on the pay-roll for any cause whatever. "How many members have you?" "Eleven hundred." Eleven hundred members, and a hundred and fifty-six on the pay-roll. It is absolutely necessary to bring into activity not to burden the faithful few that are giving now, but to interest every member so he will give. One million of our Church members are in benevolent activity. You add another million in the next year, a half a million at two cents a week, a quarter of a million at five cents a week, a quarter of a million at ten cents a week, and what would you have? Two million four hundred and seventy thousand dollars added to our benevolences. That is not theory, that is possible. Every Church that has introduced the new plan understands that it can be done.

Look again at the chart. See if it would be possible to arrange a personal canvass if the Churches support it. Would that take in the children? I asked a group of men how old a girl or boy ought to be before he began to contribute to the Church budget. One said fourteen, another said seven, but the best answer I had was this, that as soon as a boy or girl is old enough to chew gum he is old enough to help support the Church. I think when they commence to chew gum they ought to tithe their gum money and help support the Church. Let us think of the educational effect upon the boys and girls of our Churches. Do not let the boys go around talking about "father's Church" and "mother's Church" and "father's dominie;" link them up with the great work.

We must build again on a business system. I was down in Oklahoma a little while ago, at one of the stations on the Rock Island road, where there is a colored gentleman who acts as porter and calls trains. A man asked him, "Is this the Rock Island System?" "This is the Rock Island Railway; they have no system." He was slandering the Rock Island. That is not true so far as the Rock Island System is concerned, but it could be said about a good many Methodist Churches and you would not have to take it back. The plan must be built on system. That is, we must guard against money that has been subscribed for light, fuel, and music going over into New York, into Dr. Nicholson's budget for Educational Society; money that has been subscribed for preacher's salary being sent to Cincinnati, to the Freedmen's Aid Society. We must not get the money mixed up. Sometimes money subscribed for the Freedmen's Aid may go into different channels from what it is intended for. I knew of a case last autumn where four hundred dollars subscribed for benevolences got into the ministerial budget and was spent for ministerial demands. So we must have a business system.

Let us look at another chart. Two distinct superintendents in the local Church; two treasurers in each Quarterly Conference, to avoid the payment of heavy interest. The plan, to be effective, must take in the whole congregation, bring all the Church members into benevolent activity, and have them giving on a regular, systematic basis. Talking to a group of men in a Western city, I exhorted them to get the habit, and said that to get a habit you must participate frequently. The question was raised as to whether a man could ever form a tobacco habit by smoking a cigar once a year. "Why, no," one layman said; "that would make a man sick every time." Another bright fellow spoke up and said: "That is what is the matter with you preachers. You only present a benevolence once a year, and it makes us sick every time."

Then, fifthly, the plan to be effective ought to be protective in its character. Look at that next chart, that tells of that protective General Conference legislation. It is advised that no cause not recommended by the Conference Commission on Finance be admitted to the pulpits of our Churches for presentation and financial appeal. Let me read you an answer that came in to Bishop Cranston's questionaire that will emphasize that: "We have during the past year had appeals from and have contributed to the following: Anti-Saloon League, Old People's Home, the Orphanage, Children's Home, Old Ladies' Home, Young Men's Christian Association, the Training School in Cincinnati, a German Methodist institution, Mission in Russia, a German Mission Society, and one or two more; and next Sunday we are requested to make an appeal for a Protestant Orphanage in Jerusalem, but I draw the line." Any plan must, if it is protective, protect our Churches from being foraged on by non-official appeals as they have been in the past.

I wish I had time to spend on that, but I must hasten. One other thing it must do. It must minister to the social aspect. Let me give you an incident in connection with the Church that Mr. Taylor referred to. Some of those laymen that made that canvass in that prominent city Church—all of them—were at prayer-meeting on Wednesday night, which was unusual. This was their experience: they said, "We have met people who have been members of the Church for ten years whom we never before knew to be members of it." What is the plan? Here is a summary of the new financial plan for the local Church: an adequate educational campaign; a personal canvass to bring all into activity, a canvass of all the members and supporters of the Church annually; subscriptions on the weekly basis; uniform collecting devices, such as the by-pocket envelope, and two treasurers; quarterly remittances, or probably monthly.

This is the plan. Will it work? Will this new plan work? After all, that is the test of the whole business. Has it been tried and found successful? Here is a chart. "In single Churches in a whole city, in the district, in the Conferences, in the denomination." I want to show you, first, a chart of the most difficult thing in Methodism, the rural Church. I came from my Conference the other day, where motions were made to sell two churches that I had struggled with years ago when I was on the district. I dedicated one of them when the thermometer stood at one hundred and over. Brothers, we simply must get something that will take care of the rural Church if we are going to take care of Methodism. We simply must take care of the country proposition. Here is a rural Church in Iowa [shown on screen]; under no system at all they had 120 members, 25 Sunday school scholars, no Epworth League, and raised $220 for all expenses, salary and all. Under this new plan they raised $900 for current expenses, $90 for Missions, $40 for the Woman's Foreign Missionary Society; they have 150 members, 60 Sunday school scholars, and an Epworth League of 20, and when they get accustomed to the collar they will raise $1,800.

Look at this city mission Church, where there is no one that owns his home; eighty-five per cent contributed. Look at that other Church, in Denver, Colo.; the only thing that Church had was a deficit at the end of the year. They introduced this plan, and out of 186 members they had 182 contributing, and, thirty days before the year closed, all obligations met; the whole congregation went on a furlough. Wouldn't you pastors like to belong to a Church like that?

Look at this city Church, in Crawfordsville, Ind.; under the old plan all they did was $15,000. They made an every-member canvass about eleven months ago, and the number of subscribers was doubled and the increase in current expenses and benevolences was twenty-three per cent, with ten

tion. There are laboring men who spend eight or ten hours every day in heavy toil; there are pastors who are as indefatigable as any merchant or mechanic. So also the true district superintendent will be as diligent as any man in his district. Now, if we are in danger of considering our district superintendency as a sort of sinecure, this new financial plan offers a means of regenerating the whole system, for there is in it a job big enough for any district superintendent in our Church. It seems to me that this is one of the principal tasks of the district superintendent of to-day, and if I were going to put this in operation on my own district, I should begin very early in the year and familiarize myself completely with all the details of this financial plan, and by the middle of the year at least, I should, with this in view, have a reorganization in each of the Quarterly Conferences of the district. That is not so difficult a task as may be supposed. It is more difficult to get it worked out after it is adopted. We have to admit that. I know of a district where the financial plan was adopted in forty-three Quarterly Conferences, and in all of them there were only two dissenting votes. The laymen of our Church are ready for this plan. And if the preachers and the district superintendents will do their work faithfully and well, we can revolutionize the financial system of our Church in the next five years.

After this campaign has been introduced, it would seem to me that a simultaneous movement should be made throughout the district. I believe that we are connectional in our principles, but we are congregational in our practices. We do not make the best use of our connectionalism. It seems to me that every district superintendent should set apart one month for an educational campaign after the plans have been adopted. On my district, for instance, this year we shall carry on our educational campaign in February. Every pastor on my district will be asked to preach a sermon on the first Sunday of February and call the attention of the people to the literature that has been provided. After this careful campaign, on the first Thursday in March the every-member canvass on every charge on my district will be made. That is my conception. It can be done. I have an idea that the district superintendent might well go to a weak charge, where it is difficult to have this plan adopted and put into operation, and meet with the Finance Committee and the solicitors and instruct them how to go about their business, and, if necessary, go with them from house to house to put this thing on a firm basis.

I simply want to call your attention to one thing not touched on by any speaker, as to the results of this work on a given district. If the district superintendent wants his pastors to have the largest efficiency in their work, he will spend a good deal of time in releasing them from the depression of financial necessity. I do not know how it is in the Church at large, but on my district one pastoral call out of every three is a financial call. The pastor must raise the district superintendent's claim often by house-to-house visitation. And the episcopal claim in the same way, and the worn-out preachers' fund—or must supplement the public collection for that purpose. He must raise the benevolences, and often raise his own salary. One-third of the pastoral efficiency of our Church is in bondage to financial necessity. It is no wonder that in many of our great Conferences we have not added members for the last twenty years. I was in one of the great Conferences of the Middle West recently and heard the bishop say to one of the largest Conferences of Methodism, "You men have not succeeded in adding more than an average of one hundred and fifty members in your great Conference in the last ten years." I believe that much of this is due to the fact that our ministers have to give the time they ought to give to real pastoral service, to the raising of budgets. And I say to you, brethren, that if we can eliminate this thing from our Churches and free our preachers from the bondage of this financial burden, we shall set them free to go into the field and preach the gospel and minister to the sick and talk to the boys and girls about their loyalty to the Church and to Jesus Christ, and to do the work for which the Christian minister was ordained—to teach and preach the gospel, and visit from house to house, as they ought to be able to do. I believe that this is the solution of many of our great problems, and I pray God that the time may soon come when all through our Methodism this, the only financial plan now recognized by the General Conference, shall be adopted and operated.

Meeting the Demand of the Hour.

U. G. LEAZENBY.

I HAVE been sitting here these hours and my heart has been strangely stirred, and yet again and again I have found myself saying, "O Lord, who is sufficient for this task?" and here is the thought that discourages me, that this great Methodist Episcopal Church with its three and a half million members has only about one out of every five who is intelligently and aggressively interested in the task of spreading the Kingdom of God to the ends of the earth. How pitiable the condition of an army in which only one man who took the oath of loyalty to the flag was ready to fight! Or worse than that, if one able-bodied soldier was compelled to carry four other able-bodied soldiers, to care for them, and to provide their food and equipment! That is exactly the condition of the Methodist Episcopal Church. How to get these four who are not interested in the task is, if I understand it, the real purpose of this Convention.

In the first place, let me say that the every-member canvass to which reference has been made, and of which specific illustrations have been given, will do the task as certainly as I hold up my hand and declare that I believe in God the Father Almighty, Maker of heaven and earth, and the rest of the Apostles' Creed. I believe that this every-member canvass, if carried intelligently and prayerfully to every member of the Church, will solve the problem. It will solve the problem

6

of financing the Church at home, and we will never successfully finance the Church away from home until we have
financed the Church at home. Financing the Church of the
living God is like the religious life: it begins at home; and I
repeat that our first task is to finance the Church at home.
That being true, the every-member canvass, introduced in a
district and carried to the leaders of the Church in the district, will accomplish it, I have no doubt. It will rehearten
the Church. I could stand here and give illustration after
illustration of Churches that were disheartened being re-
heartened. There are men who are not stingy; they are interested in the Kingdom of God, but they have stood so long
under the crushing financial burden and come up so often at
the end of the year to meet the deficit for coal and light and
other things, that they have become discouraged and disheartened, and I say that one of the valuable things about this
plan is that it reheartens the Church. Then, it succeeds in
getting children into the Church. I could tell you of Church
after Church in the district where I am superintendent where
that thing has been proved. Now, gentlemen, I want to say
that this will do the task, provided it has a fair test. Here is
the question, and I tremble lest we may go home from this
great Convention with our hearts stirred with enthusiasm
and yet, because our hands have not been strengthened, practically forgetting this Convention as we have forgotten many
others. Something practical is the thing we need in this
practical age of ours. District superintendents, pastors, and
laymen will go away from this Convention taking one of
three attitudes toward this great plan.

The first attitude is that of opposition. I have met just a
few who have opposed the plan. If a man coolly and deliberately, if an institution or an organization cold-bloodedly lies
down before the chariot of progress, then it becomes a question of stopping the chariot or running over the individual
and breaking his bones, and in that event I think we had

better run over him as gently as possible. If he is not too old, the bones will knit and he may walk all right afterwards.

Then, the next possible attitude is one of indifference, and that I fear—just letting this new financial plan alone. It is a tragedy, it is an awful thing to be on the wrong side of a right issue. I take my hat off to the memory of Robert E. Lee for many things, but unfortunately that great heart was on the wrong side of a right issue.

I think of two other men; one was neutral concerning the great question of right and wrong. He said: "Let it be voted up or let it be voted down." But God had brought from the Kentucky hills a man who was born almost as poor as the Son of Mary, who was strong enough to be on the right side of a right issue. Here is a right issue. Let us be on the right side.

DILLON BRONSON.

JESUS said, "When you give a dinner, do not invite your rich friends or relatives or those who can return the invitation, but call in the homesick, the friendless, and the stranger," and this commandment we seem to have overlooked. I desire this morning to help you use the lower part of your bifocal lenses to study for a moment the matchless opportunity of the hour right here on our doorstep. I yield to no man in my enthusiasm for what we call foreign mission work. I have made three journeys to the Orient, and have seen as much of the non-Christian world as any man in our denomination. My ambition now is to make another three years' tour of the fields across the sea and to return the best-informed man on this work in the Church. However, we must admit that *the* great emergency is here at home, and in many respects America is now the banner mission field of the world. Some one has said that if we could make New York City completely Christian from center to circumference, it would do more for the furtherance of the Kingdom throughout the whole earth than if we sent every pastor in America to the foreign field. A few days ago we read in the papers that a desperate effort to make Confucianism the State religion in China is being fathered by a gentleman who obtained his degree of Ph. D. in Columbia University. If New York had been a Christian city while this young man was a student there, he would certainly not now be engaged in furthering Confucianism. The gathering of the nations on our shores is providential, a direct answer of God to the slowness of the Church in responding to the twelfth commandment, "Go make disciples of all nations." If we give these new Americans absent treatment only and have no relation to them except the financial nexus, often pampering them by paying their bills, the Republic and the Kingdom will surely suffer.

Not long ago I congratulated one of our pastors on the fact that so many Poles, intelligent men from the land of Chopin, Copernicus, and Paderewski, lived about his Church. "Now," I said, "get them into your vestry; give them lessons in English and American history, and gradually lead them to see what Protestantism means." With a sad look on his face, he answered, "I hate all those foreigners, and am only waiting for an opportunity to move my family from that neighborhood." Of course, he only needed to close his eyes to be dead. The Church he served was dead, and ought to have been covered up in order not to be an offense to the community. Here are these people, who are American by choice and not by accident, coming to us out of every tribe and tongue and kindred, one hundred at least every hour, day and night, reproducing themselves about seventeen times as fast as native Americans; and we need them, because they are not afraid to work. Without them and their spades the industries of the land would surely languish. What we need is honest, industrious men who are willing to do the most disagreeable kind of work. They are not the scum of Europe. They are not common or unclean. But are virile men in the years of greatest efficiency and the enormous expense of rearing them from infancy has been met by other peoples. If they are ignorant as far as books are concerned, they are ambitious that their boys learn to read and write and make good. Green foreigners they may be, but not so dangerous as some overripe Americans. When they degenerate and become drunkards and libertines, it is because of our neglect—because they are herded together like cattle where saloons are more numerous than drygoods and provision stores; where they do not get the English language, which they must have to win their way, and where the children, living in an atmosphere of American irreverence, soon learn to despise the "old man" and the "old woman."

These people need friendliness, neighborliness; they need assistance in finding decent places in which to live. They need to be encouraged to buy a little land, or a share or two in some good industrial corporation, for there is no other such cure for anarchistic notions. They must know English, and learn the things for which our Government stands. And must be told the real meaning of the Christian Church, which is the "union of all who love in the service of all who suffer." We have not dealt with the foreign-born as with the home-born. We have often exploited and robbed them, and nearly always neglected them. We have too often attempted to proselyte these people directly. We have gone at them hammer and tongs to win members for a Methodist *Statistical* Church. They need friendship. And if we show by our disinterested service that our religion is better than theirs, they will be won in due time. It would be better for many of us to have a degree of F. S.—Friend of the Stranger—than D. D. If we are to be the salt of the earth, we must be rubbed in where the corruption is. We are of no use while snugly barreled. The hope of the Republic is in righteousness rubbed into the life of common people everywhere. What shall it profit Methodism or any other ism if we gain our own puny little soul and lose the whole world?

MILITANT METHODISM.

Frank C. Evans.

I have been asked to tell you not how to do it, but how we did it, and the only excuse I offer for talking about ourselves is to present to you a concrete case and not a theory, and to prove to you and to stand before you as a witness that the every-member canvass will do the job.

In putting the every-member canvass on in the First Methodist Episcopal Church of Crawfordsville, we first took it up with our Financial Board and got their complete endorsement, and they appointed a committee of five to have complete charge of the every-member canvass in every detail. We first inaugurated a campaign of education covering fully a month. Each Sunday we had appropriate addresses from the pulpit by laymen and our pastor, winding up on the last Sunday before the canvass with a sermon on stewardship. We decided in our Board meeting that we would make this canvass in one day. We would not let the question of finances be dragged along throughout the entire year and spread its pall over our Church operations. It may not be practical to do the task in many Churches in one day, but I undertake to say that in ninety Churches out of a hundred it can be done more successfully in one than in any other given number of days. The enthusiasm engendered by getting a large body of men to work at one given task at one given time has more power than anything else you can do.

Now, we decided to make this campaign with fifteen teams of four men each, selecting the real leader as captain of each team. We did not need sixty men to make this canvass, but sixty men needed to make the canvass. In this way we enlisted the co-operation of men whom we could not have gotten into the Church work in any other way or through any other door; and when that day's work was over, we had discovered leaders and developed men that we did not dream we had. They are some of the best and most stalwart men in our congregation to-day.

Now listen, men. We did not go at this thing with any brass band or trumpets, or anything of that kind, but we went at it just as you laymen go at your business affairs. We took from a list from our official records the name of every member of our Church of school age, and the greatest trouble we had was to keep from overlooking somebody. We took that member's name and from the Church treasurer's record made up a card index of every member of our congregation. On that card index we put the name of the member, his street address, what he gave last year, both for current and benevolent expense, and what the committee thought he ought to give this year. That index was an information card. Now, these fifteen captains were coached to the last minute as to how this campaign was to be made. It was not a financial campaign. It developed in the end that the finances were really a by-product of the campaign. The real campaign was stirring up and revitalizing the men who had long been dormant in Church work; and through this campaign they were stirred up until to-day they are the very strongest and best men we have to lean on in our congregation.

ROBERT E. JONES.

IT is not a financial program or scheme that we need so much as a conviction of the need and a sense of our personal obligation, with emphasis on personal. It is not method we need, but motive. Men do not so much give by plan as by conviction.

If we faced the task before us with the consciousness that we are His and with the acknowledgment that what we have is His—that what we have is His, whether little or much—we would not need a Board to discover wealth and to blast it from our pockets by the latest methods and schemes, but our Board would become a Board of experts for spending the funds in hand the best possible way. As it is now, half of our energy is consumed in raising funds. If the men in Methodism would give to God one-tenth of their earnings, which is His and not our own, we could underwrite in five years every pressing need of world-wide Methodism. Approved business methods in our financial plan, and the zeal of a life insurance agent in pushing the plan.

An *Advocate* in every home to inform our membership on the world-wide program of the Church, the inviting doors that are open, and the marvelous results considering our resources.

Take home the inspiration and the information of this Convention.

Consecration: not an utter self-abandonment in fatal hopelessness, but a complete surrender to Him to be of the largest possible service, as He may direct.

> "Our wills are ours, we know not how;
> Our wills are ours, to make them Thine."

On our knees we should get a new conception of Christ's plan for the salvation of the world. The Lord Christ, nineteen hundred years after He completed the plan in detail for the world's redemption, sits sad-hearted as we go slowly about the task of the world's redemption. In prayer and supplication we should approach the throne of God in the interest of the great task that is before us. The physician of Tuskegee Institute, driving out one afternoon in his machine, took up in his car an old colored lady and said to her, "Mother, are you praying for me?" She responded, "Lord, child, I can not pray for myself unless I pray for you." So it is —we can not pray aright unless we pray for the other man. It is not by our might, but by His spirit that our opportunities will be met.

Go up and possess the land, for we are able.

S. R. SMITH.

MEN of Methodism, I come as a layman to talk especially to laymen. What I have to say, I think, will have the hearty co-operation of the ministers and the bishops. You have had line upon line, precept upon precept. You hardly know where to begin. Let me say this one thing: Go home and tell how Christ was with you here in this great gathering in Indianapolis; how you heard more than two thousand men, full of the Holy Spirit, upon their feet singing:

> "All hail the power of Jesus' name,
>   Let angels prostrate fall;
>   Bring forth the royal diadem,
>   And crown Him, crown Him, crown Him,
>   Lord of all."

As I heard that sung a year and a half ago by that great assembly in Minneapolis, I felt that I must give all that was in me to carry His message. How shall you do it? When you go home, bring out a surprise prayer-meeting for your pastor. He will welcome it. One man on the telephone fifteen minutes will increase your membership at that meeting perhaps fifteen per cent. Four men on the telephone for half an hour will double your meeting, and you will have a grand time and the Spirit of God will be in that meeting. I know it because I have tried it. I know that then you will think upon these precepts and these examples that you have had here over and over, and the every-member canvass will be set up. Then you will reach your Church membership. Then you will come across that blessed experience that I had in getting acquainted with the members of our Church. I said to a man: "We want you. What will you give for foreign missions?" He said, "Here is $5." "How much will you give per week?" "Five dollars." I said, "No, my brother, we want you to bring ten cents a week. We want you. The money is good, but we want you." I tell you, men, the every-member canvass will lead you to a house-to-house canvass, and you will think of these words, "God so loved the world that He gave His only begotten Son, that whosoever believeth in Him might not perish but have everlasting life." Friend, that is in your heart. You are thinking of that everlasting life. Don't forget the commandment, "Love the Lord thy God with all thy heart and soul and mind and strength, and thy neighbor as thyself." We want this work among the men of the Church to get the neighbors in to enjoy the blessed spirit of the Holy Ghost as we enjoy it, and remember that Christ died for us.

O. F. HYPES.

IN the little Methodist Church in the Ohio city where I am a member, out of something more than two hundred members who gave to the various benevolent enterprises of the Church, seventy-seven gave the same or more than they gave to themselves. This was brought about by prayer and personal presentation, and the work is only begun. The pastor of that Church, when he receives the apportionments handed down by the Commission on Finance, hangs them up, I think, in his study, and his goal and the goal of his Church is the standard adopted by the General Conference at Baltimore.

Let me call your attention to a booklet which I have been reading, "The Methodist Man's Burden," by Dr. Brewster. It is a message which I believe every man in this Convention should read while he is here, with the thought that it will possibly be of service in solving the problems which we have come here to help solve. In another Church that has been struggling along twenty-five years under a great debt, by means of the every-member canvass and weekly giving and the duplex system, that debt was soon wiped out, and Bishop Anderson came up and burned the old Church mortgage and gave that Church a commission for deeds of larger usefulness, so that pastor goes to Conference with all benevolences on the up-grade.

In adopting this new financial system, has it ever occurred to you that we are after all in that system just getting back to Wesley? You know what he said in his rules given to those united societies, "All at it, always at it, altogether at it." "All at it," the every-member canvass; "always at it," every week; "altogether at it," the benefits that come from the united effort. After all, in my humble opinion, no plan will of necessity long succeed that has not for its controlling theme and purpose the love of God dwelling fully in our hearts and in the hearts of our fellow-men. After working at all the material plans presented, we must look to Him who controls the thoughts and purposes of men and ask Him not only for the gifts, but ask Him for ourselves. Methodism so attuned will not only make America Christian in fact, but it will send the message around the world.

JOHN T. STONE.

It is my great joy to be a member of a down-town Church with all the problems that distinctively characterize such a congregation. The Church to which I belong is within one block of a brewery, which occupies a very large block of ground, and it has slopped over into the adjoining block, but we are hoping in Baltimore to slop the whole thing over pretty soon. Within two blocks there are several acres of ground occupied by railroad tracks, with the accompanying factories and warehouses. Within another block there is city market, and for four blocks we have on both sides of the street a congregation of saloons, pawnshops, and other places such as you would find in that kind of a neighborhood. All around the church there are colonies of Negroes, Jews, Italians, and other foreigners. In that great area which I have thus briefly described this is the only Protestant Church. Other Methodist Churches existed in the years gone by, scattered here and there. They have closed up. This old church, which is eighty years old, is still there; and, please God, she will always be there. Years ago when I was converted at that altar, that church was the center of the parish. For blocks around, almost every house was occupied by a Methodist family attending that Church. Now all is changed. What has kept the old Church alive? As the years have passed and the people have died off or moved away, the congregation has dwindled

91

and dwindled; but the Sunday school has kept going, and it is the missionary spirit that has kept the Sunday school alive. In that Sunday school every child has been taught to give, and to give systematically. The monthly missionary meeting has never been abandoned. A whole Sunday afternoon once a month is given to it, and as these children have grown up they have formed the old guards, sons and daughters of the old families who have kept the Church alive. Until 1910 the Church was so frequently considered as a hopeless proposition that now and then a suggestion was made for selling; but yet the Sunday school held on, and the children held on, and the missionary spirit held on. In 1910 this every-member campaign was taken up, and we called the Official Board together and said: "Here is hope for our Church; let us adopt this plan; let us go through our membership, distant as that membership is, and let us rally them around the old Church." That was the beginning. There were old ladies living at a long distance from our church who rarely came to service, and it was pathetic but beautiful to see how they welcomed our official men, going out two by two. Sometimes they said: "The pastor came once in a while; we know he has a great many people to care for, but in all the years you men are the only ones who have come to see me."

Now, what is the result financially? I wish I had time to tell the whole story. To me it is one of the great stories of my life. Briefly: In the three years that have elapsed our budget has increased for current expenses, our minister's salary has increased, and our Sunday school has grown until it is almost overflowing. It is a problem where to house the children. Our Church membership has grown from two hundred to three hundred and thirty-five—two hundred and thirty-five contributing, and there is a revival going on now, and I almost wish I were there instead of here.

THE FORCES AND THE FIELD—A SURVEY.

ALEXANDER BENNETT.

THE story I shall attempt to tell you is no miracle, nor anything that we can boast about. In the State of Nebraska, out on the prairies, one hundred miles west of Omaha, there is a little city named York—some seven thousand people. Six years ago Bishop McDowell appointed me to the pastorate. On the field I discovered a well-organized Church, fine property, and a membership of eight hundred. Why I should be sent there began to be a question to my soul, but, looking over the whole field, it became a conviction that maybe these good people needed a vision of the whole world. The Lord helped me to get the vision on their hearts somewhat, and the result is something like this: the first year I challenged our good people to contribute a full, round one thousand dollars for home and foreign missions. The year before they had given slightly less than eight hundred dollars, meeting in full their apportionment as they had met all their benevolent apportionments faithfully for many years. They accepted the challenge and paid it. The second year, I said, "Brethren, let us take a missionary, a single man somewhere, and contribute seven hundred and fifty dollars for foreign missions." They said, "All right," and so we took a man in West China. We found he was a married man at the end of the year, so it would require about $950 to support him that year. The third year we did it. The fourth year we found a man in India whose support was rather precarious, and we contributed, in addition to China, five hundred dollars for the support of an Indian missionary. The fifth year the Woman's Foreign Missionary Society thought they ought to have something doing, and they undertook the full support of a medical missionary in China. By the end of the fifth year they thought I had a missionary up my sleeve every time I came home from anywhere. Brethren, the third year before the last we endeavored to cultivate among our people giving by the double envelopes, just asking them to use them, if you please, without any more systematic form than our regular apportionment to members. They began to use them. At the end of the fifth year they let me go. But the question arising, What shall we do about all these missionaries and all this business we have? it was solved by the double envelope. We had a plan made for an every-member canvass just before my removal, and it was thoroughly worked. And this year the new pastor has undertaken it, and two weeks ago a thorough canvass was made; forty men went throughout the Church membership, and came home shouting victory. That is what the daily papers told me when I read them down in Kansas.

And so this business works. It will work in Kansas; we are at it now. I believe it will work anywhere, although, of course, Kansas will set the pace if you will give us a chance.

THOMAS LIPPY.

I COME from a modest Church in the modest city of Seattle. I want to account for this modesty in our Pacific Northwest. We have a great number of real estate men, a great number of other business and professional men, largely immigrated from the East to our Pacific Northwest. And you know that all that Northwest country is made up of the fellows of push and energy and modesty from the East. I was given a subject, and tried to prepare something along that line. Last night I was asked to tell you what we were doing and how we were doing it in the Northwest, changing my line of thought, because I was not going to speak of our modest Church in Seattle or of other things along that line, but I may give you before I close just a few thoughts along the first subject. Our Church has a membership, as represented in September, of 2,040 members. I want just to say this, that under a number of pastors, one following another—splendid pastors—the Church has increased and grown and is a strong Church and is being better organized every day for real, definite work. We have all the usual organizations, and

I think all of them are doing good work, a splendid work. You are more especially interested here this morning in the report along missionary and financial lines. I want to give you briefly what we are doing along the missionary line. Our Woman's Foreign Missionary Society, in addition to its usual work, has a representative in the field. The Church has a missionary pastor. In addition to this, supported either by the Church or by individuals, are fourteen workers along distinctive lines. There are nine students being supported in the Pekin University. And mark this: one of those Chinese students in the University of Pekin is supported by a Japanese class in our Seattle Sabbath school.

Now, along financial lines, we early adopted the duplex envelope system. It has proven a great success with us. Back of the duplex envelope system we have had for a number of years a splendid financial secretary, an enthusiastic tither, a woman of rare tact and deep spiritual life, who has been doing our individual or personal canvass through the Church largely. The result has been, up to the present year, about sixty-five per cent of our total membership of 2,040—that is, between twelve and thirteen hundred members—giving weekly through this duplex envelope system. Our benevolences have increased about thirty-three per cent in the last two years. I would like to tell you a lot more along these lines. Just before I left for this Convention, the stewards of the Church were called together and decided to make a definite member-to-member canvass.

W. F. WHELAN.

WHEN the Laymen's Missionary Movement began its operations in the United States, Buffalo was chosen as its first city. When the inspirational addresses had been made and the leaders left us, we were without a program, but upon us was laid this thought, that if Buffalo fell down the Lord's work in other places might be impeded, so it was our privilege to lead the cities of the United States. The first thing we did in every committee meeting we had, whether held in one of the city clubs or churches, whether two men or a dozen were present, from the time of the inception of the Laymen's Missionary Movement to the last meeting, we have never conducted one thing without surcharging every one of our meetings with vital prayer. If my time does not permit me to say anything else, let me say that if we are going to do the Lord's work, we must do it in the Lord's way or we won't do it at all. We next took as a text that whatever the Churches had been giving for themselves and whatever for the work in this country and whatever for work in other countries, now we would ask our Churches to come up to the goal. We went to our Churches, Church by Church, and asked the leading men to adopt this resolution: "Realizing the privilege of sharing in the evangelization of the world in this generation, we place as our goal, As much for others as for ourselves"—mark you, goal, not pledge—"and we pledge thereto our selves, our money, and our prayers," and as a result the Lord led the Methodist Churches of Buffalo, which had raised $7,000 for Foreign Missions the year before, to raise $17,000 the next year. Brethren, you saw up here on the canvas a part of my speech—that Richmond Avenue Church, which had been giving $1,100 for Foreign Missions, went to $5,000, then to $5,500 and to $6,200 —but Dr. Trimble should have told you what it cost our other Church finances to give so much money to Foreign Missions: we had a small parsonage when we started, and we have a $10,000 one now; we did not have the right kind of a Sunday school room, and we have an $11,000 one now; we had a $40,000 mortgage, but, praise God, it is all underwritten now. Men of Methodism, if you want to get rid of that load, get an objective big enough and you will lift it.

Let me speak of two things. O! in the name of Christ, do not let us try to use any sort of plan or scheme unless with consecration and prayer to Him that we do His work in His way. In the next place, do not leave this Convention to go out to raise money, but leave this Convention and go out to get your man; your money will fade away, but a man well secured repeats himself over and over again; and this new financial scheme, if you will adopt it and prosecute it in His name, must succeed.

D. D. FORSYTH.

WHEN we began to exploit this new financial plan and seek its introduction into the local Churches, I heard it said on every hand, "That plan is all right enough for some Churches, but it will not work in ours." The men in Trinity Church, a metropolitan Church, said, "It is all right in Grand Avenue, but we fellows can't fiddle around with that sort of business;" and so I made it my business early in the game to try out the system in typical Churches, taking a suburban Church, a mission Church, and a rich Church, and trying it out in all of them, and I have been asked to tell you how it worked in the three kinds of Churches. I went first to a suburban Church, having about 180 members, a small number of poor people—farmers—having moved into that section. Every time I went to that Quarterly Conference in the first year of my work in Denver, it was a regular tragedy to me. There was no financial system. There was a deficit in every account, absolutely every account; the pastor never paid—a small salary—never got it; janitor not paid; light bill not paid. It was a very discouraging situation. We had one fine old gentleman who used to get indignant, and finally one day he got up and resigned from office in the Church. He said it was an outrage. We prayed with him and let him pay the deficit, and he took his office back again at the end of the year. There were $800 in deficits in different accounts. This thing is all over. They have worked up a decent system on which to do business, and introduced it into this Church. The Finance Committee told me that all but three members made contributions systematically, and the pastor was paid every month and they made remittances every month to the various Boards. The district superintendent was paid every month, and the month before Conference everything was met. Now, under the old system the average sum of the collections was eight or ten dollars a Sunday. I am here to say that during the two years of the new plan—I was in that Church four months after Conference last year—and they had an average sum of $100 a Sunday, everybody contributing an average quota of twenty-five to thirty to fifty cents, the membership all in the game. It has revolutionized that Church. Three years ago when I went there, all they talked about was deficits; they would get mad and discouraged. Now the Finance Committee of that Church is just an incident. Now they talk about revivals and the upward, forward movement of the Sunday school and the betterment of the neighborhood, and the whole program of the Kingdom of God is upon their hearts.

I tried it out in a mission Church, where not a single member owned their homes, and we had an educational campaign so that the whole Church was on tiptoe with enthusiasm and everybody wanted to co-operate. We went out and made a canvass, and eighty per cent of that membership made contributions. The pastor said that he got twice as much salary as he ever got before, and twice as much for benevolences. It has revolutionized that mission.

Then I tried it out in a metropolitan Church—Trinity Church. The officials came to me and said, "In God's name, come and introduce some system to take care of our finances!" We went and introduced this system, and spent a month of education, every Sunday, every Epworth League meeting, every woman's meeting, and so on. Sixty men in eight hours canvassed the whole Church. Up to that time, out of eleven hundred members, one hundred and ten were the total number of subscribers to benevolences, and we multiplied it by four and one-half.

[At this point Bishop Wilson offered the prayer found on page 52. Read it again, and reverently, in the light of the foregoing addresses.—Eds.]

II. WHAT OTHER DENOMINATIONS HAVE DONE.

Southern Presbyterian Church.

C. A. ROWLAND.

THE General Assembly of the Presbyterian Church, our highest governing body, is responsible for giving the gospel to twenty-five million in non-Christian lands. I desire this afternoon, as has been indicated, to simply bring to you some of the facts in regard to this work and let you see how God has wrought among our denomination. In no sense do we wish to boast about what our communion has done, but simply tell you in order that it may suggest to you some of the ways by which, perhaps, God can use you in your Churches in bringing your people up to a greater measure of their responsibility.

One of the very first things, or rather one of the recent things that has helped our denomination to keep steadily at the task has been the fact that it assumed, along with other denominations, a definite portion of the non-Christian world. While this is very simple, at the same time it has proven a great stimulant to our people and has enabled them to take hold in a very real and definite way. It has enabled us to present to our Presbyteries and individual Churches their pro rata responsibility in this task. A still greater benefit is to keep the tremendous magnitude of this task before our people, and especially before our laymen, and it has brought them to see more and more that they have a real share in this and a responsibility which they must personally discharge.

I have here one or two charts which I want to speak from

99

briefly. This first chart gives you the world's field of the Southern Presbyterian Church. We have here clearly before us that for which we are responsible. We are responsible for five hundred thousand in Cuba, five hundred thousand in Mexico, a million in Africa, four million in Korea, four million in Japan, and twelve million in China. In a moment our people can see exactly what is to be done and determine the part they wish in it. But I am not to speak of all these fields, but will take up Korea, to show you how we have concretely taken one field. The pink part gives you the sphere assigned to the Southern Presbyterian Church in Korea. We are glad to tell you that Korea was the first field of our missions to send back to our Church a definite statement as to what was required in men and missions to evangelize our share of Korea, and when the call came, the laymen took it up, and after a vigorous campaign they secured sufficient funds to enable our Board to notify the Korean Mission that they were ready to supply the equipment. A returned missionary went through our denomination and secured sufficient to supply Korea with seventy-six missionaries and an equipment sufficient for our Church to evangelize her share of Korea. When recently we got out a pamphlet calling for a million dollars to equip our other fields, one of the most striking things in it that helped us to carry on the work was the statement, "Korea supplied."

Let us come to another field, Africa, and I will merely give you some things that have stimulated our men and enabled us to present this work in a concrete way. We have gone up in the Belgium Congo twelve hundred miles from the coast, and this red spot represents the Presbyterian sphere of influence, the territory assigned our Church, and we are endeavoring there to meet our responsibilities. Only last summer we sent twelve missionaries on one ship from Philadelphia: I am sorry I have not the time to tell you the story of how those twelve men were secured. A missionary came back and went to our seminaries and made a pathetic appeal to men to volunteer; and at a convention in Chattanooga, a year and a half ago, the laymen took up the challenge and the money was secured then and there. To-day we have almost supplied Africa with forces. That green adjoining is for the Methodist Episcopal Church, South, and I will show you how thoroughly we are co-operating with your people in the South. We have arranged to co-operate in every possible detail. For instance, we have a boat on the Congo River that takes our men up and down the Congo and carries supplies; we have arranged to do all the transporting for your people; they, in turn, have put a smaller boat on this river, which is to be the dividing line, and they in turn will likewise transport our supplies and our men to this extreme point of our territory. Bishop Lambuth is en route to Africa, carrying his quota of missionaries, and he is planning to stop at our central station for six months with his missionaries, and they will be the guests of our missionaries while learning the language, the language happening to be the same. The other day we issued a call for a printer. We searched everywhere for a printer, but could not find the man. Bishop Lambuth came to our Board meeting, and he said: ''I understand you want a printer; we have a man whom we have been training in our Methodist Training School for the last three years; you may have him;'' and he turned over to us that young man, and to-day he is on the way to Africa to fill the important position of printer to our mission. It is these things that make the foreign missionary enterprise appeal to our men, when they see that the Churches are united in a business-like way.

I did not take the time on that first chart to indicate to you that each one of those blocks represents a parish of twenty-five thousand. We consider that we have one thousand parishes to supply with missionaries, and that gives us our million of responsibility. This chart indicates that we have three hundred and forty missionaries from our Church, and the forty circles indicate that we have forty men and women ready to go. Our record has always kept pace with the demand for men. In time we hope to supply the full thousand.

Here is a chart that will indicate the progress made in the past two decades. In 1893 our receipts were $134,000, and the missionaries on the field were one hundred and six. Going to the next decade, 1903, the receipts increased $180,000 and the missionaries to one hundred and seventy-four, and this past year our receipts increased to $631,000 and our missionaries to three hundred and forty.

This rising tide of missionary interest has not come by accident, nor in any haphazard manner, but it is due largely to the fact that we have definitely cultivated our Church and tried to bring to our people the real issues involved. Our first great advance was made after we adopted what we called our forward movement or special support plan. When we offered to individuals and to individual Churches the support of a missionary, it met with a most generous response and our receipts immediately increased. This was on the basis of a salary of $500, but our assembly has changed that to full support, so that no missionary can be supported except on $1,200, and this is bringing the Churches up to $1,200 where in the past they were only contributing $500. The next step that has contributed to the advance has been the holding of conventions similar to this, the bringing to the men of the Church the vision, and it has led many men to go back and revolutionize their own lives and to revolutionize the lives of their Churches. I wish I had time to tell you a number of things that followed from those conventions. I remember the first gift of $10,000 which was made for missions; it was so unusual it seemed like a thunderbolt. While we have not as many $10,000 gifts as we want, it is no unusual thing. Only this summer I had $10,000 given me for the work in Africa for an industrial school. In connection with Korea, I must tell you of one man who is supporting an entire mission station. When the thing was first put up to him he said he could not undertake it; but after thinking it over a day or

two he decided he would, and he has assumed the entire support of that station. We sent out eleven missionaries, and
he took them all. Two more were needed this year, and he
said, "Certainly, I will supply any number needed for that
station." To-day we count on him absolutely for one of
those stations in Korea. And so more and more we are endeavoring to bring individually to men of means this great
work. We feel that they must not be satisfied and must not
content themselves with a bare contribution to this great cause
through their local Church; that many of our men have the
means and should be given a share in the work similar to
what I have indicated is being done by this man supporting
this entire station. A friend of mine spoke the other day to
a very large business man in his community and said, "Are
you going to the Laymen's convention of your denomination?" He replied, "No, I am not going; my business will
not allow me." "Why?" my friend said to him. "When
did your business get to be your boss?" He had never
thought of that. He said he had never dreamed that his
business was his boss until it was thus put up to him.
Many of us men do not realize that our business is our
boss. The business man who is unable to see anything
but business in business will earn for himself the epitaph
placed upon the tomb of a cynical Frenchman at his own
direction: "Born a man, died a grocer." So we go back to
the proposition that this missionary enterprise is to prevent
that catastrophe to many a business man. Surely of all things
it should appeal to men. Up to 1880 the graduates of Yale
and Harvard very largely went into what we call the learned
professions: the ministry, the law, and medicine. But since
that time the majority of these men are seeking a business
career. We know that the missionary enterprise appeals to
college men when it is properly presented. And this great
army of men in business to-day can be reached by this same
enterprise when the appeal is properly made; but I believe
the time has come when we should press it upon them. It

is the one thing, as I have said before, that I believe will save many a man. And men, listen! When we are able to take our business and give it its highest motive, the motive of service, we will then get from our business that sense of satisfaction which we can not secure in any other way. When men are able to say to you this, "I am working hard this year because I expect to put fifty thousand dollars in our work in China," and when a man tells you, "I am sticking close to business this year because I mean to build a mission hospital," then you may be sure that that man is getting satisfaction out of life. And so the Laymen's Movement for the coming year expects to bring this message to the men of our denomination, and why should we not, here and now, make this a message to ourselves as well as carry it back as a message to our comrades at home?

The Disciples of Christ.

A. E. CORY.

FRIENDS, it is my pleasure to bring to you the greetings of a committee which I have just been attending, representing all our missionary organizations and all of our colleges. That committee by formal vote asked me to bear their greetings to you and assure you that during the days of this convention their prayers would be with you.

It is difficult always to talk about ourselves. It is difficult always to bring a message about something which you have had a part in. But I want every man in this presence this afternoon to know that in bringing this message of the achievements of the Disciples of Christ, there is not a single word of praise for ourselves, because every man who has had anything to do with this movement which I am recounting to you realizes this fact, that we are telling the story of God's movement in our midst, and that whatever has been done has not been done because of us, but rather in spite of some of us. As your chairman has said, it has been my privilege for a number of years to work in China. I am not going to bring you a message of the world's need after the great messages you have had in the last twenty-four hours. The world is challenging as it has never challenged before. And some one has said, the world runs liquid at this hour, and it is ready for the molding of our God and of His Christ.

It is now some three years ago since one of our missionaries was taken sick in China with typhoid fever. I have never been able to decide in my own mind whether God made that man sick or not. I will leave that to the theologians this afternoon, but at any rate God used that man's illness in China, and this man, when he was finding his way back to a long convalescence, thought over a number of things in his mind; he had the burden of China on his heart and the need of our missions there, which had been very great indeed. I remember one day when I went in to this man, and he looked up at me, calling me familiarly by my first name, and said: "Abe, I want to say something to you. We have been getting about eight thousand dollars a year for buildings in China for the last number of years. In the next five years we must have forty thousand dollars every year, or two hundred thousand dollars for buildings." I remember I looked at him and said, "Huh," and he said it over again. My thought was that the typhoid fever had gone to his head, and I went out of the room and said to Mrs. Cory, "Do you know the typhoid fever has gone to Alex's head, and do you know what he is talking about?" She said, "No; what is he talking about?" I said, "He says we must have two hundred thousand dollars for buildings alone in the next five years in Central China." She said, "I do n't see anything wrong with that." I looked down at her, and I said, "Well, what 's the matter with you?" Do you know that man there in his room on his back took it up with our missionaries in China and talked it to everybody in China whom he could reach, and converted everybody except me? But I kept looking very wise and saying, "Oh, no, we must not go too fast; we must be wise; we must consider everything that enters into it.'' That is the way the devil gets a man. If he can not get him any other way, he makes him conservative on a great movement. So that was the way with me. He had me pulling back, and I could pull back harder than twenty-five men could pull forward; but God was in it. I have a high-sounding title in China, called the dean of a Bible school, and I have been working in a college about as good as the average garage in America. I am not kicking on the garage, but on the college. One night a woman wrote me, ''Mr. Cory, I have decided to give you six thousand dollars for the building of a Bible college.'' This man who had been ill was convalescing at the time. You can not know the joy that was in my heart when I read that word. I just ripped open the front door and went upstairs four steps at a time, and when I got up there I showed the letter to this man. He said to me, as he looked at it with tears standing on his cheeks, ''This is of God.'' When I found that God was in the game I got into it too. But we were not right yet. The mission seemed to think that was a stupendous task. We were driven to our knees every day. For four weeks we went down on our knees in prayer, and whatever I shall recount to you as having happened after that has been absolutely because of the power of prayer. Time went on and one of our secretaries came around the world, and we put up this $200,-000 story to him, and he looked at us very wise and said: ''Men, I have been thinking for a long time that there was something wrong with you fellows. I know what it is now: you are going crazy.'' Three days later that secretary came to us in a little town in China and said, ''Men, I can't eat and I can't sleep for that crazy idea of yours; talk to me some more about it.'' We poured out our heart's story to him, and he said: ''It is a great idea. There is only one thing the matter with it, and that is that it is for China. What about India; what about Japan; what about the islands of the sea?'' He wakened me up in the night and said: ''What we have got to do is to pool our interests and raise a great sum of money. It would take one-half million dollars.'' He said: ''It is of God. Let us go out and do it.'' We decided to go out for half a million dollars, and out there in China that seemed to be a pretty big sum of money. I was asked to lead in the enterprise, to come home and raise that amount of a half-million dollars. I went to the Philippines; I went to Japan; I went to the other fields preparing for the task; but the missionaries said to me, ''Mr. Cory, you must make it more than a half-million.'' I said, ''No; that is all you are going to get.'' And then I came home, friends, and began to study methods and consulted Mr. Mount on their great campaign. I had heard what the Canadians had done in raising money for their home and foreign missions. They told me up there I must make it a million dollars. I said, ''You do n't know our folks; they haven't got a million dollars to put in there.'' And so I went to tell the story of half a million dollars. I went to two business men in New York, and the first thing they said was that it did not strike them. I said to them, ''Don't you believe in doing a great thing for God?'' ''Yes.'' They said, ''But that is just what you are not doing.'' Then one said, ''I will give you $200 for half a million, and $1,000 on the million.'' The other said, ''I will give $300 on a half a million and $1,000 on a million.'' I said, ''I do n't believe we can do it.'' I met a man in Iowa working on a salary, not a rich man in the ordinary sense of the term. This man said to me in some surprise, ''What are you doing at home?'' I told him the half-million story. I never said a word about the million dollars. With a good deal of energy he said, ''I won't give you a cent on it.'' He said: ''You are not talking the language of this age; this is a million-dollar age. I will give you a thousand dollars on a million.'' I scratched my head and said, ''Maybe it will be a million dollars; I do n't know.'' So I went out and asked a hundred business men and a hundred preachers of our Church this question, ''Shall we make it a million dollars or keep it a half million?'' Every one of our preachers said keep it half a million, and every one of the business men said make it a million. Now men, I just want in a brief word to tell you how this task was accomplished. Back of it has been the mighty power of prayer. We have kept our methods subject to change like a railroad company's time-table, depending upon the Word of God and the power of God. A little over a year ago we went out after that million dollars, and I am happy to say that within the next five years more than one million dollars have been assured.

You want to know some of the things that have been accomplished. I went into the office of a business man in the State of New York, and when I wanted to talk to him I stood before him and he did not even ask me to sit down, and so I started in and talked right in that fellow's face for ten minutes, and he said, "You are in a hurry," and I said, "It is you who are in a hurry," and he said, "Come into my inner office and let us bow in prayer." Men, dozens of times in the great offices of railway men and of bankers and corporation lawyers I have gone down on my knees in prayer with them and never once at my request. I have come to this belief to-day, that men want to hear God talked about in a man's way. People say to me, "How do you get at these people?" We do not get at them; we let God do it. I want to put that to you again and again, and not in any pietistic way. We went into one town and had a little supper with the people. One man got up and said, "I move that this town raise $5,000 for this movement." (Afterward the town raised $25,000.) When we were going out of that building that night, a little woman met me and said, "You ought to be ashamed of yourself, asking this town for $5,000." I went home wondering if we had asked too much and were going to put the people to the poor-house. I was a little surprised the next morning when that woman called me up on the telephone and said, "I want you to come and see me." I went, and she said, "Mr. Cory, I am going to give you $500.

I have not slept very much, and I am going to make that much of a contribution." I thanked her, and asked if she wanted to sign. She said, "No, I may change my mind." I did not ask her further. That afternoon I got a note to come and see her. When I went into her presence, she said, "I have changed my mind." I said, "Why are you not going to give?" She replied: "Who said I am not going to give? I am going to give you $1,000." I never said a word to her about signing. When you get a woman going in that direction, let her go. I was not at all surprised the next morning when the telephone bell rang again, for I knew she was on the other end of the line. She said, "Come over here." I went as quickly as I could. When I went into the presence of that woman I felt I was going into the presence of an angel. Her face was radiant with the presence of God. She said: "For two nights I have been in prayer. My husband was a doctor. I want to build a hospital on the banks of the mighty Congo that will bear his name." I could tell you of dozens of people who with the power of God working on their hearts have been led to do great things. In no public meeting have we asked for money, and seldom in a private meeting. We have had but one theme, the power of God in the world.

You know when a man is doing a great task a good many temptations come to him. When we got to the half-million dollars the temptation was to stop for a while. But I went into a business man's office in Oklahoma City, and on his office door was this motto, "The man who stops on third base to congratulate himself never makes a home run." We never stopped, but went on and went on until the task was completed. But as it was nearing completion, I thought we were going to stop at the million dollars. I felt like saying, "Lord, let Thy servant depart in peace." That was the only thought in my mind. But down in a banquet in Southern California a man got up and said, "I will be one of one hundred men to give another million," and he launched at that moment another million dollar campaign. That million dollar campaign carried with it a thousand workers for America, and it went to $2,500,000.

A quiet, conservative business man asked me, "Are our colleges included?" I said, "We can not include them; this is just the missionary task." He said, "It seems to me that education and missions ought to be linked up in some way." I went to my room, but not to sleep, and all that Saturday night I battled with that question. Fifty times I decided to ask him for a million dollars, and then I said, "No." The next morning, after a great prayer-meeting in the early hours of the morning, at which he was present, I decided not to do it; but somehow it was impressed upon me to ask him for a million dollars. I went to him and I said in a quivering voice, "After an all night of prayer, God has laid it upon my heart to ask you to give one million dollars and unite our colleges and missionary enterprises." He reached out his hand and said, "Say no more; I will not say 'Yea,' and I will not say 'Nay,' but I will answer you in thirty days." I came from him a day or two ago and he has said that if our Church will raise $5,000,000 he will give $1,000,000 in the next five years. The impression upon my heart when he made that statement was, "Be still and know that I am God." A great many men have given sums like that in their wills, when they could use it no longer. I believe that God is using that man to challenge the whole Kingdom of God to do great things for Him.

There are a multitude of things that I would like to say to you. I would like to tell you about the campaign for one thousand men. I will tell you this one story. A Methodist woman in Los Angeles telephoned me to come and see her. When I went, she said, "I am going to send my daughter to China." I said, "I would like to meet her." She came in, a beautiful girl, a graduate from one of the great colleges of America. I asked her age. She was twenty-three. I turned to her mother and I said, "How long have you had it in your heart that this daughter should go to China?" Looking me squarely in the face, she said, "For nearly twenty-four years; from the time that girl was, she belonged to China." God is challenging us from the very hour of their being to give our children to the world task. Do you ask me about the influence of this world-movement on our Church? I want to say that money is the least of all. It has united our Church, and the Church can never be united by doctrine or theology, but only by a great task for God. It has united us in a mighty movement of prayer. We shall fail if we go out to get five or six million dollars unless we have created a great wave of spirituality in the Church.

Men of God, I ask you to-day, as we go to this greater task, that you will unite your prayers with ours, and I can assure you that our prayers will be united with yours and we shall all go forward, taking this world for God and His Christ.

The United Presbyterian Church.

J. CAMPBELL WHITE.

YOUR Program Committee has asked me to speak about the development of the missionary interests in the United Presbyterian Church. First of all, I want to supplement what my friend Rowland has said about the Southern Presbyterian Church. He did not tell you that they have only three hundred thousand members. It occurred to me while he was speaking that that was just a tithe of your white membership in this country—about three millions. Now, will you keep your mind on these figures? That Church gave last year six hundred and thirty-one thousand dollars to foreign missions. Multiply that by ten and see where you are. Six million three hundred and ten thousand dollars to foreign missions from the Methodist Church, if you do what should be done. Three hundred and forty foreign missionaries. Multiply that by ten and get your proportion, and you would have thirty-four hundred against your eleven hundred. You can do that, and if you are going to reach one hundred and fifty millions of people in the non-Christian world, while the Southern Presbyterian Church reaches their twenty-five million, you will have to do something like that. There is no use in talking about reaching one hundred and fifty millions of people with the gospel on the paltry sum of two or three million dollars a year. You can not do it.

And then, I want to say that Rowland himself is the chief human agency through which God has operated in bringing that Church up to that point. I have known the Church intimately for ten years, and I make bold to say to you here what I have said to great assemblies of that denomination, that Rowland, a simple business man from Athens, Georgia, is the chief human agency in this transformation. And I say to you that there are one thousand men on this floor of equal capacity with Mr. Rowland if you will go back to your community and help to work this thing out. He was talking about this to a group of business men in New York not long ago, and he said that he had for the last ten years been crowding his business into a small proportion of his time until now he is able to take care of his secular business in two or three hours of each day and the rest of his time is given to gospel work for the wide world. Then he followed this in the next breath by the statement that the last year his business was the most successful of any he had ever had. The Lord will stand by you fellows if you will stand by Him in this undertaking. He wants one thousand Methodist men on this floor, if not two thousand, who will decide to give Him a fair proportion of their time to help work out this problem among the three million of Methodists in this country, and you will never solve the problem by simply giving money. No man has money enough to discharge his obligations to the Kingdom of God. There is a man living in North Carolina into whose mind it was my privilege to put this some years ago. I had spoken in the pulpit of the church where that man attended. I wrote back to him and said: "Why do n't you take a great big corner of the world and plant the Kingdom of God there? Your Church has twenty-five millions of people to reach in the non-Christian world. Why don 't you take a corner of Korea or Japan or China and throw in a force big enough to evangelize it?" He said he was putting up a hospital just then in his own town that was costing three or four thousand dollars and took most of his loose change, but that when he got that done he would very seriously consider this other proposition. Two or three years went by before he came, last year, to the decision to send a dozen missionaries out to Korea to occupy a new corner of the land, containing two hundred and fifty thousand people. And without asking any co-operation from any one, he is supporting thirteen American missionaries in that district, and is undertaking to plant the Kingdom of God forever in that corner of the world. This is a thing that one thousand Methodist men could duplicate, if you would. Easily a hundred men here who could take a corner of India or Korea or China, or any other of these great fields, and without asking anybody's co-operation, simply tell the Missionary Board to occupy that part of the world and you would pay the bill.

Now, going on to the story of the United Presbyterian Church, which I have been asked to relate, they have been working seriously for a number of years. In 1912 they had a simultaneous canvass over the whole denomination. There are one thousand congregations and one hundred and forty-two thousand members in the denomination. This morning Dr. Hollingshead gave us a marvelous insight into the situation in your great Church. How did you feel about that fifty-three cents and twenty-three cents, and added to that the thirty-nine cents per member of the women? Add all together and you have one dollar fifteen per year through all agencies for all aggressive work at home and abroad. By the simultaneous canvass in 1912 the United Presbyterian

Church added to their highest average per capita in America one dollar and twelve cents per member to home and foreign missions. I am not talking about one congregation; I am talking about the whole denomination from ocean to ocean. Out of one thousand congregations about seven hundred and nineteen conducted this simultaneous canvass in March with that great result. The average contribution per member to home and foreign missions and the other official benevolences was brought up in that Church last year to six dollars and eleven cents per member. That includes all the Churches that are not doing anything. All those who did not have any pastor. All the colored Churches. There is a colored Church down in Knoxville, Tenn., that averages five dollars per member to home and foreign missions. Five dollars a member is only ten cents a week. Most people waste ten cents a week on something not necessary. The average to foreign missions alone in the United Presbyterian Church last year was two dollars and sixty cents per member, and to all home objects three dollars and fifty cents per member. I would not for the world hold up this denomination, even though I did belong to it once, for an illustration, unless it was a mighty demonstration of the practicability of doing that thing in almost every denomination in this country. That was a noble thought of Bishop McDowell's when he said that Methodism had no message; that it was Christianity's message. We have not got any Presbyterian message for mankind. I have belonged to that crowd all of my life, and we have not got any folks any better than you are. None of our denominations have any exclusive message in this business except that we represent Christ and His universal message. All I refer to the United Presbyterian Church for is to encourage you to believe that you can do the same thing.

I believe that at least fifteen million of the twenty-three million of Protestant Church members in this country can easily do as well as the United Presbyterians did last year. Do you know what that would make from fifteen million Church members? It would put twenty-nine million dollars into the treasury of our Mission Boards instead of the sixteen million dollars given now, and that would solve our problem and enable us to evangelize the world in this generation. Do you know what it would make if the fifteen million Protestant Church members would give three dollars and fifty cents to home missions? It would make fifty-two and a half million, and that would solve our city problem and home mission problem as far as money can solve them. The thing is practical, and if we ourselves will go into it and lift our denominations into it, we can make it a success. Now, the United Presbyterian increase did not take anything off preachers' salaries and local Church expenses. Some have an idea that we took money out of one pocket and put it in another. There is no worse lie of the devil than that. When you begin to give you enlarge the heart and the love and make giving a joy and an inspiration. After the United Presbyterian Church had added one dollar and twelve cents per member for missionary objects, it added one dollar and seven cents per member to its own local work without thinking about it at all. Their average per member for this year for all purposes was twenty dollars and ninety-seven cents against your twelve dollars and four cents. If you reduce that to a weekly average, it was an average of forty-two cents against twenty-three cents a week. I have just figured up your average since I came on the platform. You have been talking about giving a tithe—that is, a tithe of two dollars and thirty cents a week. The most ignorant Italian who lands on our shores will earn that in about a day and a quarter. Twenty-three cents a week from people like us for Church support and Christian education and home missions and foreign missions and everything else! Why, brethren, it ought to send us down on our knees in sackcloth and ashes for very shame that we are not doing more than that in view of the sacrifice which the Son of God made in order that this world might have a redemption at all.

Now, what is the explanation of the fact that this one Church has been able to make this record this last year? The pastors have largely recognized their responsibilities to lead the Church out. You will never do it in your Church until your sixteen thousand pastors get the vision of their field as the world field. I hate to hear a pastor talking about his small contracted field: he is only in a contracted field when he contracts it himself; Jesus Christ set him down in the midst of a world field. A man's Church is not his field, but only his place of work in the occupation of the world field. You will have to back up your pastors if your three million members will do the great things the Lord wants them to do. The United Presbyterian pastors have been backed up by the laymen. For twenty-five years there has been a committee of laymen who have gone here and there to help plan and educate and agitate and to back up the Boards in the strongest way possible. They have had a great deal of instruction on the grace of giving and on systematic and proportionate giving; and how much we need it! Not because God needs money. Let us get beyond the place of thinking that God is a beggar. No man has a right to beg and profess to be doing it in God's name, for God is no pauper and no beggar. "The silver and gold is Mine, and the cattle upon a thousand hills; if I were hungry I would not ask you," says God, "for the world is Mine and the fullness thereof." Why does God wait upon our giving our poor nickels and dimes for the spread of His Kingdom? I have thought of that for twenty years, and I believe that the only reason why God waits and allows His Kingdom to wait on our co-operation and our gifts is that you and I may through His likeness be partakers of His love. "God so loved the world that He gave," and giving He gave all, and He wants us so to love the world that our giving will be spontaneous and inevitable. "A man may give without loving, but he can not love without giving."

The next thing is that the missionaries themselves ten years ago got together and told our Church what was needed in the way of advance if this problem was to be solved. In 1902 they did that in India, and in 1903 in Africa, so for ten years our Church has had a great goal put before it, to rise up and win fifteen million of people in the non-Christian world. Another thing has been the simultaneous canvass; that added a tremendous power. Another thing has been prayer; there has been a great gathering of a thousand people in India every year for the last ten years, where they pray day and night for the Church at home and for a revival there, and every year in this country a group of praying people have been gathered for prayer alone, not for conference. We will never do the work without prayer. The last reason of all is that upon the Church has come the idea that our Church is only a little fragment and not all the body of Christ, only a little regiment in the army, and there has been the prayer and the hope that God would work out in that little group an object lesson proving the possibility of doing this work and in every meeting where you go you hear them stimulating each other to do this thing worthily and fully for Christ, that the whole Church may be stimulated to move out, each in its own way, to the accomplishment of its own task.

My brother men, you have been given the greatest vision that God has ever given any body of men of any single denomination. I have been trembling ever since I came on this ground, by reason of wondering whether we would do the thing that God is trying to get into our hearts to do. We have need of prayer; we need it here in Indianapolis to-day and to-morrow, that every man may set himself unreservedly to the accomplishment of God's will for your Church, for the whole Church, and for this Nation, until the kingdoms of this world are made the Kingdom of our Lord and of His Christ.

The United Brethren.

BISHOP HOWARD.

AFTER having lived among the Japanese for fifteen years, naturally you would expect me to admire their fighting spirit, and I can not express to you men what an inspiration it has been to me to have been on this platform and seen this magnificent body of Christian Samurai. What can not this great body of men accomplish if you map out a program that is truly heroic! You have the organization, and you have the constituency, and you have the opportunity, and is there not need, men, for us to make such a program? May the day soon come when men who wish to have their blood stirred will go to a missionary meeting where a great and far-reaching program is presented and where that which is truly heroic in the benefit that will be conferred on their fellowmen is mapped out!

The Laymen's Missionary Movement, started a few years ago, is just beginning to bear fruit. The careful planning that naturally followed that great movement necessitated a study of the work in the foreign field. I had a part myself in working up the statistics of the actual work needed in Japan. Just a few years ago people seemed to think that the work of the missionary societies in Japan was practically over; but as a result of the Laymen's Missionary Movement here the missionaries in the foreign field took up the study of their part anew. I was surprised myself to find that in a province of Japan lying just north of Tokio, a province that could be reached in any part within three or four hours, there were three hundred and thirty villages—some with a population of two thousand—and in not more than ten of these villages was there a regular Christian work. Two provinces lying just near Tokio offer a fair sample of the villages of Japan that remain to be reached, and as the result of the Laymen's Missionary Movement this careful study has been undertaken, and so the task in Japan is better understood to-day than ever before. You are familiar with the progress of Mr. Mott around the world last year, in India and various parts of China, as well as Japan, mapping out the general campaign. And now to come home after eight years and into a body like this with its magnificent possibilities, to be confronted by such a challenge as was offered last night, is a greater inspiration to a missionary than you can know. If to-day we map out a far-reaching program, it will be not only a great challenge to your Church, but to the other Churches. We little people could not expect to do the greater work God has clearly laid upon the Methodist Episcopal Church. If you give yourself to some great task with your organization, with your Churches established everywhere, you can lend a greater influence to the whole Christian cause in the United States than you can possibly imagine.

And not only so, but there will be a great response on the part of the native men in other parts of the world. Last night in a committee this question was asked, "How can you start a revival in Japan?" and Dr. Green, one of the missionaries in Tokio, said, "The best way to start a great revival in Japan is to start one in the United States." The influence of the Church in America is so great on the Church in Japan that if there is a great, deep, widespread interest in religion, in any phase of Church work here in America, you may certainly expect a counterpart of that movement in Japan. And what is true as regards a revival is true in any other form of Church work. If men here will give themselves loyally to the upbuilding of the Kingdom of God, to mapping out large plans, the Japanese and Chinese will respond to that movement. Three years ago some of you may remember that a Japanese business delegation visited America. Probably the leading spirit among those men was Baron Chipasawa. Up to that time he was not interested in Christian work, but in America he was struck with the vast sums of money put into Christian churches and the Young Men's Christian Association buildings, and when he went back to Japan he was a different man. A group of Japanese gentlemen, writers and business men, was called together and they were to talk about establishing a magazine to promote international good-will, which was to be launched to counteract this infamous lie about the Japanese being a warlike people. This group of men met in the baron's villa at three o'clock in the afternoon, and for six hours they talked of nothing but religion. At nine o'clock the servant came and said that it was time for the last car to the city, and they said, ''We have not said anything about our magazine;'' and they appointed another meeting, and they came together again, said nothing about the magazine, but talked of religion, and all this interest grew out of the impression made upon the baron. That was one result. Another result is found in the fact that the men of wealth over there are willing to give when they believe that the Christian Church is a going concern. A little more than a year ago the Japanese contributed three hundred thousand yen, or one hundred and fifty thousand dollars, to one university in Kioto. So it is in China; the Chinese are coming forward and are giving magnificent sums because they believe that the Christian Church can solve the social ills that China finds herself confronted with to-day.

And so, men, as you confront a great program to-day, do not think for one minute that your influence is going to be limited by the confines of your Church. Some small Church might set itself to do a great task, but the people in general would not know about it. But it is otherwise with you. Your influence is not going to be bounded by the limits of the United States, but will be tremendous on the people in China, the Philippines, Japan, and Africa. Is it not glorious to live in this day when we see the fulfillment of that prophecy in Daniel that that stone cut out of the mountain without hands should fill the whole earth? That little stone is filling the whole earth, and you are to have a glorious part in it. I congratulate you, and pray that God may bless you in it.

THE FORCES AND THE FIELD—A SURVEY.

S. S. HOUGH.

THIS present movement is the next logical step in the onward movement of the Kingdom. For if you study briefly the history of movements during the last century, and especially the last ten or fifteen years, you can see that we can not do differently from what we are doing. It was Mr. Taylor, of your own Church, together with the editor of the *Christian Endeavor World* who, following the great Student Volunteer Convention in Toronto, in 1900, started the books for mission study which have formed the basis of the great mission study courses throughout the world during the last twelve or thirteen years. After a few years the home constituency took it up and developed a series of books for home study. Then there was a necessity for catching the youth and giving them the vision and inspiration during the adolescent period. Then came the great Laymen's Missionary Movement, that challenged the adult contingent in the army of God, the men that were not enlisted. It was dealing with the generation passing from the field of action. We are fortunate to come into the Kingdom at a time like this. Let us set up standards that shall be adequate, calling to action the full power of the whole Church membership, and release on the problem of God the united force of the whole Protestant body, reinforced by the power and spirit of God.

Now, a few words of experience. We are greatly indebted to the Methodist Episcopal Church for this new financial plan that is being put before the United Brethren Church. We have three hundred thousand members in this country. A few years ago I knew what was going on in the Methodist camp, and asked them to give me some definite statement, and I got reports of the work following your General Conference. So we worked out our scheme. Before this we had the plan of having the various departments fire at the pastor separately. They were coming from every angle, until the pastor found little time for doing constructive work.

There was general dissatisfaction all over the Church with that indiscriminate separate emphasis on the part of every one of the several departments asking for the largest possible gifts, to be presented separately to the Church. We were through with that, we were tired of it; but the rank and file did not understand the way out of the desert or the wilderness, and so we went over into your camp. We saw you had worked out a plan very well, and so we adapted that to suit the United Brethren Church and we passed it unanimously at our last General Conference, and our financial scheme has a commission in the Annual Conference and in the local Church.

And now we saw the time was ripe for immediate action. How can we get this big thing in operation? It is easy to map out a beautiful scheme, but a very different thing to get it working in the hearts of the people and make it produce the result. We formed a plan by which we would have a series of institutes at our Annual Conferences, and we would ask the bishop and the men who arranged the program to grant the Commission on Finance a whole day's session in each Annual Conference, and if they could not possibly grant a whole day, grant us a half-day and a night session, so that we could mobilize our forces and present to the Conference one solid period of institute work. The result was we mapped out the right way at every Annual Conference in the United States during the last two and one-half months, and there never was a time when our presentation had such force as it had this year. Usually a team would go out, say four speakers; one would present the great thought of God for the evangelization of the world and emphasize the foreign work. That would be followed by the needs of the constructive and expansion work of the home field in a speech of twenty minutes. That would be followed by a talk on Sunday school work and colleges. In order to get a plan of campaign, we emphasized educational work and related it to the work to be done, something that is not always done, but we are getting that sort of a spirit in our institutions of learning through this united movement. We are following these annual sessions with district institutes such as were mentioned in this room yesterday afternoon in the Chicago area Conference presided over by Bishop McDowell. We have gotten to the point where we have unified our treasurers, and we have one treasurer for the entire general benevolences of the Church, and we are getting a report in blank form for the districts and for the Conference treasurers, so that the money for this combined benevolent scheme shall be lifted right through the year, and every month that treasurer shall receive and transmit to date to our general treasurer a statement of the entire amount received for the entire interests, and these are distributed on a percentage basis to the various departments of the Church activity. That is already thought through, and the printed forms have gone to press, and we expect to get the thing in operation so that our Boards will not need to borrow tens and hundreds of thousands of dollars during the year and wait for the belated money that is held back in the coffers of the Church and the pockets of the people.

What is this thing going to do? First, it will shut out the power of the devil and worldliness from our men who are enlisted in the work of the Church. It will give fifty-two blessings to every person where two-thirds of them have only had one blessing, for ''It is more blessed to give than to receive. This thing properly conducted is going to clear the decks for the most sweeping revival in the history of the Protestant Churches in North America, if we can get down to business and do it. You and I know the laws of God and the operations of spiritual laws as well as natural laws, and can we pray to God fervently and expectantly to add new members to a Church when it is already full of unenlisted members who are standing so near the door of entrance that no new member can come in without catching the spirit of stagnation and paralysis that controls those within? The call of God to the Protestant Christendom of North America is not to ask God for a single new member until we have taken care of and rightly related the extension of the Kingdom of God to those who have already been won. Thus and thus only can God bless the Church and through the Church, bless the world.

III. SECTIONAL AND EPISCOPAL AREA CONFERENCES.

The Episcopal Area Conferences.

EPISCOPAL Area meetings, each presided over by the resident bishop, were held for the nineteen divisions in the United States on Wednesday afternoon. The attendance varied from a handful of those from far-distant areas to hundreds from the area in which Indianapolis is located and the Chicago area, a near-by neighbor. The purpose of both the small and large groups was to consider the surveys and propositions as presented in the general sessions of the Convention up to this time in relation to the local situation. To this end an expert representing the Commission on Finance analyzed the statistical survey of Annual Conferences and Episcopal Areas. The discussion involved the question of the "every-member canvass" and the use of the duplex envelope, which phase of the entire matter brought forth much testimony as to the efficiency of both canvass and envelope. The general impression was that where the plan has been worked thoroughly the success has been beyond expectations. Many of these area groups made definite plans for furthering the work of the Commission on Finance after the adjournment of the National Convention of Methodist Men.

Sectional Conferences.

SECTIONAL meetings according to callings were held on Thursday afternoon. The District Superintendents' Section sought to devise ways whereby the new financial plan might be brought more effectively to the local Church. And the superintendents present committed themselves to the task of putting the plan into actual operation in their respective districts in the following resolutions:

Resolved, 1. That we, the District Superintendents of the Methodist Episcopal Church in attendance upon the Annual Convention of Methodist Men, endorse the new financial plan and pledge ourselves to intelligent and enthusiastic endeavor to introduce that plan in all the Churches under our supervision. To this end we pledge ourselves to a simultaneous educational plan and a common Every-member Canvass Day in each of our respective districts.

2. We will co-operate with the bishops in extending this united campaign to all district superintendents not present at this Convention, and we will welcome such action on the part of the bishops as will express to the district superintendents within their areas the expectation that every district superintendent will do his utmost to introduce the new plan into every charge in his district.

In the Pastors' Section the every-member canvass was studied in actual practice as presented by one of their number who had made it go. It was unanimously agreed to try it out in the home Church.

The Methodist Brotherhood Section re-emphasized its particular tasks in connection with the local Church, and received a new stimulus as a promoter of Bible study among men.

The Sunday School Superintendents' Section reviewed its responsibility in the light of the new religious psychology and pedagogy, the rise of business methods in Sunday school organization, the new sociology, and the larger appreciation of the Bible.

PART III.

Forward, March!—A Call to Advance.

The Future.

MEN are asking by the score, by the hundred, What will be the result, the concrete, practical result of our coming to Indianapolis and spending these days together? Who can fairly predict? On this one statement certainly, we will all agree, and that is that from this mountain top to which these days have brought us, there will be no turning back.

I have thought as I have seen the bishops and others of our leaders actively interested in the smallest detail that concerns this great work that we are thinking about here together, and as I have seen them in their work under the somewhat new plan inaugurated by the General Conference at Minneapolis, and that has been so acceptable to the people everywhere, that they are the leaders of a mighty forward movement in our beloved Methodism. And it seems to me that every such leader will go out of this Convention, if he did not so come to it, with no thought of dress-parade, with no thought of anything but to lead the troops and to be with them in their victorious advance.

And then as to the laymen, what of them? We who stay in the trenches, who follow and who fight. This Convention undoubtedly must have the largest message for us, because there are more of us. I do not know what action the Convention will finally take, but I think I know something of what the Spirit of God will lead us to say and to do. I live on the edge of Missionary Ridge, the Ridge that men scaled without any command. They were simply told to go to the foot of the Ridge, take the breastworks, and wait for orders. They took the breastworks, but they forgot to wait. On and up they went till the flag floated from the top of the Ridge. And I mistake the character and temper of the men who have been tarrying these days at Indianapolis if they do not forget to wait for any word of command. We see the heights, we see the enemy, but we see also the Captain of the mighty host, and we will not stay nor stop till the heights are taken and the banner of our King floats triumphantly over the mountains and the villages, over the lands and the seas that are His by the eminent domain of His love, His service, and His sacrifice.

Men of Methodism: Let us advance together!

JOHN A. PATTEN.

Forward, March!—A Call to Advance.

The Task and Opportunity have been presented; the forces and the field estimated and surveyed; now comes the call for a forward movement worthy of our Church and our day. Mere philosophizing is comparatively useless. Knowledge is power only as it is embodied in action. A message to be effective must carry with it some insistent appeal. A full understanding of the situation, need, and opportunity is instinct with an impulse to reconstruct in harmony with the new vision. In every department of life the drum-beats are calling for a forward movement. The Church, society, the State, the world are all in a mood of expectancy. The sense of humanity bulks large and God is speaking out of the skies. It was evident that the compelling power of such convictions rested mightily upon the Convention during the presentation of this thrilling topic. Speakers and hearers were keyed and kept at the point of high tension. Every one realized that mountain peaks of vision, responsibility, and privilege had been attained. The land of opportunity was before us— a field for conflict and for conquest. Forward, March!

I. THE CALL OF OUR LEADERS.

"The Circulation of the Scriptures."

W. I. Haven.

It is the conviction, brethren, of every one who speaks to you this afternoon that the burden resting upon his shoulders is the great burden of the Church. I am no exception, for it is my confident conviction that the circulation of the Scriptures lies at the foundation of all our Christian advance. The Bible is the great missionary. That may be controverted, but I wish to assert it again: The Bible is the great missionary

129

because it is the most unsullied mirror of the perfections of Jesus Christ. In its origin it is the fruit of the Church inspired by the Holy Ghost. Holy men spake as they were moved by the Holy Ghost. In its outgoing it is, as Bishop Parker has said: The seed corn of the kingdom. Wherever it goes, Churches spring up. It is everywhere the inspiration of missionary advance.

Now, I am bringing to you a truth you do not realize. For nearly a century the Methodist Episcopal Church has officially recognized its obligation to circulate the Scriptures among the people of this and other lands. For a number of years it had its own Bible Society, but in 1836 the General Conference disbanded the Methodist Bible Society and adopted the American Bible Society as one of the official institutions of the Church. For seventy-seven years then, brethren, we have been your servant. During this period we have sent forth to the ends of the earth 96,279,287 volumes of the Scriptures. What will the harvest be?

I am not to speak, however, of the past, but of the call to advance; and lest my time runs out before I get through, let me say that I am going to put my final word first, and say that the most important call to advance is the call to advance in offerings on the part of the Churches for this cause. In 1857, the first year of which I find a record in the official benevolent offerings of the Church, you will be astonished when I tell you that with a membership of 820,519 members its offerings were as follows: For missions, Home and Foreign, $226,-697; for Sunday schools, $13,250; for the American Bible Society, $46,610. That was fifty years ago. It ran up to $90,000. Then it went down to nearly $30,000, and during the first period of the last decade it went up until, in 1910, it was $46,000, and now again it has gone down to $34,000. Brothers, do not forget that the foundation of all our work is in the circulation of the Scriptures.

1. *We need to advance in order to keep up with ourselves.* During seventy-seven years the average output of the Scrip-

tures by the Society has been 1,200,000 volumes a year. But the last decade the average was 2,500,000 annually. But the last year of record it was 4,049,610 volumes. The world is hungry for it, and we will have to advance or stumble over ourselves. What is true of your Society is true of our elder sister in Great Britain, whose circulation last year was over 7,000,000. Add the circulation of the three Bible Societies of the English-speaking nations of the world, they sent out over 14,000,000 volumes to the ends of the earth as a missionary agency. But all this could be put into one nation; for every volume could have been used last year in China alone if they all had been in the languages of that Republic instead of the five hundred polyglot languages of earth. I wish I could make you realize what the New Testament is worth to that people over there who are trying to build up a Republic, a free and staple goverment, while the Scriptures are unknown to millions of their people. No wonder Bishop Bashford said: "Modern inventions have so reduced the cost of printing the Bible that a single gift of $4,000,000 will enable the American Bible Society to produce 50,000,000 copies of the Chinese Bible; at an additional cost of $1,000,000 these could be distributed by missionaries and pastors and colporters. Thus it is possible for $5,000,000, a gift within the power of one Church alone, or even some wealthy man, to evangelize China within the next fifteen or twenty years more fully than Europe was evangelized before the Reformation."

2. I pass to the next point. *There is a demand for advance in the circulation of the Scriptures in our own land.* A careful statistician of the Home Mission statistics has said in 1607 the first immigrants landed in this country in Jamestown, a company of 109, and that in the twentieth century, for the last thirteen years, that number or more has come into this country every hour of every day, year in and year out. That company was, so far as we know, homogeneous so far as language was concerned; but your Society two or

three years ago sent a man to spend his entire summer in the Southern capitals of Europe to find what Bibles were used by the people there. Then we enlarged our warehouses and stocked them, full, and last year we sent out into this country alone Scriptures in seventy languages and dialects. You have no conception of what it means to people coming to our land to give them the gospel in their own tongue. Some one has said, "There is no menace in this immigrant population except the menace of acquiring a population not brought up in the ideals of the New Testament."

Our own American stock is in a condition in this country which we do not imagine. We sometimes plume ourselves on the peril of the foreign born; if I had time I would like to argue with you that the peril is equal if not more than equaled in the decadence of our own American stock and the loss of its religious life. In one of the great agencies where our colporters are at work, they went among 63,000 American homes last year and found 24,000 without copies of the Bible. We must go out among these people. I saw the other day a statement made by a French Jesuit concerning Wesley; he said: "Newman never went among the people; Wesley, on the other hand, was pre-eminently an apostle to the multitudes; thus after his preaching millions of farmers and workingmen have remained and still remain Christians; religion for the masses is the problem of problems; Wesley's example ought to strengthen and enlighten those who wish to stir into life the religious apathy of France." It means getting close to the people. We sent out among these people last year 428 messengers; the number ought to be doubled immediately.

3. *But we are here to look the world in the face this hour.* I spoke of China a few moments ago. On last New Year's day the strange thing happened of the Gate of Heaven in Pekin being thrown open to our superintendent and his colporters, and for ten days they sold the Scriptures at the Gate of Heaven to the people gathered there; and in another community at a great fair for twelve days they sold the Scrip-

tures, a thousand a day, to the people who crowded those places. We made our heaviest appropriation last year to China; it seems to go beyond our resources. We put more than $65,000 into China alone, but we had orders for more than 300,000 copies of the Scriptures that we could not afford to manufacture because what the people could afford to pay for these volumes in their poverty was so much less than the cost of manufacture. We had operating in China in all the eighteen provinces 265 colporters going from village to village. They visited 13,000 villages last year, and we ought to have 1,000 colporters at work immediately.

I have here in my hands the decree passed by the Legislature of Peru on the 5th of October last decreeing religious tolerance to all religious bodies and giving them the right to build their churches and worship in Peru. And I have, what is more significant, the action of the 15th of April last in which they put the Scriptures into their public schools in Peru. By exchange with our British sister, we have given her our own work in Northern Persia, and they have placed in our hands all other work in Central America and on the Panama Canal. We have sent our agents to Port Said to study methods used there. We expect as soon as the Panama Canal is opened to give the millions coming through that gateway the gospel in their own speech.

We have to-day in the world 1,238 colporters. A few years ago when I talked to the people I said, 400, and I said, "It is the 400;" now we have three times as many, but where we have a full regiment, we ought to have an army going from door to door. Dr. John Butler, of Mexico, who is here, told me that nearly every preaching place in Mexico that we Methodists have was opened up by a Bible colporter, and that is true in all Latin America and in many heathen lands. These men are the sappers and miners and open the way for the army of the Cross.

4. I have no time to speak of the work needed *in advance in perfecting the versions of the Bible.* Dr. Drees

and Mr. Balz are over in Spain on a committee perfecting the version of the Spanish Bible for 90,000,000 of people. Over in the Philippines, McLaughlin, another Methodist preacher, is at work. Do you realize that the translation of the Old Testament into Greek, what we call the Septuagint, prepared the soil for Christianity throughout the Levant? Do you realize that Jerome's translation of the Vulgate prepared the way for missionary advance all over Europe? Do you realize that Tyndall's version of the New Testament prepared the way for advance into all lands where the English language goes? Last Sunday they dedicated a monument to him in Brussels, where he was strangled by the order of the English king. Let us be ready for those who come after us.

Advance in Temperance.

CLARENCE TRUE WILSON

THE century-long contest between the organized liquor power and Christian civilization is culminating. The conspiracy of silence which has lasted fifty years in the Nation's capital has been broken, and the Webb Bill, after thorough discussion, was passed by approximately a two-thirds majority. Then the President waited until the last minute, and announced in his Cabinet that there was not time to reconsider it, and then vetoed it. It was reconsidered and passed by a three-fourths majority over Taft's veto, and the administration went down beneath an avalanche of indignant protest which never had a duplication in the United States.

Now we have a Temperance man in the White House, and no intoxicating liquors are served to guests upon the White House table. We have a great Temperance statesman as our Secretary of State. Former Secretaries of State have written to all the American consuls when the breweries were to have a big convention and asked them to find out what they could do to increase the amount of American beer exported to other countries, making every American consul a beer-maker's agent. William Jennings Bryan will never do that until the sun grows cold. When the representatives of the nations gathered around his table, he set before them the same kind of grape juice that they used in Palestine in the days of Jesus, the kind that was used in the institution of the Last Supper. And Bryan's grape juice and Emperor William's lemonade are becoming as popular as buttermilk. When somebody pointed the finger of criticism, Mr. Bryan made a temperance speech that has been heard around the world and is echoing still. A few days after that memorable event, the Secretary of War telegraphed down to the Canal Zone and on June 30th every saloon was closed and no more licenses issued. Not a week passed before the Secretary of the Navy sent word to the Navy Department that the law against the keeping and the use of intoxicating liquor on shipboard must be strictly observed, and the navy went dry.

The last State that voted on the question of prohibition carried it by a 94,000 majority, and West Virginia wheeled into line with her prohibition sisters. Now ten States have outlawed the liquor traffic, thirty-six other States have given the people the right to exclude all rum shops through local option. Better than all this, the unseemly division of temperance forces is at an end. The temperance forces of the New World have gotten together, not by passage of resolutions, but by putting up an object big enough to draw all eyes, and when they started for it they found themselves together. They stood together, and swords were turned to the enemy and not to each other. The National Anti-Saloon League is called to meet on the 10th of next month in Columbus, Ohio, the greatest convention that ever assembled on the temperance question in the history of our world. It is called to announce a slogan and to consider a campaign that is going to mean an amendment to the Federal Constitution prohibiting the manufacture and sale and transportation of alcoholic beverages throughout the United States. The Prohibitionists started that campaign forty-four years ago, and though it will not be won by their methods, they will be there in line to help push the final battle. The Woman's Christian Temperance Union will be there, the Good Templars will be there, the seventeen organized Church temperance societies will be there in force, and they will be for all time a united force against the liquor power. That amendment to the Federal Constitution is going to pass the Senate and House and be passed on to the States in such a surprisingly short time as to take the breath of the people who have not kept their faith up to their wishes. There is more prospect of carrying it through Congress to-day than there was the Webb Bill two years ago. One of the most strategic movements of the temperance reform has come almost without observation. It is this: The seventeen great denominations of the country have organized themselves at last into Church temperance societies to make sentiment among their own millions and publish literature for Sunday school and Young People's organizations, to inspire the ministry to lead the reform in every community, and to fill the Church press with information about the rapidly changing issues of the temperance reform. I name it as the latest evolution of the temperance reform that the Church of Christ has at last ceased to carry prohibition by resolutions, and instead has organized for it as it organizes for Church Extion and Freedmen's Aid. Brethren, if you want literature for distribution, books for study, speakers for campaigns, programs for your quarterly temperance lessons in the Sunday school, studies for the young people of the Epworth League, I want to announce that the Temperance Society of the Methodist Episcopal Church was organized for this purpose, with headquarters at Topeka, Kansas. Glorious old Kansas, that has shown to the other States of the Union for thirty years that a State can thrive through droughts and everything else without the aid of license money!

FORWARD MARCH!—A CALL TO ADVANCE.

The whole license system is lame in logic and a failure in practice, wrong in principle and powerless as a remedy, foolish as a financial investment and a Judas Iscariot in morals. It has put human souls up for sale for revenue only. We ought to cry out against it in this body in such a way that our voice would be heard around the world.

"The Call to Advance in the Sunday School."

EDGAR BLAKE.

I REALLY wish at this moment that I had a temperance section in my speech. There are a number of dry periods in it, but none that deals with the liquor problem.

The papal delegate, the official representative of the pope in this country, in addressing a great Roman Catholic gathering in the city of Chicago some weeks ago, said: "Whenever there is a decline of faith and in morals it can be restored through the training of the children. From one child rightly reared, a whole generation of Christians can come. What they receive to-day, they will give fifteen years hence," and then, he added, "The great task of the Church of Christ is the training of our children." I have been looking over this body of men this day assembled to face the central task that confronts the Church of Christ to make our Master regnant in the thought and life of the world, and as I look I note the fact that the average age of the company is about forty years, which means, brethren, that the final conflict in this war of Christ is not to be fought by you and me, but by our children and our children's children. While we do what we may, and please God that it may be much, to advance the interests of the Kingdom of our Master in our day and generation, the most strategic proposition that fronts us this hour is the training of the generation that shall be inspired with the thought and thrilled with the purpose to make our Christ the Master of the world thought and life.

Now I am going to speak to you in this period upon the

137

call to advance from the standpoint of the Sunday school. At the beginning of 1908 we had three and one-third millions of men, women, and children in the Sunday schools of our Church. At the close of the year 1913 we have four and one-half millions. In the six years from 1901 to 1907 the membership of the Sunday schools of our denomination increased by about 350,000. In the last six years, 1907 to 1913, the increase has been 1,150,000. The increase has been three and one-half times as great in the last six years as in the six years immediately preceding. In the six years from the beginning of 1907 to the close of 1912 the Sunday schools of our Church have reported the conversion of 952,000 of their scholars to Christ. In the same six years our Sunday schools have placed upon the altars of God to send the gospel into the uttermost parts of the earth more than four million dollars. We are in the midst of the most striking and remarkable advance in the history not only of the Methodist Episcopal Church, but in the history of the Church of Jesus Christ in the past century. In the last four years the Church has made an increase of $19,000 in the annual offering to missions. In the same period the Sunday schools have increased their annual offerings by $118,000. The increase in the Sunday school offering to missions has been six times as great as that in the Church. If we should suddenly deprive our great benevolent Boards of the support they now receive from the Sunday schools of the Church, four out of the six great Boards of our denomination would be face to face with absolute and almost hopeless bankruptcy. If it were not for what our Sunday schools are now giving to our Church membership, that membership would show a net decline of 100,000 members a year. The year 1928 would have a membership in our Church cut clean in two, and inside of a generation, if it were not for the recruits that come from the Sunday school, our Church would almost have ceased to be. The future of our Church is not worth more than one generation's purchase, apart from the great body of childhood and youth and the work being done in our Sunday school department. And sometimes I think we have not appreciated it. I picked up the budget of one of the leading Churches of our denomination, and appropriations made by the Official Board of that Church for the year included for the Sunday school $850. I thought that was fine. But I found the Church music appropriation $4,500. They have eighty-five officers and teachers and they have five members in the choir. That great Church is spending ten dollars per person a year upon the equipment of its men and women to teach its childhood and youth religion and morals, and is spending nine hundred dollars upon a soprano to entertain the congregation on Sundays only. That is an extreme case in this respect, that the vast majority of our Official Boards make no provision whatever for their Sunday schools. The Methodist Episcopal Church is devoting less than eight per cent of its total expense to this department from which eighty per cent of all our growth comes. We shall never have a generation pervaded by the spirit of Christ and held in the grip of spiritual ideas, motives, and purposes until the Church makes a vastly larger investment in the training of the childhood and youth in spiritual things.

I met one of our ministers; he said to me: "Some time ago my people desired me to look after a certain wayward man about sixty-three years old. I camped on the trail of that man for nearly three weeks, until I finally ran him down, brought him to church, got him to the altar, and he was converted to Christ. It was worth all the effort I made." Then he said, "With the time and effort it took me to win that one man to Christ I could have won fifteen lads to the Master and saved them from that man's career." I sat in the East Maine Conference with Bishop Burt when he called the class to be ordained as deacons and elders. Out of the fifteen fine fellows who came forward to be ordained, fourteen said that they found Christ before they were sixteen years old. Here we have a magnificent body of men, and I venture the vast majority found Christ when you were lads. Does that teach us nothing? Has not the time come for our Church to shift its methods? Is it not worth as much to save a lad from becoming a drunkard, as it is to save him after he has become one? Is not formation worth as much to the Kingdom of God as reformation? Is it not the business of the Church of Christ to minister to lives beginning as well as to lives closing? The thing that I stand here to plead for this afternoon is not that the Church shall do one whit less in behalf of lost men or women who have strayed from God's home. I would that we might do vastly more for those who have strayed from the Father of us all. But the thing I plead for is that this body of Methodist men shall speak to the Church of Christ in America and around the world, sounding a note out across the country and the continents and the seas that shall summon our Church to care for her childhood and youth, to lead them to the Church and to Christ. The future of our land is in hands of that Church that makes the largest investment in and the most successful venture which childhood and youth.

In the United States this hour more than 20,000,000 of children and youth under twenty years are receiving no ministration whatever in the name of Christ, either Protestant, Catholic, or Jewish, but are growing up absolutely unministered to in the name of our Master. Gentlemen, there is a field white unto the harvest ready for him who will glean therein. If you will give us the backing of this Convention and the support of our denomination, and will double the resources of the Board of Sunday Schools, we will lead a movement in America and in the world such that inside of seven years it will put seven millions into the Sunday schools of our Church, and will put a million dollars annually into the coffers of our Boards of Missions—Home and Foreign. I look into faces that represent the brain and brawn and genius of Methodism in America; and I challenge you to meet the offer that our Board makes this afternoon.

The Need of Advance in Our Educational Work.

Thomas Nicholson.

LAST week one of the great New York "dailies," perhaps the one of them all the most sympathetic and friendly to the Church and all that the Church advocates, said editorially:

"What is the matter with the preachers? Have they lost their fire, their inspiration, their grip on the people? They seem to be busily engaged in confessing that they have. In every denomination we hear the complaint of inability to get the people into the Churches, and of the difficulty in inducing bright, brainy young men to enter the ministry. Of course, this impression must be false. The Churches are operated by sincere people, firmly convinced of their possession of a great saving truth. It is proper to say, however, that the searching of hearts now going on among the shepherds of the flock is entirely timely."—(New York *Evening Mail* for October 22, 1913.)

No thoughtful and well-informed person will deny the increasing difficulty of attracting the masses to the Churches or of bringing them into hearty co-operation with the program of Christianity. The reasons for this difficulty are manifold. The changed conditions of our civilization; the insane lust for money getting; the negative influence of the press itself; the rage for pleasure; the possible failure of the Church to adjust itself quickly and safely to these modern conditions, and numerous other reasons may well be studied earnestly. Mature reflection, however, convinces me that no single cause is so potent as the negative attitude of our whole system of public education to the religious element in education and life. As a Nation we are constantly saying to successive generations of youth: "The three R's, the fundamentals of a liberal education, are of vital importance. If you do not willingly avail yourself of their benefits, they are so essential to life and good citizenship that we have compulsory education laws. We think so

141

much of our system of secondary education that we now spend $43,000,000 a year upon it; and our system of State universities is of such worth to the State that last year it cost us over $72,000,000. But religion is an optional. You may take it on the side lines if you wish, but it is not even an elective in our course. As a Nation we have no concern about it. The Churches in their voluntary capacity are supposed to be concerned about it, but if they fail to reach the problem, let the subject take care of itself."

Now, gentlemen, do not misunderstand me. There is not a man on the floor of this Convention more loyal and devoted to our great system of public education, from the little red schoolhouse on the hillside to the great State university in the valley, than am I. I simply, as its friend, point out to you, its friends, that the system is not yet perfect; and I point out to you its gravest defect. Education, wherever one gets it, is the chief formative force in a man's development. To omit religion from the training of our youth is to insert the germ which will result in the lingering death of the Church, and which will, I believe, lead to National deterioration. George Washington told the new Nation, in his "Farewell Address:" "Of all the dispositions and habits which lead to political prosperity, religion and morality are indispensable supports. Let us with caution indulge the supposition that morality can be maintained without religion. Whatever may be conceded to the influence of refined education on minds of peculiar structure, reason and experience both forbid us to expect that National morality can prevail in exclusion of religious principle."

Gentlemen, I stand here not merely to urge your interest in a little group of schools and colleges operated by the Methodist Episcopal Church. I come to urge upon you the larger duty of joining a movement which shall never cease until we see the religious element restored to its proper place in our great National system of education. It is not a question of maintaining a few schools as a denominational propaganda.

It is the larger question of finding a way to let the breath of God breathe through the bones of a life withered and dry without that vital breath. It is the question of the preservation of National morality on an eternally safe basis. And I make bold to say that no greater question can or will engage the attention of this superb body of men. It is of supreme importance, and this Nation is not at this moment alive to its deepest significance. What is the use of sending millions of money every year to foreign lands to Christianize alien people, if we can not make the program of Christianity effective in the noblest Nation of them all? Is it no concern of this body, is it no concern of this Nation that, by figures compiled with scrupulous care by the present private secretary of John R. Mott, we are shown that in the five-year period from 1904 to 1909 our own Northwestern University at Evanston furnished four-fifths as many recruits for our foreign missionary service as all the State universities in the United States combined? Is it of no significance that two of our smaller colleges in the same five-year period furnished us more missionary recruits by five than all those State universities combined? Look at facts like these. We have perhaps not less than 20,000 Methodist students in State universities, yet they return to us but four per cent of our ministers. One great State university, with a thousand student members of the Methodist Episcopal Church and with three thousand members of other evangelical Churches, and with a body of alumni numbering eight thousand, is said in half a century to have given less than twenty ministers to all the evangelical Churches combined. Of the college men entering our ministry, moreover, twenty-two per cent testify that their call to the ministry came to them, not before they went to college, but while they were students in our own denominational schools, showing the vitality of the religious influence existing there.

I am not making an attack upon State universities. Let

143

that be clearly understood. I am sympathetic with their problems. Many of their presidents and professors are devout Christian men who deplore these facts as much as I do. Many of them would give their right hands if they could cure these things. They implore our aid in meeting the grave situation. They know that a series of conditions and circumstances in the history of this Republic, which they did not create and for which the Church itself was not wholly guiltless, begat an eagerness to be free from sectarianism, which resulted in leaving the Bible out of our education, but, what was and is of greater moment, led to a narrow method of instruction in history, in literature, and in the humanities generally. The movements of God in human history, the influence of religious conviction born of the study of the Bible, the influence of the moral ideals inspired by the Man of Nazareth can be discussed in many class rooms with far less freedom and sympathy than can the philosophy of Hæckel or the opinions of the promoters of the French Revolution. Almost any new or novel subject could be introduced into the curriculum easier than could a course in the literature of the Bible or a sympathetic study of evangelical religion. It is the paramount duty of the American Church to bury its sectarian differences and unite its rival bodies in an effort to create a public sentiment which will correct this defect and which will put the religious element in its rightful place in our public education. In my judgment, for the public school age we should intensify the responsibility of the home and the Sunday school for the culture of the religious life of the child, and we should aid to put in the public school curriculum some such course of moral and religious instruction as has been worked out successfully in two or three of the Western States.

There is another consideration. This is an age of institutions, and the Christian spirit must be institutionalized if it is to prevail. A Nation becomes neither permanent nor strong until it develops settled institutions. If Christianity is to survive, if it shall become powerful enough to influence the coming generations, it must voice itself through the institutions of the Nation, and our great problem at this hour is how to preserve the benefit of training and of culture, how to preserve the great institutions of modern civilization without letting them go to destruction for lack of moral and spiritual direction, how to have them rich and powerful without having them selfish, self-centered, and the creatures of arrogant oligarchies. Only the great, commanding, life-giving force of divine love, breathing through them and permeating their whole being, will accomplish this. And for this purpose we must strengthen and broaden our denominational colleges as we have not yet dreamed of doing.

THE STATE STARTS ITS EDUCATIONAL POLICY from the doctrine of duty, growing out of the child's right to an education; on the inherent responsibilities of citizenship; THE CHURCH STARTS HERS from the Christian impulse of the love of God and of men. The Church believes that duty can never be fully met while there is indifference to the underlying forces that develop men and perpetuate civilization. To the Church spiritual ideals are supreme. The denominational college is and will remain her great fort where the freedom of religion will be maintained with the same courage as in the State institutions the freedom of science will be defended. I insist that the Church college must never falter in its insistence on these moral and spiritual essentials. The fact is that not all these Church colleges are as pious as they might be. Not every college we have is just now a veritable copy of the Kingdom of God come down to earth, nor of the perfection of wisdom in the use or disposition of moral and spiritual forces. They are struggling with great difficulties. They are in the midst of great temptations. Their presidents are diverted from educational and spiritual contact and leadership by the stern necessities of finance. They are doing a great work for the Kingdom as it is, but they must go on to perfection, they must ask no pardon for giving prime consideration to these vital religious concerns. But, gentlemen, I want the Church college to be less and less a denominational propaganda, and more and more the defender of these Christian ideals and the champion of the rights of the vitally religious element in all education. I want the Church college to lay less and less stress on religiosity, cant, and churchianity, and more and more stress on the great Christian fundamentals. I want them never to surrender on the incontrovertible principle that we can not get ultimate and final truth if we leave out the moral and spiritual element in the culture of the men who seek for the truth. I want these colleges to be cautious not to take a querulous and antagonistic, much less a villifying attitude toward State institutions. Our mission is to help and not to hinder, to supplement and not to supplant, to create a public opinion which will demand perfection, and to perfect ourselves that we may the more forcefully demand it. We must consistently place the perfected education by the side of the education imperfect because of the lack of the religious element, until the world realizes the lack and supplies it. I therefore want these Church colleges to be well equipped and well endowed. They can not do their great work if their libraries are composed only of antiquated books, if their laboratories are absent or ridiculously defective, or if their teachers are narrow traditionalists, bigots, or weak and nerveless men who expect to be protected by ecclesiastical or religious sanctions from the searching tests of truth and efficiency which come to other men. Their equipment must be of the best. Their Faculties must be composed of noble men of proved and accurate scholarship, reverent toward God, devoted to their fellow-men, and incapable of an ethical twist for the sake of securing personal advantages.

The Church must accept the responsibility for the support of these institutions, but I believe we have a right to ask for them free and liberal contributions from citizens generally. The skilled workman demands the best tools. The man who works beneath his ideals soons degenerates. Great teachers will not and can not get along with inferior equipment. The days of the omnibus professor are ended. Lifelong education, critical knowledge of a specific subject, power of original research, scientific accuracy, spiritual insight, personality, and moral fiber are the demands. Men who acquire these must forego many of the prizes of business and professional life, and they have a right to demand adequate compensation and retiring allowances. Such teachers have supreme opportunities for molding world civilizations. The schools under the auspices of our own Church are counted by the score. With a very few exceptions they are strategically placed and in communities where they are needed. They have an abundant wealth of students. The number constantly increases. But look at these facts. In 1911 the statistics show that the average cost per student of such education as we gave was not less than $140; in some institutions it was considerably higher. The total amount received in tuitions and all student fees was a little over $90 per student. Personally I have not much sympathy with the movement to increase fees and tuition excepting to cover the actual cost of board and such expenses. We want democracy in education. The Church should make education with the religious element as free as the State makes education without the religious element. But, be that as it may, when we add to the average fees paid by each student the average amount received from all income, from endowment and rental of property, from room rentals in dormitories, from Conference collections, we find the average total amount received from each student from all sources combined is only $99.14. In order to pay the actual present cost of education, we must supply an average of something like $40 per student in their current income, and that means that they must have an increased Sustentation Fund of well on toward a million and a half of dollars per year. The Board of Education deserves the dignity of a great benevolent Board of the Church; every member of the Church in every

State should be interested and enlisted. We can not do the work of supporting and supervising these colleges properly if we leave it to local pride or prejudice, or to the confines of single municipalities. A National society has the advantage of opportunity to study country-wide phenomena. No local agency can possibly have the outlook upon the field which a National agency may have. If the National agency is scientifically conducted, it gives valuable advice in regard to methods, and it has the opportunity to aid in the saving of very large sums of money.

A recent report of the United States Commissioner of Education places the average cost of education per student in the universities and colleges of the country at $303. It would take an added endowment of $167,000,000 this year of grace 1913 to bring our endowments up to the point where their income would equal the average amount per student which the higher institutions of the country have expended. But fifty cents a member would add that needed current income; fifty dollars a member for a single year would supply all that needed endowment.

THE BOARD OF EDUCATION therefore urges upon this great Convention the necessity for an immediate advance in support of educational institutions. It urges the placing of the apportionment for public education at a more liberal figure, and earnestly insists that the amount should be raised in every charge. It urges your loyal support of our denominational colleges, not only because of their vital relation to the sources of supply of our workers at home and abroad, and also because they are a vital and necessary part of our great system of public education. It urges the co-operation of these institutions with those in charge of the administration of our system of public education to the end that the religious element may find its proper place in all education everywhere. The aim of denominational life should be the larger Christian life which will tend to make all men everywhere love and serve our Christ.

Advance in Freedmen's Aid Society.

P. J. MAVEETY.

IN the city where I live they have recently put up the largest skyscraper on the face of the earth outside the city of New York. A little while ago a company of the members of the Board of Managers of the Freedmen's Aid Society, through the courtesy of the vice-president of the institution that owns it, were invited to visit it, and we were taken to its top, nearly five hundred feet from the pavement. From the top of that great structure the city stretched out in every direction. The great river swept and twisted and wound its way in the distance. The hills rose covered with beautiful homes, and the hum and buzz of the city rose like the swelling of a great organ. Everything was beautiful from the top of that huge building, and as we visited it from story to story and saw the beauty of the offices and the magnificence of display on every hand we were charmed, and we were inclined to go away feeling that everything must be as beautiful as this. Now, the men who have been on this platform to-day have lifted us to the top of a great building, and from this top we have looked out over Methodism. We have seen its winding way through the centuries; we have seen its hilltops of success; we have heard the busy hum and murmur of its millions of men and women working for the advancement of the Kingdom of God, and we have been delighted and pleased and, I have no doubt, fascinated with the beauty of the prospect. But most of the people who go to the top of the building forget that this building has a cellar, and very few of them go down to visit and see the man in the cellar. But I am going to take you for a few moments this afternoon and show you the man in the cellar. Christianity is not to be judged by its hilltops—it is not to be judged by what it does for the rich, although this is a hard task; it is not to be judged by what it does for the great masses of the people, for, thank God! they are mostly religious anyhow, and they need only to be guided and directed. But our Christianity, the Christianity of our day, is to be tested by what it does for the man in the cellar. I do not mean in the slums. No, no. The man in the slums may be a hobo or he may be an idler, or he may be a drinker. But I mean the man in the cellar, the man with grime upon his face, the man of the strong hand, the man of the brave heart, the man without whom the top of the skyscraper and without whom the beauty and the comfort of all that lies between the pavement and the top would be utterly impossible. Our civilization has its cellar, and the man in the cellar of our civilization in our country is the man with the grimy face, with a hard hand, with a strong heart, and with a musical voice as you have heard this afternoon. This man is the man in the cotton fields, the man in those great sections of the South that furnish our civilization so much of its comfort, so much of its satisfaction, so much of its joy. And I come this afternoon, in the few minutes I have, to this great body of Methodist men gathered from all over the land and ask you, my brethren, What are you doing to-day for these black men in the cellars of our civilization? I take it for granted that Christianity is for the men in the cellar as well as for the men in the rooms above. I take it that when Jesus said to a handful of fishermen and farmers on a hillside in Galilee, "Go ye and make disciples of all the nations," that He excluded none, and therefore the white man and the brown man, the yellow man and the black man are all embraced in that great commission. I suggest also, what has been suggested previously to-day, that this religion is a universal religion; that it is for the white man and the black man, the king on his throne, the noble in his palace, the business man in his office, the farmer in the field, the artisan in the shop, and for the humblest sweeper on the stairway or the street. If that be not so, if there be any section of our world, any race of people for whom it is not adapted, then we must cease preaching and search for the universal religion that reaches all men. But we do not have to do that. We have the demonstration of it everywhere, for earlier Methodism reached the men in the cellar. It began with the man in the cellar in English life, and it went up through every grade, because the man in the cellar may become the man on the throne. Kingdoms and empires may be swayed and moved by the power of his mind and the strength of his hand and his heart.

Now, this black man in our country is ten million strong. At the close of the war four millions of them were freed from slavery, and from that time until now they have been multiplying and increasing until they number ten million. And we in our egoism have presumed to say that because this man is backward and because he is poor and covered by the grime of centuries, that therefore he is a problem to us. Forgetting that all men are problems to God, and that the great problem, after all, is not the black man, is not the brown man, is not the yellow man, or any other man, but the problem is the man ignorant, the man poor, the man backward, the man who is vicious and who has not the opportunity to correct and control those evil tendencies. The Methodist Church, in response to the call of this great home missionary problem, has at this present time twenty-two schools among these black people in the South, where nearly seven thousand boys and girls are being trained to be preachers and teachers and Christian leaders among their own people. Some of the brainiest and strongest and holiest men and women that the Church ever produced have gone down into that Southland to train and teach this man in the cellar, that he might be able to come up into the light and go out on our streets and enjoy the sunlight. Thank God that he may do so! These men and women have given to the Church its ministers, its teachers, its preachers, and its members. Out of ten millions of these black folks four millions are members of Christian Churches and one and three-quarter millions are members of Christian Sunday schools. They have thirty-five thousand Christian Churches, and they have about the same number of ministers to minister to them. These churches have a seating capacity of ten millions of people, so that all the people who choose to go to church on any occasion would have seats ready for them. This property is worth $56,000,000. They also have imitated us in another thing, that these properties are in debt. They have $5,000,000 of indebtedness; but, deducting it, there is still $51,000,000 gathered as the result of fifty years' work, and that is at the rate of a million dollars per year of every year of freedom.

The call for advance is based on two or three things. First, the demand for better and stronger preachers, teachers, and Christian leaders. The South is awakening to its duty and its responsibility to the black man. While here and there there are still individuals who are living in the Middle Ages or in Russia, or in Florida, where, on the 9th day of June the governor of the State put his pen to an act of the Legislature forbidding white persons to teach colored pupils in a colored school. If that were spoken of Russia, we would feel that it was commensurate with the ignorance and backwardness of the land of the Czar. The South, however, as a whole, is waking up to the fact that this black man must be educated, trained, else he becomes a menace to himself and a menace to the people among whom he lives. Popular education is extending wider and wider, and there are school teachers enough to supply the great demand, but there are not preachers enough who are trained and educated to supply the demand caused by the better training and the larger vision of the colored people. Therefore it belongs to the great Churches of the North, whose schools have been down there for nearly half a century, to provide those Christian ministers and Christian teachers and Christian leaders for the service which they will be called upon to do in the training of this colored population during the next twenty-five years. The larger call comes from the South, from our colored Churches. When we mention the name Africa: Mohammedanism like a tremendous wave is sweeping over Africa from the North, and it has reached almost half way towards the South. If we are not to stand still and see Mohammedanism stretch its awful pall of ignorance, polygamy, and licentiousness over Africa, we must hasten to prepare the ten million blacks of the United States with consecration and knowledge enough to send representatives into that dark continent and bring it to Jesus Christ.

The demand for the education and training of the black man comes from our own needs. You heard from the first speaker this morning how small the world has become and how the dividing lines have disappeared. There never was a time in the history of the world when it was so true that no man liveth to himself or dieth to himself. for if we live to ourselves we die miserably, and if we die we can not die without bringing some one down to death with us. If they have the plague in Shanghai, the rats bring it over to New York or to San Francisco by the first vessel. The newspapers said a few days ago that the plague had been found in rats in New York City. We live in the same house with the men of China and of Africa, and we can not help ourselves. It becomes necessary, then, that Christianity join hands with the scientific man to rid the world of vice and ignorance and everything that would cause any race to die lest in its death it bring down all the other races with itself. We are under the necessity of training the black man in the South in order that we may be free from the consequences of his ignorance and poverty and the diseases that come upon him. Statistics tell us that he is three or four times more liable to tuberculosis than the white man because of ignorance and unsanitary surroundings and inability to take care of himself in sickness. In order that we may protect ourselves we must bring these men into a larger life for themselves. We must help the black man out of the cellar, for the man in the cellar will breed disease for the man in the skyscrapers to its very top. The black man comes to you not as a man in the slums, but in the

153

cellar. He puts the fire under the boilers that run the machinery of civilization. He goes out into the cotton and cornfields and everywhere to contribute his share towards the great conglomeration of human beings which we call civilization, composed of men of every type. And only as the Church goes forth with the gospel of Jesus Christ in its hand and with the love of Jesus Christ and the love of manhood and womanhood in its heart, will it serve itself or its God in this day and generation. If we do that, we have before us the prospect of training and educating the largest section of the humblest Protestant people on the face of the earth. This great Negro population is almost entirely Protestant, and of that Protestant population a very large section is Methodist or Baptist. The responsibility that rests upon us is tremendous. It is a critical time with our black brothers. They have not yet secured a foothold in property or a foothold in society; they have not yet secured a sufficient foothold in the Nation to take care of themselves; they are still dependent upon us for love and sympathy, and for money that their teachers may be paid and buildings erected and their work carried on.

Brethren, our work commends itself to those who are outside. The largest single gift to the work of the Methodist Episcopal Church during the last five or ten years came from a man who is not a member of any Church, Mr. Andrew Carnegie. The second largest came from a Presbyterian woman, $12,500; and the third largest gift came from a Unitarian of New England, who gave $35,000 for the building at Orangeburg, South Carolina. And the next was from a Jew of Chicago, and another from the aforesaid New England Unitarian. So that Jew and Gentile, bond and free, Methodist and Presbyterian, Englishman, Scotchman, Irishman, and American have all joined together in this great work, and they see the need of it, the need of bringing to these colored people of the South the uplifting, the humanizing, and the constructive processes of our Christian civilization.

Advance in Home Missions and Church Extension.

WARD PLATT.

THE needs of the Board of Home Missions and Church Extension are as manifold as the forty nationalities that crowd our shores and till our soil. America is the fountain that waters the earth. If the fountain be pure, the streams will bring life to the nations. As a nation thinks, so it is; its Churches determine the character of its thinking. The man of God officiating in the place of worship is the center of things which tend to the regenerating of the community and the building of a new earth. To aid in building more than 15,000 such churches and to extend help to the maintaining of four thousand preachers is the work of this Board. And every such church is a new center of supply for every benevolent cause, and every such preacher is the agent for every benevolent Board. In a single quadrennium, the last, Churches were helped to the number of 1,775, and four thousand preachers, in making their appeal for all good causes, were subsidized by this Board to the extent of $2,600,000.

Then, this appeal of the Board of Home Missions and Church Extension is as fundamental as our Methodist propaganda. This Board of Home Missions has its responsibilities as I have indicated in a world sense. We, the most popular Protestant body, numerically the largest, have our proportionate responsibility in our National life and influence. Situated as we are in the North Temperate Zone, we have the ideal climate. Our soil excels in natural fertility. Our mineral deposits are rich and various. We have vast forests and mighty rivers. Stupendous as are our material achievements, they are but the foregleaning of an output from stream and soil and air and wealth which is hardly above the horizon of dreams. We inherit the best blood and genius of a select ancestry. We inherit ideals. We are still under the thrill of the Puritan who endeavored to realize the Kingdom of God in his community and Commonwealth. We inherit the best

155

Christian civilization upon which the sun has thus far shone. That is evidenced by our Christian propaganda that leads Christian forces in the world evangel. We inherit the good-will of the nations yet to be Christianized. Historically our relation to them gives America an open door more fully than comes to any other people. Truly our call is a world-call. We have untold millions of people in different portions of the earth turning from worn-out civilizations and exploded religions and they are endeavoring to approximate the institutions of these United States of America. In short, we are so scrutinized and studied that if we, through missionary and other aid, may set up in the United States of America the Kingdom of God adequately, in the next few years it is certain to go clean around the earth.

If you ask what the Board is doing in a particular sense to help this Nation realize its world mission, we might specify and say that $473,000 have been appropriated in a year to white English-speaking peoples; $57,000 to be spent among ten million Negroes. The American Negro tends to hold leadership in his race, and if in a brotherly sense we aid this man to come to his own, we therefore set up a standard for the lifting of the whole African continent. We have among ten million Germans an appropriation of $53,000 in a year. One German immigratn cared for on American soil gives us sixty-three thousand; and we have a Bishop from this wing of the Church who has spoken to us eloquently this day, and an overflow of more than thirty-seven thousand in Conferences in Europe. Among four million Scandinavians the appropriation is $60,000. One Scandinavian cared for in the city of New York gives us an outcome of twenty-eight thousand sturdy Scandinavians organized into Methodist Conferences, and an overflow in Europe of more than thirty thousand. Two and a half millions of Spanish-Americans received about $50,000 appropriation; and four million Italians, the work just beginning, an appropriation of more than $50,000. If you will take the Japanese, seventy-five thousand of them, with an appropriation of $30,000; seventy-five thousand Chinese, with an appropriation of $20,000; and the more we understand about these, we come to regard these Orientals from the East the more highly. They come here to study and to absorb and to form their conclusions concerning present-day Christianity at its best. They return and tell us to wait until they tell their countrymen their impressions of our American Christianity. Those are the missionaries with whom we have to reckon. If you will take the Southwest, that will grip the world. It holds the waterways that are to feel the products of two hemispheres. Our own acres will produce abundant crops for the Orient and thus bind us closer to the Far East. You take the Northwest, pouring out its harvests by the way of the Golden Gate, pouring out its products for the sustenance of the Asiatics; this Pacific Sea is certain to become a great American Ocean. We only see yet the shadow of it; but the time certainly is coming when we must answer the question, What shall be the moral and spiritual character of this Nation as effected through these channels? It is a world question. Let us answer it by our supply of Churches and preachers in this Northwest and on these far frontiers. If you will study the map you will find that those people fronting Asia are paying twice per capita what we are in the East, and they are giving about twice as much for the other fellow as we in the East are giving.

There is no time, of course, to tell this story, but as you reinforce this Board you are standing by an organization that faces and helps to solve the problems that you face. It is the uplift of this country that means the salvation of the world. O men of America, who turn not back from any material enterprise, no matter what awful front it wears, to you is committed the biggest man's task of the ages, the salvation of America! That is your campaign. A nailèd, pierced Hand points the way. A streaming, blood-red banner tells where the Man of Nazareth leads, and do you not hear His militant call, "If any man will be My disciples, let him take up his cross and follow Me?" O men, with the possibilities before us, and our appropriations nearly on the level of a bare sustenance, lacking the efficiency that we ought to have, let me ask you this, Is it not time that because of financial limitations you no longer keep this Board in leash? Loose it and let it go.

C. M. BOSWELL.

I WOULD rather be anywhere else just now than on this platform to make a speech. It is pretty hard to get away from the thought that our colleague, Dr. Robert Forbes, who has been with us in so many glorious campaigns, was this day laid in his grave. I can not help feeling that had he been here he would have warmed your hearts and won your spirits by the presentation of this cause. I am asked simply to speak a word in regard to our Board and the American city; and through that we trust to get a greater support for the cause we represent.

We need a larger support because of the great responsibilities you have placed upon us in regard to the American city. A little while ago we were startled with a statement in the *Christian Advocate* that in the seventeen large American cities with a population of three hundred thousand and over we have less than five per cent of our Methodism; and in the two hundred and twenty-eight cities with a population of twenty-five thousand and over we have less than fifteen per cent of our Methodism; or, in other words, we are out of the cities. Now, I do not know whether it is because of reasons sent to the office not long ago like this or not: We have been sending out letters asking for information regarding rural Churches. This answer came back: "You have tampered with the city Church until you have ruined it; for God's sake let the country Church alone." I do not know whether that is the reason we are out of the big cities or not, but we are out, and the statesmanship of Methodism is being concentrated on getting into those great Commonwealths. We must be in there, and get the population to get the money that we need in our business, to get control of the institutions that are influencing religion and other things, to get religious control of the newspapers that are wielding power everywhere throughout the land, to get control of amusements that entertain the people, to get the influence that the big city wields in the United States of America and through the world. We must get in by wise, timely, and tested methods and agencies, and the Board of Home Missions and Church Extension is expected to co-operate with these and never stop until we plant our flag on the largest and most influential of the Commonwealths in this country. To do this, we have to get back of the city missionaries. There are many of them who are doing work in American cities, and if I can believe the reports that they are sending into our office now, Methodism must go out of business if we do not give them the money they seek. Listen to me: New York, supposedly the richest city in the United States, with over five million people, one million and over from foreign lands, sends this word: "Give us twenty-five thousand for New York, or Methodism is doomed." Multiply that all over the country, and you will see the burden you have given the men who are governing the affairs of the Board of Home Missions in its relation to cities.

We must get back of the district superintendents. They are the key to the situation religiously, as far as Methodism is concerned. I have been with them in the city of Portland, Ore., in Tacoma and Seattle, Wash., down in Atlanta, Ga., and the cities between, and I have been with these men when they stepped on the ground, when they had located churches, planning to combine structures for the betterment of the work that a Church organization ought to do, and when they are through, they turn around and say, "How much will the Board of Home Missions and Church Extension give us?"

We are co-operating with the bishop. Thank God that

these men under the new régime are getting the American cities with their varied population and their changing conditions on their hearts. They are studying the questions as to population, as to progress, and as to needs, and when they make their wants known to the Board of Home Missions and Church Extension, it has to get back of them and give them just as much money as it can, and tell them to go ahead and when they run out to come to us and we will give them more. All we want is to have sufficient funds to let the men who are our leaders go into these cities as generals of an army, meaning business, and when they need munitions of war, give it to them, provide men, build churches, plan battles, and we will back them up until we win every place we see.

We want to get back of the new Churches getting in before the saloons; put up the Methodist flag, start meetings, organize a school, build a church, and enlist soldiers for the Lord Jesus Christ. Go into every new neighborhood and hold it for Christ, for Methodism, and for man. On my desk in Philadelphia there is a paper which says one city has eighty-five per cent foreign population; another, seventy-five per cent foreign; another, fifty per cent foreign; and so the Board of Home Missions is getting back of that proposition, establishing a Church, and getting a man that can speak another language than the English and putting him in there to tell the story of Jesus and His love, and converting the stranger. Forty thousand dollars goes into the Italian work. Then, the rescue neighborhood Church. Methodism can not forget the pit into which many of the wayward are falling, the evil of gambling houses and other places of vice. We are in this world to fight sin, and to fight it with the gospel of Jesus Christ, and I know of no better place to do it than to go to a drinking hall in a tenderloin district; put a Methodist minister in there, a Methodist singer, and a Methodist deaconess; start them going, and they will tell the story that will regenerate that neighborhood. In the city of Philadelphia, on the edge of the tenderloin district, a place is open every night in the week, and fifteen thousand of the hardest drinkers have been led to Jesus Christ through this place. O, the American city! What an appeal it makes! Let the answer to that appeal be, "God helping, I will give so much to the Board of Home Missions and Church Extension that every city may be supplied with money to bring the erring to Christ."

Advance in Foreign Missions.

W. F. OLDHAM.

Brothers: You have heard many eloquent pleas this afternoon, and are to hear several more through the days urging "Advance"—but the only voice distinctively raised on behalf of the 150,000,000 of unevangelized souls committed to the Methodist Episcopal Church in non-Christian lands is the one you are now hearing. The Board of Education and of the Freedmen's Aid, the Board of Home Missions and of Sunday Schools, except for some recent devisings, and all the other Boards are all working at different parts of the same home problems. They are all subdivisions of Home Missions. And I and those I stand for rejoice in all these and would have them doubled. When the Board of Foreign Missions is named, that is the agency which is trying single-handed to do for the pagan and Moslem and semi-Christian world what all of these others unitedly are trying to do for our share of the United States of America. And if a high appreciation and gratitude force me to name as a great co-worker of the Board of Foreign Missions the Woman's Foreign Missionary Society, it would be necessary also to introduce the Woman's Home Missionary Society, the Church Deaconess Board, and a multitude of other co-operative woman's agencies working at home. With this in mind I present at once the cause of Foreign Missions under the three-fold aspect of their *reasons, successes,* and *present opportunities.*

MILITANT METHODISM.

I. Why should there be any call at all to Foreign Missionary endeavor?

1. The obligation of obedience. Whatever other reasons may or may not commend themselves, here we reach bed-rock. Said a young lieutenant to the great General Wellington, "I do not believe in this new enthusiasm for Foreign Missions." Said the General, "Sir, what are the marching orders?" Soldiers of Christ, I read to you the marching orders, "Go ye into all the world and preach the gospel to every creature."

2. The obligation of gratitude. Remember the pit out of which we were digged, and who they were that found us. Foreign missionaries reached us when our forefathers were wild savages. We received Christ and took the upward path. Here we are. What was done for us we owe it to do for others.

3. The moral condition of the unevangelized non-Christian world. I would not subtract one tittle from the good that is found in alien religions and among alien peoples. The great heart of God loves all men, and the mighty power of the Holy Spirit ceaselessly endeavors to illumine all people. Nevertheless, making all concessions and giving all credits, the condition of the pagan and Moslem world may be characterized by the opening words of Milton on his own blindness, "Dark—dark—dark." Admitting all existent values in the non-Christian world, yet in the main it may sadly be said that manhood is without rights; woman is practically a slave or a toy; childhood is dwarfed and stunted by superstition and ignorance. Thirty years ago I saw a great feast at a sacred shrine in Mysore, India, at which were gathered perhaps a thousand mothers with their children. The idol god was the seven-headed serpent, representing power. Presently there stepped from a dark recess a Brahmin priest bearing brass trays covered with chipped eggs and small pans of milk. He rang a bell as he placed the trays before the idol, and immediately there swarmed into view scores of deadly

162

cobra snakes to eat the offering. Among them stood the priest unharmed. I saw the fright in the onlooking children's eyes. The mothers, however, were gently forcing the children to bow down and worship the gods—the Brahmin and the serpents. And eighty per cent of Hindu India would thus have bowed to them. The Moslem world stands over against us, howling defiance, practicing slavery, degrading womanhood by polygamy, saying our Scriptures are garbled, and DENYING our CHRIST as the Divine Son of God. And these are the sunlit peaks of the pagan world. What shall I say of the cruelties and the sorrows that are found in the darker areas still? As the Great Son of God looks down upon this welter of sin and cruelty and superstition, can you not see the breaking of His shepherd heart and hear Him say, "Other sheep I have that are not of this fold—them also I must bring?"

And to these, *their* deep needs, add this of ours. We need to see world problems. *We* need Foreign Missions that we may have wider horizons. Only a world-girdling and world-conquering Church has in it a real dynamic, a potent call, a stirring life. It has been well and truly said, "Whether the heathen will be lost unless we come or not, we are *already* lost if we are not moved to go or send." We will never take America if we do not bend ourselves to take the world. Only the Christ-passion in us will enable us to win at home. We can never have the Christ-passion if we refuse the Christ-vision.

II. The successes of Foreign Missions.

Methodist Missions at the oldest are but eighty years old, and the bulk of our foreign enterprise is from fifty to sixty years of age. The agency employed has been comparatively small. For the evangelization of the 150,000,000 assigned us by the enlightened and deliberate judgment of the world's missionary forum, we had last year but 400 ordained foreign missionaries and 650 ordained native ministers—or about 1,050 in all. While here in Indiana, for Methodism's proportion of the three millions there are about one thousand ordained men. The ratio of agency runs about one hundred to one. Yet this slim handful, met at first by misunderstanding and racial prejudice, by open opposition and stony indifference, has kept patiently, steadily at work. They have had but about a brief half century. During that time, working from five to ten thousand miles from home, contending with strange languages and stranger customs, debilitated by unfavorable climates, harassed by disease, criticised abroad and till lately often sneered at at home, they have overcome initial difficulties, broken through the apathy of great masses of ignorance, have withstood the organized opposition of aroused priesthoods and the militant frenzy of persecuting fanatics. In the face of mobs and riots, of revolutions and wars, and above all, in spite of powerfully intrenched religious and hoary superstitions, they have inaugurated changes, they have altered civilizations, they have witnessed the reformation of peoples and the rebirth of nations; they have planted schools and school systems; they have built churches and established Christian homes and Christian worship, and have already gathered in a membership who number one-tenth of the whole Methodist Episcopal Church. Behold, what hath God wrought! If ever there was written a page that speaks at once the divinity of our faith and the virility of our Methodism, it is the record of our foreign missionary achievement.

In nominally Christian lands have been planted Churches of such evangelical fidelity and aggressive methods as to command the esteem and quicken the life of all around them, and in the pagan world what marvels have been wrought! Japan has launched her autonomous Methodism. Korea shows, perhaps, the most aggressive Church of personal Christian workers in the world. Malaysia exhibits a program of effective social help largely self-supporting, hard to parallel. Africa emerges in part from the darkness of the ages and is pierced with shafts of light. India turns away from her myriad gods and adds 30,000 baptized Christians to Methodist ranks this very year. China, great China, thrills with new life and publicly holds out beseeching hands, saying, "Pray for us, O Christians; we long to find our way into the light." In the span of a single lifetime has come a change which betokens the approaching rebirth of half a world. And while not we alone but all the great Churches of Christendom have brought this about, Methodism has had a large and commanding place in the program, under the direction of what Dr. Harlan P. Beach, of Yale, terms "one of the greatest missionary organizations on earth, "the Board of Foreign Missions of the Methodist Episcopal Church.

III. But, brothers, great successes bring great obligations, and often still greater opportunities. And the call of commanding opportunity is now added to that of appealing need. I name only a few of the outstanding opportunities:

1. The Mediterranean basin is the theater of a new life and the scene of a most dramatic and fateful contest for empire over the souls of millions of men. Here Islam, jostled out of the complacency and self-sufficiency of thirteen centuries, develops a new spirit of inquiry. North Africa and Southern Europe are both involved. Ours is no part in carnal military or commercial contention, but the call is for the planting of those ideas and the proclamation of that gospel which assures renewal of life and permanence of progress. How manifestly opportunity beckons to Hartzell in Africa and to Nuelsen in Southern and Southeastern Europe! How shall they answer? They wait to hear. Will this Convention, speaking for Methodism, say: "Go forward. Take opportunity at the flood. We are with you. *Advance?*"

2. Here are the Latin lands—our neighbors and some our wards. What are we to say to Butler, who comes out of Mexico City, where, after forty years, only recently "stormed at with shot and shell, bravely he stood and well," and, in company with his bishop, quietly caring for the interests of the mission? And what word have we for the eloquent and forceful leader of South America? What shall we do with the

new opportunity that opens on both banks of the Panama Canal and among those potent States that we must link up in closer unison of heart and democratic purpose? Shall not Methodism say to Stuntz and to Eveland, in that gloriously successful mission under our own flag in the far Pacific, "No more hesitation and parley—Forward! The Church orders are, 'Advance!'"

3. India and its dependencies are rocked with spiritual stress and agony of soul. That great, passionate, religious heart is strangely stirred by the manifest and felt presence of her Lord—the Light of Asia and of the world. No greater religious opportunity has been put before the Church since Methodism was founded. The opportunity in India is to actually gather into Methodist membership a million converts in ten years if the right word be sincerely spoken here. These numberless thousands are now being held back. Let us but say to the gallant leaders Warne and the Robinsons: "Let the people come in. School, preach, baptize, Church—go forward. We'll stand by. More men, more means are on the way." What a shout would answer that word! "Jai Prathu Jesu," "Victory to Jesus," would be sung by tens of thousands of new voices in a few brief years. The glories of Pentecost would be revived, but over wider areas and under ampler skies.

4. And China! Who can gauge the size of opportunity as it is written over the portals of that greatest gate ever opened for the gospel to the hearts of men? O brothers! what word shall we send Bashford and Lewis, those two great hearts who face a continent, bearing burdens beyond human strength to carry? There they are, with strategic union educational projects, in which Methodism is shamed by not being able to do her part and meet her share. Hospitals there are without doctors, and schools without principals, vast stirring areas without missionaries, preachers, and leaders. A great nation comes to a new day. In the midst of it stand these mighty men of God, loved, honored, trusted, implicitly fol-

lowed, and yet in this home of tremendous opportunity, in a situation which beggars all description, when the Presbyterians are sending one hundred new missionaries, and when *all* the other Churches are devising larger things, Methodism, whose impact has been strongest, whose fruitage is largest, Methodism is not sending a single added male missionary on its regular budget. And what is more, the bishops write that unless $32,000 are added to their budget this year they must send home several missionaries, for they positively refuse to incur any debt.

I cease specifying. The fact is, we are in the midst of the greatest movements of all time. Christianity began in Palestine, and was in danger of being merely the cult of a small Syrian lake. Its foreign missionary passion burst through those earliest bonds and carried it a conquering force to the Mediterranean basin. Thence it sped its forceful missionary way through Europe and gallantly flung itself across the wide ocean till it occupied the north Atlantic shores. Now, in this latest day, comes the last challenge and the greatest. The mightiest ocean, the Pacific, fronts us with great lands and great races—for Christ. These lands, already moved by the loving efforts of Christendom, are being stirred to the depths. All life wakes to nobler ideals. Home life, intellectual life, life social, industrial, and political, are all in ferment. The crowning day towards which all the days have worked is at hand. Our Christ comes to His final enthronement when He shall be declared Lord of lords and King of kings. What does opportunity like this call for, my Brothers, on our wide-flung mission frontiers? We are starving our institutions, we are overweighting our men. There sits in our midst a missionary district superintendent trying to struggle back to life and health. His was a district of 60,000 square miles, with a population of eighteen millions. On the failure of his neighbor's health there was added to him the oversight of a second district; to these later, a chaplaincy. Why? Because the Board could not send more help. He nearly died under the pressure. He did nervously collapse. And all over the fields men are being crowded to the last ounce of their strength. Everywhere is comparative arrest of movement because of poor equipment and because the existing agencies have gone as far as they can.

What shall be the words of this Convention and of the great Church behind this Convention to these resolute but overburdened men in this greatest day of all time? We will be true to our heritage and our traditions. In the name of John Wesley, who started us with the great motto, "The world is my parish," and of Coke, our first great missionary bishop, whose dead body touches every shore, pledge of the coming of his successors to help occupy and redeem the lands —but, above all, in the name of our Divine Redeemer, "who by the grace of God tasted death for every man," and bade His Church in its earliest hours of insignificance and weakness to "Go disciple all nations"—hearing the voices that call to us from the historic past, from the wide spaces of earth, and from heaven above, will not this Convention answer back so our word will reach a waiting world and an expectant heaven, saying, "We hear the call and by the grace of God we pledge ourselves to heed the call and *advance* the work of a world's redemption?" In the name of the Lord, "Go Forward."

II. THE CALL OF SOCIETY AND STATE.

American Cities and the City of God.

WILLIAM F. ANDERSON.

IN the city is the crisis of national life the wide world round, and as goes the city so goes the Nation. One of our leaders has written a significant volume, entitled "The City the Hope of Democracy." I came upon it for the first time a little while ago, after my pathway had led me through the red-light district of my own city. I said to myself, "If this which I have seen is the city, and if the city is the hope of Democracy, then God pity democracy." My inference would be perfectly correct if in the red-light district of the city we found the best features of the life of the city. I am glad to believe, however, that this is not the case. You will remember Burke's definition of the State. He declared that the State is a partnership in life representing all the interests of its members.

It is encouraging that among civic leaders in this country and in other parts of the world there has been during the last twenty or twenty-five years a remarkable quickening of effort to make the city a partnership in the life and interests of the people. I wish to bring you two or three notable instances. A few months ago, I picked up one morning in the city of London, the London *Times,* and I found a very interesting article concerning a municipal movement in the city of Edinburgh, looking toward the better housing of the poor in that favored municipality. With characteristic American nerve, I wrote to the Lord Mayor and told him that I was to be in his city in a few days, and should esteem it a very great favor if he would put me in the way of information as to that movement. He replied promptly, stating he had handed my letter to the chief of the Health Department, and further, if on arrival in Edinburgh I would notify that gentleman, he would be glad to receive me and give me the information desired.

Upon my arrival in Edinburgh, I wrote to that gentleman and made an engagement to call at his office. He told me about the work that had been going on, and then after we had talked for an hour in his office, he said: "Come along with me; I want to show you what has actually been done." We walked along for a few blocks and passed a certain building. He said: "A few weeks ago there were thirty-six hundred people housed in this single building. Now there is not a human being within its walls." We went on further and he showed me the modern, sanitary buildings that were erected under municipal direction for the housing of the poor, and stated that the city undertook to make about four per cent profit out of that enterprise. I said to him, "Well, Doctor, how long have you been engaged in this kind of work?" He answered promptly, "For fifteen years." "How many houses have you condemned as uninhabitable in the course of a year?" He replied, "Certainly, hundreds of them." But I said, "Without any respect at all as to the ownership of the property?" "Certainly," he answered, "without the slightest respect to the question of ownership." Then I said, "I should like to ask if in your experience of fifteen years the thought of graft has even been suggested?" "Graft, graft?" he queried; "I do not know that word. Is that an American word?" I was sorry to have to confess that it is. Then I replied, "Now, in your condemnation proceedings of this large number of houses, has the suggestion ever been made to you by any one, that if you would pass by certain houses belonging to certain prominent citizens, they would make it a consideration for you?" He said, "Not at all, not at all, not for a moment. No citizen of this municipality would insult me in that fashion."

FORWARD MARCH!—A CALL TO ADVANCE.

This is no isolated case. This Christian conception of the city, making it a partnership among its people, has spread throughout the world. Let me bring you some very interesting statistics. Among the fifty leading cities of Great Britain, thirty-nine own their own water-plants; twenty-one own their own gas supply; forty-four their own electrical supply, and forty-two their tramways. In Germany the average is higher. Out of fifty leading cities of Germany forty-eight own their own water supply, fifty their gas plants, forty-two their electrical plants, and twenty-three their tramways. This idea of the city is more and more impressing itself upon civic leaders in our own land. Among the cities of this land there is a call to real patriotism which the leading citizens of these great municipalities are recognizing as never before. There is in St. Louis a young man, a college graduate, worth thirty millions, who devotes his energies as Park Commissioner to the city's welfare. The Superintendent of Parks in that city is authority for the statement that it is not an unusual thing for him to be on the job in the park at six in the morning, and for the munificent reward of two hundred and fifty dollars per month. How is that for a man who is worth thirty millions?

Now it is unfortunate that the progress of the Church has not kept pace with this development in civic affairs. American Christianity has not been grappling the saving of the down-town portion of the city as it ought to be doing. We have found ourselves very frequently excusing ourselves. In what contrast are we with the English Wesleyans? They plant themselves right down in the most thickly populated part of a great city in a way that is impressive and masterful and in a way that commands attention, and they are solving the problem of the saving of the city in Great Britain perhaps as Methodists are doing nowhere else in the world. When we have contrasted our conditions with theirs, the common answer has been, "O well, our conditions are different." Of course they are different; that they are more intricate we must concede by virtue of the fact that instead of having to take the gospel to one language only, we have to take it to men of many languages; but when the problem of the different languages is solved, our work is no more difficult than theirs. Every earnest approach which we have made to the foreign-speaking populations has been abundantly rewarded. Countless thousands from all parts of the world are eager for the gospel message. Here is a field which is white to the harvest. God help us both to see and to improve the great opportunity!

Just what is our problem? Let us come to it in a rather indirect fashion. Whenever any side of the life of a man becomes stronger than his moral and spiritual life, he begins to deteriorate and decay, ceasing to be a man and becoming a mere thing. What is true of the life of the individual is true of the community, municipality, or Commonwealth. Whenever any side of a city's life becomes stronger than its moral and spiritual side, it is facing towards paganism. Now, the city represents intensity of life as nothing else does, and the problem that rests upon the Church of God is the making of the moral and the religious life of our cities stronger than their business, their political, their intellectual, their social life. It is the business of the Church of the living God to permeate all of these aspects of the life of our modern cities and to mold them in the fashion of the divine ideal of life. You say that is a terrific problem, and I grant it is, and you say that is too much to be expected of the Church of God. I tell you no. The Church must do that or else it must confess failure and go at last out of business.

Now the fact is that we must get at this problem in a larger way. We must attack it in bigger fashion. We have been content to make a fairly good impression in some sporadic communities. It is the business of the Church to take hold of the entire problem. I do not know better how to bring to you the thought that I have in mind than by a very interesting historic incident in connection with the great metropolis

of this country. Among the men interested in the redemption
of New York City, who have been giving their best study and
efforts to it, is the Rev. Bishop David H. Greer, of the Protestant Episcopal Church. You know the Episcopalians received large grants many years ago that have made them
occupy a very advantageous position. Bishop Greer has
studied the problem with deep earnestness. Above the Har-
lem River, he found that in the last ten years the population
had increased nearly forty per cent. There were great business blocks devoted to money-making. Every here and there
was a great temple erected for the gratification of the love of
pleasure so characteristic of the people of to-day. He said,
"If we do not get into this game in larger fashion, the first
thing we know the Borough of the Bronx will become pagan."
So he began to think about what he could do to relieve the
situation. He said, "If I can find ten men in the Protestant
Episcopal Church who will give me each $10,000 for the re-
demption of the Bronx, I can do something worth while."
The more he thought of it, the more that seemed to him a
practicable proposition. He put at the head of the list the
name of a great banker down in Wall Street. He said, "It
is hardly worth while for me to speak to that man; I know
I will get his check, but some day I will step in and tell him
that I have put him down for $10,000." One morning, being
in the region of that banking establishment, he sent in his
card and was ushered into the private office of the president,
who soon came in and with cordial greeting said, "I am
glad to see you, Bishop Greer; if there is anything I can do
for you I shall be very happy indeed." Said the bishop:
"I will come directly to my point. I have been studying conditions in the Bronx. We Episcopalians are not doing what
we ought to be doing up there. If we could raise $100,000
we could do better. And I have conceived that there are or
ought to be ten leading Episcopalian business men who would
give me $10,000 each. I have put your name at the head
of the list." The banker said: "No, you will have to excuse

173

me. I am not interested in that proposition.'' ''What?'' said the bishop; ''I did put a question mark in my mind after some of these names, but not after yours.'' ''No,'' said the banker, ''I am not interested.'' The bishop began to think how he could get away with as little embarrassment as possible to his friend and himself, when the banker said: ''I will tell you, Bishop Greer, the kind of a proposition I would be interested in. I have been looking over conditions in the Bronx. What is $100,000 for the Episcopalians to give for the redemption of the Bronx. If you had started out to find ten men who would give you each $100,000 for the redemption of the Bronx I should be interested in that sort of a proposition. That would command my respect.'' And the bishop grasped him by the hand and said, ''Thank God for a layman who has such a vision of the building of the Kingdom as that.'' And the banker continued, ''What is more, Bishop Greer, if you are interested sufficiently in this proposition and it appeals to you, I will give a day in the near future and go with you and we will see if we can not find the other nine Episcopalians who will give each $100,000 for the redemption of the Bronx.'' A friend of mine told me that one of the bishops of the Protestant Episcopal Church told him that he saw Bishop Greer with eight checks for $100,000 each in his hand and two letters from responsible business men in that communion inviting him to call at their offices and saying that they would be glad to draw their checks for that amount any day he would come in. I have been trying to imagine what a bishop would feel like with a lot of papers like that in his hand, and I am authorized to say to you in behalf of my colleagues that every one of them would like to have that sensation. And if the laymen of Methodism will put into the hands of every bishop of the Methodist Episcopal Church $1,000,000 for city redemption, some things will be happening in this country and the wide world around that will make glad the hearts of men and of angels.

174

Now, my brethren, I do not believe that we can ever hope to win in this contest simply according to the old methods. The old introspective conception of Christianity is not big enough to meet the demands of this day. We have a gospel that includes the whole life of man, and we must preach it in its entirety. A few years ago I was pastor of a downtown Church close to the Judson Memorial Church, established by that good man, Dr. Edward Judson. The Institutional Church was then a somewhat new development. One day, soon after beginning my pastorate, I said to him, "Dr. Judson, will you characterize in a word or two the chief features of the Institutional Church?" Said he, "It is simply a Church of organized kindnesses to the individual." I tell you, my friends, the Church that gives itself in organized kindnesses to the individual is the Church against which hell itself will not be able to stand. Note the putting of it in the Gospel according to St. Mark: "And He ordained twelve, that they should be with Him and that He might send them forth to preach and to have power to heal sicknesses and to cast out devils." Here we have the inspiration and the method of Christian evangelization. The inspiration—presence with Christ Himself; the method—prophecy and philanthropy, evangelism and every-day brotherhood linked in noble balance. By this method, with this inspiration, through the power of the Lion of the tribe of Judah, the cities of America shall become the city of our God, and the kingdoms of the earth shall become the Kingdom of our Lord and of His Christ.

The Call to Civic Righteousness.

ADNA W. LEONARD.

THAT there is a summons to civic righteousness is included in the very wording of the subject, and that there is need of civic righteousness no intelligent person will question for one moment. Great as has been the history of our Nation, marvelous as has been the achievement of the immediate past in social work and in social affairs, there is still a loud, clear call to civic righteousness in this Nation.

The sky of our political life is not without clouds. We can but mention a few. There is political corruption. Not so much perhaps as some pessimistic folk may declare, but that there is commercialism in politics no one will deny. There is a cloud in the National sky. There is not yet complete independence for the voter; the independent voice of the voter is not yet clearly heard, for vast numbers of people do not cast their votes with independent judgment. They cast their votes at the dictates of the boss and the politician. Great as has been the history of our public school system, we are sometimes appalled at the vast volume of ignorance that is abroad in our land.

Not all of us have descended from Anglo-Saxon ancestors. Not all of our people have come from those nations that have achieved the true standard of self-government. And increasingly large numbers of people know not what it means to live in liberty under restraint of law. Great cities have come into existence. We have seen them grow. And with their growth there has come the unsanitary slum—men, women, and children dying prematurely.

Then there is yet another cloud in the sky. Little children are being robbed of their childhood with a robbery that is truly cruel. Girls and women are compelled to work, not only in physical environment that causes the outbreaking of terrible diseases, but in moral environment in our factories and mills and stores that too often exposes the white flower of American womanhood to moral peril enough to make the lightest heart sad and the stoutest quake with fear. There are in this country of ours vast problems. The city becomes a forcing bed where every vice grows into abnormal proportions. Here we find too often our system of justice a system of injustice, so that every now and then poverty becomes a crime, while the rich man, though a criminal, is

176

given his liberty. I can not pause beyond the mere mention of these subjects. Suffice it to say that if the problems are to be solved, it will be necessary to create wholesome public opinion for civic righteousness. Mr. Bryce has said that public opinion is the conscience of nations. It is in two forms. Crystallized public opinion is statutory law. It marks the ethical advance of a community or a nation. There is another, and that is the liquid form of public opinion; it is ever supplementing, ever-changing, ever making its inroad on statutory law. Abraham Lincoln said that if you would change the law of the land, you ought to change public opinion, and you change the law in proportion as you change opinion. In order that we may have wholesome public opinion three factors are essential. These are the pulpit, the pew, and the press. Let us consider them.

By the pulpit I mean the Christian ministry. The man with a true vision of the ministry will know that he must preach the gospel with all the passion of a moral physician, for he knows that sin is a deadly curse and not a mere term of the school men. And the average man will go to church, not that he may hear some particular philosophy or some literature or the history of some poem, but he goes into the church of the living God because he is hungry for the bread of life. Alas for the ministry or the minister that gives to the hungry soul a stone when he asks for bread! Now, I recognize the fact that all the methods of the past can not be used in the present. The gospel of Jesus Christ, like our Divine Lord, is the same yesterday, to-day and forever, though it is progressive. The methods of yesterday can not be employed in the work of to-day in the Church of God, any more than the methods of yesterday in the business house can be employed in the business house to-day with the maximum of success. We are living in days of momentous changes. And the minister of the gospel of Jesus Christ owes it to his day and generation not only to interest himself in all the problems of the times, but to be in sympathy with every throb and pulsebeat of society that makes for the uplift of mankind. Therefore he can not be silent when he comes to the great subject of social service, when it comes to the great subject of the congested district of great cities. He can not be silent in the presence of that awful problem, the un-American saloon. He can not be silent in the presence of any moral problem that is sapping away the life of the people. He must be in smypathy with his day and with the time. But while this is true and he feels his way into all these things, I believe the minister of the gospel who wisely studies these matters, when at the right time he exposes the corruption of a city council or opens up to the public gaze the graft of a police force, or shows that officials in political positions are the recipients of the manifold bounties of vice interests, he is doing as much of the Lord's work as when he invites the sinner to the altar that he may find pardon and peace.

The next is the pew. By the pew I mean the Christian manhood and womanhood of this Nation. It is a sad fact, but I believe it to be true, and I am not unmindful of the magnificent laymen of the Christian Church who are doing their best constantly for civic righteousness in increasingly large numbers; but it is a fact that is worthy of our prayerful consideration that so many of our Christian men are unwilling and afraid to put themselves on the firing line for moral reform. Some of them have not in the least realized their responsibility for the moral conditions that surround their community. What is necessary is that Christian ministers and Christian laymen face the great evils of our cities and by the grace of God endeavor to seek their solution. If we are to have public opinion intensified through the laity, it will be necessary for the laity to make sacrifice. I have found it very difficult for men, because of their inter-relationship in business, to come out strongly on the side of moral reform. They are interested, but they are not interested enough to make sacrifice. They are willing the preacher should stand on the firing line and receive the filth and the abuse of the

said, "No, this other business is too profitable for us; we can not do it." I say to you the business men can direct very largely the policy of the daily press. Now, this same paper, when we were having that war on the red-light district—we recalled Mr. Gill—there has been but one recall election in Seattle, and we recalled the man who stood for the saloon and who stood for the red-light district, and ever since that time we have had noble Christians as mayors of the city of Seattle —notified one minister that if he kept up that fight he would have to leave the city in ninety days; the minister sent back word that if he left the city he would leave it feet first.

There came a time for the revival, and here is where I want to close by showing the connection between the evangelistic work on the part of the pastors interested in the civic affairs of a great city and in social service. Four Churches—Baptist, Presbyterian, Methodist, and First Congregational—came together. We had 10,000 members as an aggregate of membership in those Churches. We held four weeks' revival services. We spoke every night on the streets to 3,000 men while we stood in automobiles. I have seen strong men kneel in the streets of Seattle, yielding their lives to Jesus Christ and finding Him as their Savior from sin. This paper came to the business men's committee and said, "We want you to place us on the same footing as these other papers," and the business men said, "No, you have been fighting our ministers, you have been declaring them immoral, you have lied about them; we will give you no recognition." They said, "We will give you the best write-up in the city." So they put on five reporters, two of them court reporters, and every sermon preached was taken down verbatim and printed in that particular paper. When it was over, that paper sent word to me as president of the Ministerial Federation of Seattle—I have the letters on file in the office, "We want to let by-gones be by-gones; we are not going to knock the preachers any more; give us the recognition that you are giving the other papers, and we will never again attack the ministers of Seattle and the Churches and that for which they stand.'' These are the three factors in developing public opinion that is to be crystallized into statutory laws, but I am not unmindful of the fact that every inspiration that helps a city, a State, and a Nation finds its source in the cross and emanates therefrom.

The Call to Social Service.

FRANCIS J. McCONNELL.

IT requires only a very ordinary power of discernment to see that there is all over the world a movement of society toward the emphasis of a larger social control. The social economist says that it is because the free land of the world is rapidly becoming exhausted. In our own free country we no longer have free land as our fathers had it, and that is practically true all over the world. Because the tide of emigration has been turned back, the problem of congested population forces upon us this subject of social control. The social economist also says that the rapidity of communication of ideas in these days is so great that men in all lands quickly find out what is happening in the thought of men in other lands, and are very anxious and willing to try out any social scheme. I do not know what the cause is, and I do not pretend to say what the cause is, but it is very significant that every one who looks upon this problem sees that it is a movement that goes forward and not back. There will never be a return to conditions of other days. We may not know what is going to happen in the future, but we certainly shall not go back. There is an enormous turmoil and commotion and we can not tell what is ahead of us, but we are moving on towards stricter and stricter forms of social control. It is true in England. It is true in France. It is true in the Balkans and the Far East; true everywhere. Let this fact sink into your consciousness for a minute. I do not appear to-night as an advocate of Socialism. I simply bring Socialism

forward because, as you know, it stands for social control—
that is to say, society is an organization and is controlling
and ruling itself. I have seen on the statement of reliable
authority that there are more Socialists in the world to-day,
more men who in their various countries vote the Socialist
ticket than there are belonging to any other human organization under the sun except the Roman Catholic Church when
it counts as a communicant every one who is really attached
to the Church. Think of that! More practical Socialists,
standing as they do for social control in perhaps an extreme
form, under the sun than any other organization except the
Roman Catholic Church. It illustrates the tendency of which
I speak. No man can tell what the future is to bring forth.
I do not wish to trifle with the dignity of this occasion, but,
to use a slang expression that is really descriptive of this
situation, we are not very certain of just where we are going,
but we are mighty certain we are on our way. Nobody can
tell what the future is to be in view of that world-wide movement. More important, it seems to me, than any strictly intellectual movement or philosophical movement, more important than any other single movement of this kind in the
world to-day is this trend all over the world towards increased
social control.

What shall be the attitude of the Church, and what
summons is there to us as an institution? The summons
to us is for a very deep type of personal piety, of sanctification and redemption of life in all our contact with our
fellows round about us. There have been some statements
of the doctrine of entire sanctification which I could never
understand, but I heard a definition of entire sanctification
once that struck me as being fairly satisfactory for practical
purposes. I heard an old man say once that he was a little
bit confused about the doctrine of sanctification, but he proposed to make it mean that he would sanctify to the best of
his ability everything that he could get his hands on. We
must have a sanctification of all personal contacts in every

realm of life. Of course, we are getting beyond the dividing line between secular and sacred, but we have not come yet to see, perhaps, the wild tracts of land in us that need to be redeemed. Nominally we are Christians, but tracts in our political and commercial and social relations are not yet entirely sanctified; there is a lot of wild land especially around the edges; and while the land near at hand in industrial contacts seems cultivated, look out into the jungle and you will hear the wolf calling, and that kind of thing needs redemption mightily. Some man says, "Let us not get away from the individualistic personal gospel." I am not trying to do that; let us stay there, but remember, after you have got a man clean, everything cleansed and pure at its source, we will not have solved the social problem and all problems. And some man says, the moment you talk about this, "You are talking impersonal forces." I am talking about personal sanctification, and when you talk about environment, remember there are two kinds of environment: first, the environment of impersonal forces, and second, personal environment, which consists of persons, and if you do not believe in that kind of environment you do not believe in the Christian Church, for it is nothing but personal environment in religious principles. We need to sanctify environment in that sense. A good, pious man called upon me one time to see about getting a pastor for a Methodist Church a good many hundreds of miles from here, and unless you locate it nearer, a good many hundreds of miles from Denver. He said, "We must have such and such kind of a man." We sat up until eleven o'clock Saturday night, and he got his man. Later I found out that every time the preacher in that town tried to clean out dives and do something for the good of the town, somebody called him off. In my innocence I went down there one day and I asked this layman who called him off, and he gave a gasp and said, "If that man talks about dives and disorderly houses I will have to surrender my business position." Now, I do not say that that man should be turned out of the Methodist Episcopal Church, but I do say that he should not be on a committee to seek a minister. I will say this also, that if I ever hold that particular Conference again and he comes to me on the Pulpit Supply Committee, we will not talk until eleven o'clock, but we will get through comparatively early in the evening. The point is this, that that Churchman was the personal environment of practically everybody in that town, and they were suffering from these evil influences and he sat there and said what he wanted was a preacher who would preach the pure gospel. He was superior to them, but the thing to do was to rise superior to him by putting him in his proper place. We need that doctrine of entire sanctification of the practical kind, the doctrine of a sanctified life. We need emphasis on the social consciousness coming out of sanctified social lives that will make a different social climate. We can not overcome some things by direct attack, but we can melt some things down by the Christian consciousness of the Nation and transform some things.

Take the home mission problem—say, the problem of Mormonism. What is the trouble with it? Is it anything especially dangerous in its theology? Not at all; if you want to keep a man from becoming a convert to Mormonism, let him read the Mormon Bible. Of all nonsense, that is about the worst. If you want to separate him still further, let him look into its theology. The danger is not in polygamy. I have been trying to find specific cases. The marriage has to take place in secret. The priest has his face muffled, and if anybody is caught in the thing he has to be willing to plead that he is guilty of unlawful cohabitation. What is the trouble? In the old days there was a strong social feeling against it; but what is now the trouble? About two trusts and a railroad or two. You send missionaries out there, and they do the best they can; and about all they do is to keep the people from becoming good Mormons, and that is worth while. I am not afraid that anything that happens in

MILITANT METHODISM.

Utah is going to transform the United States. Utah had a very fine chance in the last Presidential election to show what she could do if let alone. Even with the help of Vermont she did not get very far, and that is no reflection on the man she voted for. The trouble is that Mormonism is absolutely un-American. Think of two or three million tithes turned into one man's hands, with practically no kind of a check! That amounts to political domination. The right kind of atmosphere will make a transformation, but we will have to keep our mind on that railroad and the trust or two. How did those great monsters of other ages die? Because somebody took a weapon and smote them? No; they died because the climate changed; and there are a great many things in this country that will die one of these days because the climate changes, and our children will look back and see some things we now have in this country, and wonder how we stood them. Maybe we are not correctly informed about the social consequences of these things; I am not talking about any particular scheme. Some profound reorganizations are coming along as the nations pass from one crisis to another.

We talk about the home mission field and the foreign mission field; what is the great hindrance in these days to the spread of the gospel? James Bryce in his book of "University and Historical Addresses" makes this statement, that clear up to the present time contact between the so-called favored nations and nations less favored in certain respects, and especially material respects, has very little to redeem it from being an unrelieved horror. That is practically true. We have looked upon the material resources of other countries simply as something to be exploited. We have looked out on the human beings of other countries as something to be exploited; and the traveler and the diplomat that the missionary in the foreign field has to contend with are the ones most completely in his way. I know what I am talking about, for I have been to Mexico. I have a speech on Mexico that I have been giving all over the country. I am

186

going to put in a paragraph of it here. We send Dr. Butler and his faithful and noble band of men and women—as faithful and noble as you can find anywhere—down there, and then ask them to contend against almost insuperable obstacles in the contact of the two nations. Let me be very accurate. A Mexican, when he has a chance—and a very few of them have had a chance, living on ten cents or less a day— the Mexican, when he has a chance, is just about as good a person as you would care to find anywhere. Here is an incident. An American was sitting, just before this last outbreak, in his office in Mexico City. A nicely-dressed Mexican came in, and he turned and said to his secretary, "Send for an interpreter until I find what this damned Aztec wants." That's what he said. The Mexican said, "It is not necessary to send for an interpreter; I understand English." What kind of an impression was made on that particular Aztec's mind? I was on the streets of Mexico City the day before Madero was shot, and one American said, "I hope to goodness they will get him soon." I was on the streets the day Gustavo Madero was killed, and another American said, with a profane and obscene expression, that he was glad they had got him at last. I was in communication for two days with the former Secretary of the Madero government, whose statistics may have been colored a little; but he told me that there is one whole State in Mexico, every square foot of land in which is held by a foreign corporation, and not one foreign corporation pays one red cent of taxes to Mexico. He said the Peninsula of Lower California can be divided into six strips, each of which is held by foreigners paying no taxes. Mahogany forests are given away as foreign concessions. Sixty million acres of land, which one government brought back to the public domain, given away by graft concession. That is friendly contact; that is peaceful penetration. And I have to say it gets pretty far in; it is successful. There is not much that has more of an edge on it than this. I have been reading in the papers a lot of talk about American honor, but I have yet to see many magazine articles on this question, "What is the best for Mexico in this whole matter?" We hear a great deal about the honor of the United States. I heard a wise man say this, that it is hard to treat anything with respect unless it is respectable." And when you hear people talking about the honor of the United States, we think of the Master's words, "You know not of what spirit you are." Nobody is asking me for any light on the Mexican question. But I want to say this plainly, that the consideration of the contact of the so-called higher class with the so-called lower class has been an unrelieved theme from the beginning until now, but when the question is studied through and through, in the light of right social and political relationships, the nations will come to the glory of God with a spontaniety that will be beyond description.

There is one further point I wish to make and that is this, that when we get the right kind of social consciousness we will have a new understanding of Christianity. I do not believe that the foundation of the Book ever stood firmer than to-day. I do not think the Church was ever looked upon more favorably than to-day. And men are searching after all these things that will transform the Nation. It has been done in the past, and if we can lead this world-wide movement into the right channel, it will be an argument that can not be shaken. Is that radicalism? If it is, it is the radicalism of going down to the root. The Master told a parable of a man who cut down a tree, and I suppose he left the stump, and another man came with a spade and moved the earth and let in the sunshine and dropped a seed in, and lo! a great change. The radicalism of the Lord Jesus Christ is just this, of giving things a chance by getting down to their roots. There are certain institutions that never yet have had a chance. Splendid as the family is, it has not had its best chance. Has there ever been any kind of organization or institution that has had its best chance? Christian radicals should come not with the ax to destroy things necessarily, but with spades to give things a chance. Heaven is just an improved environment. A wise old thinker once said, "All the Lord does here is to start the plants and then He puts them in a place where the personal environment is better," and this is the thing we have really been standing for in Christianity from the beginning. Starting with the individual soul, and realizing the fact that there are things we can do better together than alone, recognizing the fact that there is a kind of birth of consciousness that is better than the individual consciousness. What is the law of social movement? That two and two make four? Not at all. Two and two make half a dozen or a hundred. We have been working for that from the beginning. It is no new doctrine. I remember that Bishop Foster, standing once before a convention of ministers of Baltimore, said one great trouble with the Christianity of the world is that we have not proper conditions in our social life at home. How can we go out to preach the Christian gospel to the nations with a cancer of intemperance burning in the bosom of our Nation? There are some other things besides that. The thing for us to do is to try to go clear down to the depths of the gospel of the Lord Jesus Christ and insist in all our dealings with the outside world that the influence of the Lord Jesus Christ shall govern. The summons of the age comes out of the fact that there is a world-wide movement for the Church to register itself and stand squarely face to face with these issues and try to guide this movement in the right channel.

III. THE CALL OF AMERICA AND OF THE WORLD.

New Americans for A New America.

Edwin H. Hughes.

New Americans come to us through three gates: the gate of immigration, the gate of birth, and the gate of character. The problem with immigration is spiritual assimilation. The problem with youth is spiritual education. The problem with character is spiritual regeneration. If we are to have a new America, it must arrive from these three directions.

That adjective "new" has played a huge part in all our American life. Its use began in colonial days. The hope for the future as well as the reverence for the past was expressed by its recurrence even in geography. New England, New Hampshire, New York, New Brunswick, New Amsterdam, New Orleans, New Rochelle,—all these names, whether English or Dutch or French, were symbols of expectancy as well as reminders of fond experience in the lands beyond the sea. In truth, the adjective "new" has been used in a wholesale manner; and we speak of our country still as the "New World." More than four hundred years have passed since Christopher Columbus touched these shores with the cross of our faith. Yet our National hope is so large and bright that, in spite of well-nigh half a millennium of history and the passing of about twelve generations of human beings, we persist in calling America the "New World." The emblem of our Nation is not tottering age, nor even staid and completed mid-life; it is rather youth,—buoyant, eager, glad. The visitor to our land is not treated to the sight of many ruins, but he is regaled with the vision of many

190

castles in the American air. We still look here for a "new earth wherein dwelleth righteousness." The mood of the New Testament is in our blood.

The ever-present danger is that we shall think of new Americans as creations rather than achievements, and of the new America as an inevitable happening rather than as a holy and serious task. The pillars of State are not flung into their places by the lazy fancy of men, nor are they pushed beneath the temple of State as structural accidents. They are shaped and cemented in the sweat and blood of men. It is nearly three hundred years since Plymouth Rock became historic, and nearly a century and a half since the Liberty Bell became musical. The dust of millions and of hundreds of millions is lying beneath the sod of valley and mountain. Still do we speak of the "new land," and "new Americans," and of the "New America." We toss these phrases upon a program as if the normal American heart needed no explanation of their meaning. It may be said that Christianity as a religion and the United States as a Nation have this in common: that both hear some adequate power saying, "Behold, I make all things new."

It is our duty as Christian men to see to it that America shall turn to Jesus Christ for all its newness. Those who come to us through the gates of immigration must be met in His spirit. Those who come to us through the gates of birth must be received as His immortal charges, to be kept as His own forever. Those who would seek the gates of regeneration must be persuaded out of the hostile country and the neutral ground until the touch of Christ's power shall make them new men and, therefore, best Americans. At whichever of the three points we meet our problem, the method and spirit of Jesus are our only hope. God stations us at all three of the gates through which the new Americans come in order that, by ushering them into His life, we may likewise usher in the New America.

I. What, then, is the command that comes to us from

191

the spirit of Jesus as to our attitude toward those who arrive through the gates of immigration? This is not the occasion for debating the wisdom of our immigration laws. Among Christian men there can be no possible controversy on one point: If our laws give men and women and children either invitation or liberty to come to our shores, they must here be fashioned after our political life, and they must be met and conquered by that free gospel that is alone the safeguard of our Republic. If each year a million new faces turn eagerly to our ports, it will be national idiocy and religious apostasy for us to withhold that sympathy that is the very beginning of spiritual assimilation. Let it be said without sentimentality that the great assimilator is love. In the long run, that section of the Church of Christ that most loves the immigrant will most claim the immigrant. Physicians will tell us, in their medical vocabulary, that very often the immigrant is afflicted with "nostalgia." He longs for the vision of the native hills and valleys and of the dear faces of his family and friends until at last his heart breaks for very loneliness. The steerage of the ships and the files of Castle Garden are filled with the germs of homesickness. Christian men must furnish the antidote. Jesus would do just that. His heart would yearn toward those newcomers. He who said, "The foxes have holes, and the birds of the air have nests, but the Son of man hath not where to lay His head," would enter into sympathy with those homeless arrivals. God put the "stranger" into the Ten Commandments and allied the dispensation of law with the treatment of every newcomer. Jesus put the "stranger" into the tests of the judgment and allied Himself with every foreigner whose anxious eyes really look for the face of Christ in the American welcome. Those who know best will tell us that the stranger is peculiarly susceptible to Christian friendliness. Our Lord knew this when He identified Himself with him and said, "I was a Stranger, and ye took Me in." The Christian attitude toward this candidate for Americanism is not

192

simply that he represents Cæsar or Savonarola, Luther or
Goethe, Huss or Copernicus, Shakespeare or Milton; it is
rather that he represents Christ. Long ago four Greeks
came and said, "Sirs, we would see Jesus." In their coming our Lord beheld the coming of His own Kingdom. Out
of a vast hope He said that those fragments of the outside
world were prophecies of His wide reign over all the world.
Already our Lord has given us these tokens of optimism.
Already many thousands of immigrants are walking the ways
of loyal Americanism and likewise the ways of a free and
spiritual religion. Some of them are in all our Churches.
In a union Thanksgiving service of our denomination in San
Francisco one would have noted the Japanese here, the Chinese there, the Scandinavians on the left, the Swedes on the
right, the Germans in the center, and a little group of Italians sitting, shy and modest, in the front seats. He would
be dull, both in his American faith and in his Christian faith,
who would not see the significance of such a scene as that.
My brethren, every year God gives His Church in America
a million opportunities in as many immigrants. William Nast
was one of those opportunities in the not distant past. We
seized that human chance for Christ, and to-day many thousands of voices, both German and English, bless the event,
while a fine stream of Teuton blood helps to make both the
New America and the new Methodism. God give grace to His
Church that we may more and more make Castle Garden one
of the entrances to His Kingdom and that we may turn the
Panama Canal into a river of life along whose borders will
grow the trees for the healing of the nations!

II. We must not, however, neglect that other road along
which wee feet walk into our National and Church life. Far
more than a million little people come annually out of the
everywhere into the here. Around each of a thousand cradles
men and women stand daily saying, "What manner of child
shall this be?" George McDonald makes this dialogue to
occur with each blessed and breathing arrival:

MILITANT METHODISM.

"And how did you come to be just you?
God thought of me, and so I grew.

"And how did you come to us, you dear?
God thought of you, and so I am here."

It requires no great strain on faith to say that this is quite as true in the National and in the Church sense as it is in the family sense. Every child is God's thought for the future of the Church and the Nation. Those eager feet romp on to take our places. The boys that shouted on their way to school this very day will run the Men's Convention twenty-five years hence. The chairmen of those coming sessions to-day gave the mystic signals on the gridiron. The speakers of that coming program to-day exercised their vocal powers in shouting teams onward to the goal. He is an infidel who does not believe that those boundless powers belong to Christ, and he is a new betrayer of our Lord who takes no earnest part in keeping their feet in the path everlasting. These are the new Americans that will fashion the new America, these the new souls that will make the new Christian Republic.

Nor can there be any real doubt as to the attitude of Christ toward the subjects of this problem. To rich men Jesus showed a differing mood. To the adults who sought His teaching He gave widely differing commands. But to children He was ever the same,—gentle, hopeful, and utterly dogmatic in reference to their spiritual standing,—saying: "Take heed that ye despise not one of these little ones;" "Whosoever shall offend one of these little ones;" "The Kingdom of Heaven belongeth unto such." We will search the words of Jesus all in vain for any utterance that did not distinctly claim all childhood as His own. Beyond the earthly parenthood He saw the Heavenly Fatherhood. Above the family tree He saw the eternal reach of ancestry. The children's names were written in the Lamb's book of life ere they were penned in the family Bible of earth. Jesus on

194

the streets of Jerusalem represents God, gathering the children in His arms and saying forever, "Suffer the little ones to come unto Me and forbid them not." They will come if they are merely *suffered* to come. They will come if they are *not* forbidden. The time may arrive when they will walk the byways and highways and when the Lord's word will be, "*Compel* them to come in." It is not so now. Children are the primary opportunity of the people of God. They are the hope of America and of the Church.

It might not be amiss for us to imitate the splendid dogmatism of Jesus with reference to the spiritual standing of children. We forbear to do so. Whether our problem be that of keeping them within the Kingdom or of gaining them for the Kingdom, their plastic lives will answer to our touch. Among all hopeful signs for our Church of the present time, this is the most hopeful: that there is a loving Children's Crusade in the plan of the Kingdom; not a crusade that sends wee marchers to die on the plains of Italy in a wild attempt to recover Jerusalem from the Saracens; not the hysterical leadership of Nicholas of Vendome and Stephen of Cologne; not a glaring track of small skeletons whitening beyond the passes of the Alps and southward; but rather a crusade which seeks to claim every young life as a recruit for that army that is led by the Son of God as He goes forth to war against strongholds mightier than a walled Jerusalem. If we knew the far and high issues and the sure tokens of progress we would hail the large increase in Sunday school scholars as the prophecy of new Americans, new Methodists, new soldiers for Christ. Here in a Men's Convention Jesus would still place the child in the midst. Directly we shall know that nothing more truly represents Jesus than a proper attitude toward the little people. When that attitude claims us wholly, we shall put child labor to death and the two million pairs of small feet that even to-day stood in the mills and factories of our Nation will walk out to their God-appointed places of preparation in the schools and Churches of the Nations and to their God-appointed play amid the daisies of the field. The Christian conception of childhood will soon or late reach the hand of the modern Herod and stop forever the modern slaughter of the innocents. It will do more than this: it will translate the children from the dust of mills and factories, not only into the sunshine of natural childhood, but even into the Kingdom of God. We shall hear the march of that glad and alert procession of children as it moves through the beautiful gate of the temple. When we allow the Good Shepherd to gather the lambs in His bosom, He will be compelled to make fewer journeys out to the wild and bare mountains that He may recover the lost to the safety and peace of His blessed fold.

III. But there is another gate through which new Americans may be brought to the New America. Immigrants may become our anarchists and saloonists. Children may grow up to be grafters and blasphemers. Immigration is not regeneration. Assimilation is not sanctification. Education is not a new birth. The inspector at Ellis Island can not see the heart. The public school teacher may not officially use the penitent form or the mourner's bench. If we but knew it, the hope of America lies with the men who proclaim a redeeming God. A revival of religion is necessarily a revival of assuring Americanism. Crowded altars are the Republic's best hope.

For, after all, we need a frequent return to the commonplace statement that a Nation is not made up of hills and valleys, but rather of human souls. Every good man makes a better America. When the preacher sees his convert walking the ways of righteousness and service, he can say, "I have helped my country." Rocks and rills and woods and templed hills get their meaning from men. Mrs. Browning does not overstate it in her "Aurora Leigh:"

FORWARD MARCH!—A CALL TO ADVANCE.

Government, if veritable and lawful
Is not given by the imposition of the foreign hand.

*   *   *   *   *   *   *   *

Genuine government is but the expression of a people,
The loud sum of its silent units."

The unit of America is an individual heart. Every renewed heart lifts the moral average of the Nation and is a contribution to the new America. It is the business of the Church, both as a matter of patriotism and of religion, to keep open the gates through which men and women walk the ways of genuine penitence to the peace and pardon and purity of God.

This, my friends, was the message of Methodism to the eighteenth and nineteenth centuries. It must be our message to the twentieth century. It may be that at times and by some persons the doctrine of conversion has been held narrowly; and it is doubtless true that we have confused many good hearts by the preaching of a typical experience. But our main message remains intact: God Almighty by the Holy Ghost sent down from above and by the free grace revealed in Jesus Christ, does save men from their sins and does give them new hearts. That conception has found its way into literature, both polite and philosophic. William James celebrates it in his "Varieties of Religious Experience," and the Harvard professor leaves the prime contention of Methodism in possession of the field. Harold Begbie celebrates the same spiritual fact in his two books that, recounting actual experiences, none the less read like heaven-inspired romances of the soul. We may well submit, that when the philosopher and the novelist begin to exalt the doctrine of conversion, it is a poor time for a Methodist Episcopal preacher or layman to slur or modify or discount the first and foremost article of our creed. The whole modern movement in religion swings back to the position of our fathers and admits, however falteringly, the gospel of a regenerating God. In that gospel is revealed the one sure process of making new Americans, and from that gospel alone can come a new and exalted America.

Years ago Sir Edwin Arnold visited America and spoke to the students of our oldest university. One memorable and even unforgettable sentence seized the memory of every hearer. He gave a succinct and epigrammatic description of the great wars of our past and of the greater contest of our future: "Gentlemen of Harvard," he said, "in 1776 and in 1812 you conquered your fathers. In the years from 1861 to 1865 you conquered your brothers. Will you permit an Englishman to say that your next victory must be over yourselves?" It is small wonder that the sentiment wins for itself frequent quotation. It approaches the heart of our present American problem. We need not ask for that control over ourselves that is represented merely by cool diplomacy that seeks advantage in commercial or political contest. Rather should we ask for the control that is large enough to yield to God and wise enough to choose His way. We boast of the Anglo-Saxon blood. We forget that our ancestors were the wild men of the North until Jesus found them and made them the mightiest people on earth. If America goes back on Him, we will make choice of suicide. One who is from the Pacific Coast may be allowed to say that the only "yellow peril" is a white peril. If America rejects Jesus and if China and Japan accept Him, the yellow man will seize our crown. But if America shall keep Christ and more and more live in His spirit, and if China and Japan shall accept Christ and shall walk in His ways, they will simply become the Eastern and Western partners of the Prince of Peace.

By this program America may become the servant of God for the world of God. Claiming the immigrant for our free religion as well as for our free Republic; claiming the child for the Stars and Stripes only more because we claim him for the banner of Immanuel, and claiming every sinner for a cleaner Nation and an ampler gospel—we shall make our country great by the greatness of God Himself.

The Challenge of An Awakened World.

Homer C. Stuntz.

I AM to ask you to-night as I shall be helped of the Lord to look at an open world as the challenge to our Methodist men. And the feeblest understanding can see at once that that opens a theme for which I would require not thirty minutes but thirty days of five hours each to adequately treat. And I will cut out the conventional introduction and say that we began as a foreign missionary agency, we began our work in Africa, and I will begin at Africa.

And I begin by saying that when we first sent Melville Beveridge Cox to Africa, the work that was possible for the evangelical Churches upon the continent of Africa was about in relation to the bulk of Africa of a very small wren's nest under the eave of an immense barn. It was just a little point on the western edge of a common five thousand miles long and nearly as wide, a continent containing to-day one hundred and sixty million souls as near as may be known. And the years have gone on since 1833 until it is now 1913, and we lack but twenty years of a century since our first foreign missionary died crying, "Let a million fall, but let not Africa be given up." And what do we behold in Africa to-night through the leadership of God as seen in schools and Church work? We see Africa not like it appeared to Melville Beveridge Cox when he first entered it. We see an Africa which is almost entirely patrolled from the pillar of Hercules right away to the cape and from Liberia right away to Eastern Africa by the representatives of a Christian Nation, and you can take your train at Capetown and go north fifteen hundred miles, and take your train and go to Khartoum and find a college at Khartoum with four thousand students in it away down there two thousand miles south of the Mediterranean Sea. And when the Italian flag fluttered from the masthead in Tripoli some months ago practically the last foot of Africa under the control of heathen government came under the control of Christian nations and to-day Africa is an open Africa. And our own Brother Springer, away in the heart of the interior of Central Africa, is controlled and under the flag of and policed by those who come out with at least the higher ideals of Europe.

You go over to China, our next field to be occupied. There is the miracle of the world, the most stupendous illustration of the theme of the evening, not only that can be found to-night on the face of the earth, but that was ever seen upon the face of the earth since Jesus Christ hung on the cross to redeem men by His efficacious atonement. I say, there never was such an open country, considering the country, considering the size, considering the resources, considering the strategic relation to what lies out yonder in the great deeps of heathenism, as is presented to-night by an opened China. I need not take your time nor attempt rhetorical devices to make this thing clear to you. I simply set it before you as an opened China, where one quarter of the human race to-night are as accessible to Christ as are the people in the wards of Indianapolis or Evansville or Kokomo or Des Moines or any other part of the world. All that country that they told us, when I was a boy, could not be opened, into which we could not enter, is wide open, free territory for all those who will go in to preach Jesus Christ among men. Furthermore, not only is it true of Africa, but it is true of China, that every part of that country is covered with at least a skeleton force of those who are out yonder for the proclamation of the gospel of the Son of God. You can find in the Congo Land, in Algeria, in Bechuana Land, and among the Kaffirs, and everywhere in that land, a network of Christian agencies. The barriers have been torn down. A skeleton force is there, from the Cape at the South to the Mediterranean at the North. And so you will find it in China. You can go right away into the extreme northwest, about Chentu, and beyond, clear over into Tibet, and begin at the borders of Tibet in the extreme west and come down the sea and find that Central China and South China and North China and all China are covered with a network of Methodist and Baptist and Presbyterian and Congregational and Episcopalian missions, and every considerable province and town, while we have not evangelized them, yet we have a beginning everywhere in the whole country. It is open, wide open, to the work of Christ.

The next great country that our Church took up was India. We began as a Church rather feeble as to the number of men whom we sent. Thomas Coke, when he went to India to begin his work in 1813, took six men with him from England. He had greater courage than we had when we undertook foreign work, for when we looked at Africa we sublet our part to one man—he was a single man and a consumptive; and when we let the contract for China, we sent only two, and when we undertook to evangelize India, we sent one, but if any one concludes that we were feeble as to the four, let it be remembered that we were courageous as to the size of the field, for when we undertook our third missionary task, we laid our hands upon Africa, China, and India, with their populations of over eight hundred and fifty millions of people committed to us for evangelization. That was courage, for we did not have resources to send as many workers. The reason we did not have resources was because of that condition to which Bishop McDowell alluded this morning when he spoke of a class of men whose benevolent impulses were under perfect control. When we went to India, India was under the control of the British East India Company; and I am profoundly impressed with the guidance of God in our missionary history, for He sent us into India at precisely the right moment. Other missions had been there, doing a blessed work, but He sent us there just at the right time, when Great Britain through the crown assumed charge of all India and threw down all the barriers and let us into a country that was wide open. We did not have to waste any time. I speak with profound reverence: I think that the Almighty saw that we had too much to do to go there and sit down and wait, so He did not call on the Methodist resources until He was ready to turn us loose in that country, which was policed by Great Britain, with British judges on the bench and the British army keeping peace and British engineers making roads and British officials running postoffices so that we could send our invitations to Christ and give the dates of our Conference sessions and plan the itinerary of our missionaries. What has happened in India? India is opened in a way that fairly staggers the imagination.

Our own magnificent Thomas B. Wood, still living—he is from this State and from your own great Greencastle—for the last eleven years he has been sitting down before the gates of Peru, and he has gone down to Paraguay and Uruguay, planning and working and speaking for laws that would guarantee religious liberty. And one by one Paraguay has opened its doors, and Uruguay, Argentine, Chili partly, Bolivia utterly, Ecuador utterly, and now, when I was in London the other day I picked up the *Times* in the morning at the home of the man whose guest I was and I read this telegram, and I was so lifted up in spirit that I had other meat to eat than the breakfast. I had been in Lima last winter when we were asking for religious liberty. I had preached sixteen times with two policemen watching me. Romanism is stronger there than anywhere else on the American continent. This is the telegram:

"Lima, Saturday, October 4, 1913. The Chamber of Deputies has this forenoon passed a bill granting complete religious tolerance by a vote of sixty-six to four."

And the last wall went down. By the blessing of God a Methodist knocked it down, and by the special grace of God he was an Indiana Methodist that knocked it down. Now, there is South America wide open to you, and I affirm that I would sooner be in the place of Wood than to have any other honor that men could give me. To have opened the door of religious liberty to twenty-five million people is a bigger work than most of us will ever accomplish. That is done. That man is fitted for his place with John G. Paton and the other great leaders of missionary work.

Now, I affirm that this open world is a challenge to Methodist men. It is a challenge that ought to appeal to us in a concrete fashion. How shall we meet that challenge? Let me put my argument wrong end first. I had an Irish ancestor. Let me say this. First, I want to get clearly before you the magnitude of the challenge. Take Africa, for instance—what are we going to do for Africa? What does the challenge mean to Africa? We have a skeleton force in Africa, we are giving five thousand a year to North Africa—clear across that great country. Let me stand here and put forth a suggestive budget for North Africa. We ought to provide for North Africa a mission force of thirty trained men from North America in addition to the present force. We ought to have fifty workers there within five years. I am not ballooning. I am a veteran. An amateur might say we need one hundred at once. You have to digest missionaries. If you feed them to us too fast, they do not break in well. Send us out five or eight good men a year to North Africa. Then provide us a training school; and do not, for the Lord's sake, send it to Jerusalem, but to North Africa, right in the heart of our job. That is my opinion. Let us be where the job is. Let us train the workers where the work is. Some Methodist layman has a chance to put it there. It should be established with buildings worth one hundred thousand dollars and endowed with two hundred thousand dollars; and if you will do that we will give you a half-million converts in North Africa within not many years. We will make the first real breach in that land. My hopes soar when I see the first attack of the unlimited doctrines of free grace on the Mohammedan proposition. There has never been one before. Our advance upon the Moslem situation has been an advance more or less weakened by a background of thinking about a limited atonement. This is the first chance the Wesleyan doctrine has ever had at a solidly Mohammedan population, and I have great hopes that if it be adequately backed we can see mighty results. For I have never been persuaded that a Mohammedan was harder to reach than any other sinner, if you offer him Jesus Christ and do not quarrel with him because he is a Mohammedan. I have no quarrel with a Mohammedan. I go to a man because he is a poor, heartbroken captive of sin, and I preach the gospel that can open the door. That is our mission.

Now go down to West Africa. Let us take that Liberia mission and give it a budget of about fifty thousand dollars and a plant worth about one hundred thousand dollars. Then go down to Angola and give them the same budget, and then go on up to East Africa. And by that time you would have a budget of about two hundred and twenty-five thousand dollars to give in Africa instead of a beggarly little budget of seventy or eighty thousand dollars. Here is a challenge to Methodist men, a definite proposition of what we will do in open Africa.

Go to China—what is needed there? I will tell you. We ought to put into each of our five colleges in China at least two hundred and fifty thousand dollars. I was greatly pleased that Bishop Anderson told us of that story about the rich layman in New York. We must get through expecting to do great things on the foreign field with nickels. We must move out of small things if we expect to do our work. We must move up to a great program. In China we ought to have at least a million dollars for our educational work, right off. That is safely and sanely within the facts. We ought to have an increase in our annual budget of about twenty-five thousand dollars a year for five years, and then stay there.

In India we ought to put into Reid College a big endowment and double or treble our part, and then go down to our five theological schools in India and put them on their feet with buildings and men.

Now, what will you do in South America? What do you need in South America? We have not in all South America as much money spent annually as they spend on the Wilkes-barre District of Wyoming Conference under the two heads of pastor's salary and incidental expenses; that is all you are spending in the endeavor to convert seven Republics in South America wide open to you. Let us have one hundred and fifteen thousand dollars next year, one hundred and twenty thousand dollars the next, one hundred and twenty-five thousand dollars the next year, and put us up to about one hundred and fifty thousand dollars in ten years, and give us a million dollars in Buenos Ayres, the greatest city in the world south of the equator. The Church that depends only upon evangelization will be a spent force within two generations of the time it is born. We must find and put into leadership such men as have come out of Northwestern, De-Pauw, Allegheny, Old Wesleyan, and out of our theological schools, if we are to keep and maintain leadership in the evangelization of that continent.

Just this last word: we are never going to meet this challenge by talking about budgets. Just this last sentence—O brothers, will you hear this? We will never get the budgets I have been talking about except from hearts that are entirely filled with the Holy Ghost and the love of God. Our fathers were driven over these prairies and went to India and to China with hearts aflame with the love of Christ. Let us not imagine that the adoption of budgets or the proclaiming of plans is going to save the world. It is only by a Church that is all penetrated with the spirit and love of Jesus Christ that we are going to find the money and the young men and young women who will lay their lives upon the altar and lead this whole open world to a saving knowledge of our Lord and Savior Jesus Christ. God grant that we Methodists may be worthy of our place in this vast plan of God.

The Call to World Conquest.

J. CAMPBELL WHITE.

I HAVE been speaking for ten years, since coming back from India, to representative gatherings of men in practically all the great cities of North America, but I declare to you that never in my life have I had a greater sense of responsibility than I have to-night in view of the outreach and possibilities of the great gathering of men here related to your own Church with its millions of members, and through that Church to the whole of Protestant Christendom. I hope I may have your prayers that I may be guided in what I say.

The plan of redemption was a necessity with God, and missions are not any subordinate part of the Church of God. "If you would make the greatest success of your life," some one said a great many years ago, "try to discover what God is doing in your time and fling yourself into the accomplishment of His purpose and will." I know of no better rule than that for attaining certain success in life, and if I am any judge at all of what God is doing in our time, and it has been my main study for twenty years to find out, I believe the thing He is doing unmistakably is opening all the avenues of the world to the spread of His gospel, and asking His Church to be His messengers to speed it to the last nation and the last man on the face of the earth. And deeper and deeper grows the conviction in my own soul, and it has been growing for twenty years, that the only rational interpretation of the great commission is that when Jesus Christ said, "Preach the gospel to every creature," He meant His people in every age to undertake to do it. And that means that we of our day must plan the universal propagation of this gospel in our time. I was profoundly impressed by the statement of Dr. Barber, the secretary of the American Baptist Foreign Missionary Society, after a trip around the world, that the thing that impressed him most in all the lands he visited was the vast unnumbered multitudes, and he said, "I did

FORWARD MARCH!—A CALL TO ADVANCE.

not see one person in all the lands to which I went that
I thought could afford to wait until some future generation
to meet the first messenger of Jesus Christ.'' They can
not afford to wait, but they must wait until we go, for the
world is redeemed but it does not know it, and it never
will until some human messenger tells it of the redemption
that Christ purchased for all mankind nearly two thousand
years ago. Up across the great National Convention some
three years ago was this, ''This is the only generation we
can reach and we are the only people that can reach this
generation,'' and the obligation is squarely upon the men
of our day to plan the universal propagation of Christianity.

Now, I have absolutely no sympathy with any separation
between the different classes of missionary work. I believe
that whoever sets home mission work of any kind over
against foreign missionary work, or foreign missionary work
over against home missionary work, thus dividing the forces
and bringing them into conflict and competition with each
other in the extension of the Kingdom of Christ, is the enemy
of the whole cause. Our Lord gave us a universal program
when He said, ''Ye shall receive power after that the Holy
Ghost has come upon you, and ye shall be My witnesses in
Jerusalem and Judea and Samaria and unto the uttermost
parts of the earth.'' He said it stronger than that, ''Both in
Judea and Samaria, and unto the uttermost parts of the
earth.'' Divine resources are promised for a universal
program, and no man has any right to claim the power of
God for a part of that program. And only when we undertake the plainly revealed will of Christ for the world have
we any right to come into His presence and claim any of
His resources with which to carry out His program. We
shall fail except as we have divine energies released through
us. Human energies are incompetent to deal with the problem of any single sin-sick human soul, even in our Western
so-called Christian lands. Divine power is necessary for the
salvation of any man anywhere, and when you get into the

207

realm of Divinity, God is able to carry out the plan that He Himself has made. We must undertake, therefore, His whole program. If there is anything that ought to be inspiring to us in this Convention, it is that the whole aggressive official forces of your Church are here on a united program asking you to carry out what is indicated in Acts 1:8, and receive the power from on High that is promised and then be His witnesses in Jerusalem—both in Jerusalem and in Judea and all Samaria and unto the uttermost parts of the earth. And it is a great encouragement to me that we are getting together on this program as denominations. I believe it is one of the indications of surely coming victory. For my Lord prayed, away back in John, seventeenth chapter, "That they all may be one; as Thou, Father, art in Me, and I in Thee, that they also may be one in us." Why? "That the world may believe that Thou hast sent Me." In view of that great high-priestly prayer were wrought these two conceptions, the unity of His spiritual body and the universatility of His gospel. And they are going to come together in history, and they may come together in your lifetime and mine if we do our duty.

Out yonder on the mission field they have got to the point where they are able to divide up great sections into districts and trust the various evangelical Churches to preach an adequate gospel in those districts. Colonel Halford was at the head of the Evangelical Alliance in the Philippines that sliced up the whole country as you would slice up a pie, and gave the Methodists one section and the Presbyterians another, and so on clear around the circle. A splendid way to divide up all our mission fields. I have a map of Korea showing where the different denominations are at work. They have divided the territory and straightened the lines so that each denomination may know exactly how much its obligation is. Bishop Harris told me, in the capital of Korea two years ago, that in order to do this the Methodists had traded off twelve thousand Methodist converts to the Presbyterians, but he went on to say in the same breath, "I think we got the best of the trade." I do not know whether he did or not, but I know it is an enormous advantage in Korea for a native Christian to be a member of whatever Church he happens to be nearest to. When he moves from one province to another his Church membership changes automatically and he does not keep his letter in his trunk for five or ten years, the way so many people do in this country. It may take us a little while to get to that point in this country, but the men face to face with heathenism have felt that the difference between all our evangelical Churches is so small in comparison with the difference between any particular forms of religion and heathenism that we simply must get together in order to publish the glad tidings around the world. And so, even in theological seminaries, they have been able to unite four or five denominations and two or three nationalities on the foreign mission field. In one city of China the Northern Methodists are in the southern part of the city and the Southern Presbyterians in the northern part of the city; and some of the Chinese said, "You can not teach us religion; you do not know even the points of the compass."

Now, it is possible that Bishop Stuntz has attended a theological seminary that would enable him to define free grace in a way that would not be satisfactory to me, but I would like to see him try it. I have been in missionary councils of all denominations and all nations for twenty years on a half-dozen continents, and I have yet to hear from any missionary representing any of these forces the first echo of doubt about the fact that the love of God is strong enough and the grace of Christ is broad enough to include all humanity. I do not believe that Presbyterian or Dutch Reformed or Episcopalian any more than Methodists are going to spend their lives in Africa or China or India unless they believe that Jesus Christ gave Himself a ransom for all and that God so loved the world that whosoever believeth on Him may find eternal life in Him. Why, when they got a half-dozen denominations over there in Nanking, China, they decided they would keep the Chinese a couple of weeks at the end of the year and teach them the denominational tenets of the different Churches that were co-operating. That worked out all right until the end of the year, and then the Chinese insisted on going into all the classes so they might find out what all the denominations believed. These Chinese can make their own theology if we give them the Bible, and I am not so much concerned to have the Presbyterian Church or the Methodist Church established as that all may come together to work for all the world. My dear friend, Dr. Watson, who has been a leading foreign missionary man in the United Presbyterian Church of which I was speaking this afternoon and which is getting a good deal of publicity because of his missionary record, said a very subtle thing to me the other day: "I am not sure that God can afford to let one Church get very far ahead of another in this business. They turn Pharisee very quick when they get a little ahead of some one else. I do not believe any of our Churches should get far enough ahead to have any chestiness about it. I believe we all ought to work in harmony, we ought to get together that we may not lose anything in friction, but may turn all the friction into energy for the propagation of the gospel."

Now, there are some great outstanding problems, some of which Dr. Oldham referred to yesterday, and one is the call of the world. They have given me the same topic tonight, and I want to just touch three or four of the outstanding problems and bring them in review before you, calling attention to some of the things that challenge us. First of all, I want you to recognize that there is tremendous improvement. The man who said the Laymen's Missionary Convention at Chicago was all "ration, oration, and evaporation," did not know the power, the inspiration and vision that came through that gathering. I have met men all over this country, from the Atlantic to the Pacific, who have been leading a different life since the Convention in Chicago.

FORWARD MARCH!—A CALL TO ADVANCE.

I will meet men from one coast to the other, if it is my
privilege to live five years, I believe hundreds of men—I hope,
two thousand men—from this Convention who will look
back to it as a time of mountain top vision when they saw
things more clearly and put themselves more irrevocably into
the purposes of God. The fact is that the last six or seven
years have witnessed the most wonderful growth of missionary
interests and contributions recorded in human history. In
1907 the foreign missionary contribution of America was
$8,500,000, last year (1912) it was $14,942,000, and this year
it was nearly $17,000,000—an increase of more than a mil-
lion dollars each for the last seven years on the part of our
Protestant Churches. Now, that is an unprecedented advance.
I can not give you so accurately the increase for home missions, but it is very much larger than the increase in foreign
missions, and, more than that, the increase in the contributions of Churches in this country for the last year has
been far greater than the increase in the amount given to
foreign missions and to home missions. That God is putting
the seal of His approval upon this agitation is evident from
the financial returns in the various Churches, and I want no
man to be discouraged with the progress that is made. We
are just getting ready to do tremendous work in the next
few years. It has been five or six years since the leaders of
the various denominations were persuaded to try the new
plan. Your own Church only got to the point of adopting the
method that will solve this problem at the last General Conference. Other Churches have only just gotten to the point.
There is not any large denomination left on this continent
that is sticking to its old, outworn annual collection system.
That is a tremendous thing to be able to say: that in the last
ten years the financial methods of the Churches of this continent have been revolutionized. That is true absolutely.
And the next ten years will be required in order to see anything like the proper full fruitage of the change in the whole
financial system of our Churches.

MILITANT METHODISM.

Now, there are two tremendous problems facing us. One of them is the problem of immigration, to which that wonderful reference was made last night by Bishop Hughes. Just a fact about immigration: about a million people coming, in round numbers, and about a quarter of a million a year returning. Let us not fail to put emphasis on the fact of this great army going back each year. Why do I put emphasis upon it? Because it is the shuttle between our civilization and the old, effete civilization, in many cases, of the continent of Europe, and the steady stream going back constitutes a marvelous opportunity of getting back new streams of life into these old civilizations. It is, therefore, our National peril or opportunity, this immigration problem.

And along with that is the other great problem of Christianizing our whole civilization, social, industrial, political, economical, not only for its own sake and our national future's sake, but in order that our Nation may have a testimony among the other nations of the earth of which it need not be ashamed. It is a terrible indictment of our so-called Christian civilization that Japan has learned to put her children in the factories from us. Not until she sent her men scouting all over the world to see how things were done in the most advanced civilized nations of the earth did she have the horrible practice that has grown up among us of putting these tender little children—who ought to be in school—at work in the factories. Now, the whole impact of our civilization upon the rest of the human race must be Christianized, so that we shall not belie with one mouth and with one voice what we are trying to enforce with another. God has opened up to us very marvelously the Mohammendan world, and there are two hundred millions of people in it; they have been humbled by these recent wars as never before for many centuries, and they are open as never before to aggressive missionary work. The United Presbyterian Church, which has been at work for fifty years in Egypt, has not until within the last year been able to go out in open evangelistic preaching on the streets, but this year it has been able to do that in country districts, among the Moslems, without creating riot and bloodshed. The whole Mohammedan world is open to our preaching and influence as never before. I am very glad that your Church among others is enlarging its work for Moslems. Do not get the idea that we are not accomplishing anything among them. There are two hundred native preachers in India who are converts from Mohammedanism. There are forty thousand converts from Islam in the island of Java alone, and up the Nile Valley there are Moslem converts some of whom are marvels of knowledge, graduates of the great Mohammedan University at Cairo, who have come into contact with the missionaries in that Nile Valley and now challenge the Mohammedans in debate; one of them, Monseur, coming back to the shadows of the Mohammedan University from which he was graduated, challenges all comers to debate the merits of Mohammedanism and Christianity, and the greatest building they could get was packed night after night, and so marvelously did he debate Christianity to the great Moslem audience that they, being the judges, acknowledged that he completely outwitted any man who would stand up against him, so that the daily Mohammedan press in Cairo sent out a challenge, saying, "Is there no man in all Egypt who can stand up and put this man to shame in public debate?" It is true that the Mohammedan world is being powerfully influenced, but the few that have had the boldness to come out and confess Christ are only the advance guard of the great army that has been prepared spiritually and intellectually to take that step in the next few years. Right across the heart of Africa we have the great problem of deciding whether Mohammedans are going to reach those fifty million pagans before the Christians reach them. In that continent of one hundred and fifty million people the central problem is whether those pagans living in the heart of the continent are going to be made Moslems before we get there with the Christian message. Mohammedan traders are moving down across the heart of Africa at a hundred points, and every Mohammedan trader is a propagator of his religion, not because he desires the spiritual benefit of those people, but because the larger number of converts he makes, the larger is his constituency. A friend of mine went down to Nigeria twenty years ago; at that time in its greatest city there was only a Mohammedan now and again, and no Mohammedan mosque; to-day there are sixty-six Mohammedan mosques in that city, all built and patronized by Mohammedans. The Mohammedans are advancing across that continent, and the men of our decade must decide whether those fifty millions of people are going to be Moslems or Christians in our lifetime. We had a striking picture last night of India, the land to which I gave ten years of my life, and I feel that in some ways it is the ripest field in all the world, with three hundred and fifteen millions of people, with this great low-caste movement involving sixty millions of people, about whom Dr. Oldham and Bishop Stuntz told us yesterday. When I was in India ten years ago, they put tremendous emphasis upon every man who really believed in Christ to come out and confess Him, and to the people it meant the severance of family relations, disinheritance, and the risk of life. A little bit later many missionaries encouraged these individual converts to wait until they could bring their whole families with them and thus be the point of contact between the missionaries and the gospel and their own loved ones. A little later, instead of encouraging a family to come out from its community and to be ostracized, some missionaries who have been far-sighted have been encouraging them to remain, that they might impregnate their whole community with the gospel spirit and lead them to come out on the Christian side.

The most marvelous message which I have yet received from the mission fields, I received the other day from one of your own missionaries, with a paragraph from a letter just received from Bishop Warne, and I have additional evidence of it in the *Indian Witness*, that comes from Calcutta week by week. Bishop Warne says that the Methodist missionaries in the Delhi District in India have just been meeting two hundred "head men" of two hundred communities, and these two hundred men, with the consent of their communities, have promised the missionary forces that their communities, as communities, would surrender their idolatrous practices and cut out all their heathenish methods and put themselves definitely under Christian discipline and instruction if the missionaries were prepared to take them in. And messages coming week by week through the *Indian Witness* are that there are a hundred thousand of these low-caste people at this moment knocking at Methodist doors in India. When Bishop Thoburn went out to India there was just one Methodist convert on your rolls. To-day there are two hundred and fifty thousand, and one hundred thousand more asking admission. Yesterday Bishop Oldham and Bishop Stuntz independently, without hearing each other, on this platform made this statement, that the Methodist Church could take in a million converts in India in the next ten years if you would take in those that were coming and asking for admission. Gentlemen, if any voice from the open sky could move a company of men like this, ought not such a statement do it? I believe these men have made conservative statements in what they have said, that a million people might be added to your Church in that single field in the next ten years. Will we do it, or supinely go away and close the doors on these tens of thousands of earnest seekers? I asked Bishop Stuntz what it would cost to look after this additional million that ought to be taken in. He said, "Somewhere from one hundred thousand to a hundred and twenty-five thousand dollars a year." Think of it! For a million dollars we could probably turn the tide in the next ten years and take in that million that we are not prepared to take in now. And for something like a dollar apiece! Dr. Goucher during twenty years invested one hundred thousand dollars in a district yonder in India. At the end of twenty years there were fifty thousand Methodist converts in that district. I believe now, with India in the dead-ripe condition it is in, it would be possible for men ready to make gilt-edged investments perhaps to bring in this extra million of people at an average cost of not over one dollar per convert. I am willing to join the Methodists to this extent, of being one of a thousand men who will give out of their own pockets a million dollars to make that thing possible. I do not see how, in the presence of an opportunity like that, backed up by your own experienced and responsible leaders, we dare sit here in the presence of God and do nothing.

The situation in South America—instead of the paltry fifty thousand or one hundred thousand dollars that Bishop Stuntz is asking, they ought to have a million dollars. Mexico, Central America, Cuba, South America, have seventy million people, more than one-half of them of illegitimate birth, and far more absolutely illiterate; and the Methodist Church is the leading Christian agency among the seventy million. All Protestant Churches put together have only five hundred and thirty-one ordained missionaries among the seventy million, or only an average of one to every one hundred and thirty-one thousand of the population. You can not afford to invest Bishop Stuntz in Latin America unless you put several hundred missionaries alongside of him and a million dollars for the redemption of that continent. But North America must solve the religious problem of this hemisphere. We have kept out other nations by our Monroe Doctrine, and by our spiritual Monroe Doctrine we have to enlarge our missionary forces and save this whole great continent.

I have not said anything yet about China, which is, I suppose, the leading nation in the appeal to the world, where one-fourth of the race is in transition and holding out pleading hands, praying to Heaven and to us, saying, ''What have you to teach us?'' And we can turn the tide in China in this decade if we will. My brethren, are we ready for this responsibility, or are we going to plead the idea of saving the world and then let somebody else do it? Mr. Taylor was talking this morning about four million dollars for missions. I have made a life study of the forces needed to occupy and evangelize the field. I want to say to this great Methodist company, to whom I have no responsibility except the responsibility I owe my Lord, that you can not evangelize the people in your fields unless you multiply over and over again the amount you are now giving. I want to say to you that I believe the Methodist Episcopal Church with three million of members ought not to rest day or night until you have adopted a policy of raising at least an average of five dollars per member per year for home and foreign missionary work combined. That would be fifteen million dollars a year. That would be less than half you are spending for your own congregational expenses. That is entirely possible to any congregation that really desires to see Jesus Christ made King of this world; and you can not face Christ, and I do not see how as sensible business men you can face each other and talk about this problem, and offer to Christ less than two street car tickets a week for the redemption of these people in China. Two street car fares a week is five dollars a year, and it would be fifteen million dollars a year from your great Church; that would be seven and a half million dollars a year for foreign missions and as much for home missions. Are there any of you good business men who will tell me how long it would take by spending seven and a half million dollars on each of the one hundred and fifty million of people in your parish abroad? How do you calculate that? Seven and a half millions a year among a hundred and fifty millions of people would take about twenty years to spend one dollar on each of the people who wait on the Methodist Church for their first news of Jesus Christ. If you want to do the thing any cheaper than that you will have to get somebody else than me to give you counsel about it. You want to do it and you can do it, and if you do it—hear me—if you do it, the

Churches of Christendom will follow you in that great first crusade. No body of three millions of people in this favored land can move out to its world problem in that way without shaking the earth on its foundations and filling all the realms of glory with hallelujahs.

The prayer of years and years has been answered since I came to this meeting. For ten years at least I have been praying that soon somebody would see the vision of the world open and decide to give at least a million dollars to spread the gospel in it, and yesterday my friend Cory, who spoke on this problem, told me of a dear friend of mine in this country who has been the first man to step up and say, "I will put down a million dollars for the spread of the gospel." If I had been asked six months ago what the comparative probabilities of the Disciple Church raising five million dollars or the Methodist Church raising twenty-five million dollars, I would have said without hesitation that the Methodist Church would raise twenty-five million dollars before the Disciple Church would raise five, but they have raised their first million and started on their two-million campaign, and now one of them says, "For the glory of God I put a million dollars down at your disposal, and I want you to raise five million." I heard a man on this platform say to-day that there are twenty-five men at least in the Methodist Church each one of whom could give a million dollars in a single lump to the spread of the gospel in the world and never know the difference except the difference in his bank account. Brethren, with wealth like that in your hands and with millions of people who can give their systematic amounts week by week, shall we hesitate on the threshold of the world's most marvelous opportunity to go forward under the leadership of the Son of God to capture this world for Him?

PART IV.
Actualizing the Program.

The New Day.

OF course, the New Day can mean only a new mood in men. The sunshine smiling upon an uninhabited desert does not make a new morning that has human significance. But when that sun glows upon a city filled with people moving out to their play and toil, the new day has come in the larger and deeper sense.

No man present at the Indianapolis Convention could fail to feel that many hundreds of men had gained a new relation to the Sun of Righteousness. This figure seems to me to represent what has happened. The Convention is not represented by a cyclone or an earthquake, but by the steady strength and warmth of the sun that makes the seasons and brings the harvests. Three things especially impressed me:

1. The spiritual tone of the speeches made by laymen was a real feature. I say "real" thoughtfully. There was no parade of spiritual phrases, but there was a sincere and penetrating piety in it all. In the old days I heard laymen whose spiritual purpose in a local sense was earnest indeed. But the spiritual note here was broad and even universal. These men seemed to love not simply a town, but a world in their hearts. It is fair to claim that the laymen struck fully as spiritual a note as did the preachers. There was a democracy of responsibility and priesthood that boded a new day.

2. A second related impression was that this spiritual mood on the lay part was not merely a relic and reminder of "the good old days." The vast majority of men present was made up of comparatively young men. Counting the sections of seats in the hall, one would note that not more than one head in eight was crowned with white. I do not think that the croaker would have had much chance at Indianapolis. Those splendid men, young and middle-aged, were hopeful prophecies of the future. The Church has a new day, and she will have new day after new day, until Christ owns the whole calendar.

3. But, most of all, the Convention impressed me as relating itself to the wills of men. There was emotion, deep and fine. But the mere hunter of thrills would not have been at home much of the time. Everywhere I heard men saying, "Now we must do the work. The spirit of this wonderful gathering must be carried home with us!" Indeed, often I detected a holy fear lest the power of the Convention should somehow escape. I liked that holy fear. I felt that the final effect of the meeting was not pride or emotion, but work!

These impressions being correct, it is not too much to say that the Indianapolis Convention was both the token and the helper of the New Day. God help us to greet its dawning with gladness and consecration!

EDWIN H. HUGHES.

Actualizing the Program.

No GREAT program can be carried to successful issue in the Methodist Episcopal Church without full co-operation among the various agencies held responsible for its many-sided activities. The connectional idea, which is the very root of our Methodist polity, asks that every great plan be linked up with existing means of contact in the local Church. Such a program as that adopted at this Convention must bring its message to the great membership of the Church in terms of the various activities which are now a part of our Church life. That this is practical and that our present leaders in applied Christianity are in hearty sympathy with such an effort is seen in the methods presented in this section of the report, for making the program actual and vital in every part of the field. Of a truth all this is a sign of the new day that is surely dawning. Social reform, Christian citizenship, evangelism are receiving such reinterpretation as makes them a part of the normal life of every human being, and not something thrust upon the individual from without. It is not a minister's task alone. That man who characterized our time as "the laymen's day" did but place fresh emphasis upon the need for thousands of our laymen to put their shoulders under the world's burden. Indeed, if the new program for the Methodist Episcopal Church is to go beyond the point of "vision" the hosts of Methodist laymen the country over must very quickly learn that he who professes himself a disciple of Christ thereby takes upon himself a part of the responsibility of bringing the world to the foot of the cross. Men who have prayed for opportunity for service, here is the answer to your prayer!

I. A WORKING PROGRAM OUTLINED.

Message to the Church.

THE Methodist Episcopal Church has birthright in two outstanding characteristics of present-day Christian consciousness—world vision and world brotherhood. John Wesley's words, "The world is my parish," and those other words in our history, "I desire a league offensive and defensive with every soldier of Jesus Christ," affirm the faith of Methodism to have a world vision, its hope to be a universal hope, and its love to be an all-embracing love.

This first National Convention of Methodist Men has been assembled because men of official and commanding relationship in the Church specially need to be aroused to larger initiative and service for the establishment of the Kingdom of God throughout the world. This body of men, representing every State of the Union and practically every Conference of the Church, manifests the presence of an awakening which is a part of the rising religious consciousness of universal manhood.

The responsibility of the Methodist Episcopal Church for the evangelization of non-Christian peoples is self-defined, and has been accepted as 150,000,000, among which number of such peoples the Church has elected to serve. Its responsibility for the Christianization of the United States is in like proportion to the unchurched and unevangelized in our ninety millions of population. This whole service must be undertaken and forwarded in harmony with other existing Church agencies. "Together" is the watchword of the twentieth century. Unification, co-operation, co-ordination are the recognized principles to secure economical and efficient service, not only in the sphere of secular business, but equally in the business of the Church.

To meet this responsibility adequately requires the quadrupling of life and supply to missionary agencies. One person out of every thousand of the membership of the Church would add thirty-three hundred to the missionary staff, and an increase in missionary and benevolent giving set by the General Conference of 1908—"as much for missions and benevolences as for our local budgets"—would afford ample revenue. This Convention repeats the challenge of "at least as much for others as for ourselves" as the lowest goal for final attainment in view of the second great commandment.

This standard of giving is easily attainable if proper apprehension of the stewardship of life and of money can become the *impression* of the entire membership of the Church, and if Scriptural methods can become the regular means for the *expression* of their religious life.

The "New Financial Plan"—nothing other than these Scriptural methods—embracing continued information and education, the acceptance of the principles of stewardship and of systematic methods of proportionate giving, and the steady practice of prayer in daily life, should be actualized in every Methodist home and congregation. To secure this there must be carefully planned and cordial co-ordination and correlation in the methods and work of the several agencies charged with missionary and benevolent responsibility. Business intelligence demands and the best interests of our benevolent work require that there shall be no unnecessary duplication of programs or multiplication of agencies. The direction of the General Conference of 1912 for the "unity and efficiency of financial plans," and for the protection of our Churches and of the official connectional benevolences from the confusion and harassment of multiplied financial appeals, must be carried out in the spirit which prompted the legislation.

The Methodist Episcopal Church must ever show itself the Church of the people in the spirit of Him whom "the common people heard gladly." The desire for true Christian social service is everywhere prevalent. In the words of Frederick William Robertson, "We must socialize our Christianity and Christianize our social life." No civilization can be permanent unless based upon religious principles. The evils and wrongs so sorely afflicting society must be overthrown and remedied through an aroused public opinion that will register itself in righteous laws and just administration. The Church must ally itself sympathetically and aggressively with all that commends itself to its judgment and conscience as essential to the perfection of the Christian state.

The necessary leadership of the Church and the continued maintenance of an intelligent, active, and consecrated membership depends upon education, Christian literature, and the training and direction of young life. Our schools, colleges, and seminaries must be kept adequate to their task; the literature of the Church must continue of the highest quality and be increasingly circulated and read; and all agencies for the nurture of youth into strong Christian manhood and womanhood must receive fullest sympathy and support. By its birth and history Methodism is committed to the broadest educational program, to the largest mental development of its people, and to sacred care of the home, from the precincts of which must come the saving influences of the Church, State, and society.

In all the work of the Church the laity have equal resources and privilege with the ministry. Particularly is the demand upon "Christian business men to give the same energy and intelligence to the work of the Church that they now give to their own private affairs." When this is done the Kingdom of God will have come upon the earth. The General and District Superintendents, Pastors, and several missionary and benevolent agencies are the natural and appointed leaders. They must lead and the Church must follow.

No work for God can be done successfully unless undertaken in His spirit. Nothing can be so essential as that the

Church go forward with the courage that comes through prayer. Men everywhere must be brought into its fold and be made to flame with the evangel of His Word. This Convention commends the work of the Commission on Evangelism to the entire Church. Methodism must maintain itself as "Christianity in earnest." If the note of evangelism be hushed; if the work of the Church be attempted by mere organization, however perfect and comprehensive; if reliance be placed upon societies and agencies, however numerous and well equipped; if there be attempts to lay other foundation than that which is laid, the Church will be powerless and its work futile. "Not by might nor by power, but by My Spirit," saith the Lord. If the agencies and membership of the Church be transformed and transfused by His Spirit, and be uncompromisingly loyal to Him who hath purchased it with His own precious blood, it will be "fair as the moon, clear as the sun, and terrible as an army with banners" to aid in the accomplishment of His divine purpose in the world.

In solemn consecration and in the spirit of humble obedience, the representatives of the Methodist Episcopal Church, in Convention assembled, pledge this great communion of the Church of Christ to endeavor and achievement for Him in whose name we pray, "Establish Thou the work of our hands upon us, yea, the work of our hands, establish Thou it."

A Working Program.

The Convention of Methodist Men, assembled at Indianapolis, Indiana, commits itself and calls the entire Church:

First: To a program of personal evangelism at home and abroad which shall enable the Church to reach effectively the last man with the message of redemption; and that we set as a goal an annual minimum gain of ten per cent in the full membership of every local Church.

Second: To the principle of social redemption in all lands and the application of the spirit and teachings of Christ to the total relations of men.

Third: To the bringing of our youth everywhere into real Christian life and to their training for effective Christian service by all those agencies which the Church has created for this high purpose.

Fourth: To the practice of the principles of stewardship by every member of our Church as defined by our Discipline. This recognizes God as Giver and Owner of all things; man as a steward, holding as a sacred trust all he has; the systematic application of a portion of our income to the advancement of God's Kingdom, and the dedication of one-tenth of our income as a minimum.

Fifth: To the universal introduction of the every-member canvass and the weekly offering by every man, woman, and child of our Church, with these two principles always in view:

(1) The standard apportionments met in full as a minimum achievement.

(2) At least as much for others as for ourselves, as our near goal.

Sixth: To the hearty and full support of those Boards which are created by the Church as the proper instruments for the application of the benevolence of the Church to the world's need. And we emphasize the paramount claims of those regular causes established and approved by the authority of the Church.

Seventh: To the loyal and loving support of all those forms of Christian activity, in all lands, as expressed in our educational, philanthropic, and evangelistic institutions, looking everywhere toward the care of the sick, the aged, the orphan, the unfortunate, and toward the training of our youth in the spirit of Christ.

Eighth: To an inspirational and educational campaign, having in view our full relation to the civic, industrial, social, educational, philanthropic, and missionary problems of our age—and to the enlistment of the unused energies of the men of the Church under the leadership of the Son of man.

Ninth: To an emphatic reaffirmation of the action of the

General Conference on the subjects of higher Christian education and the imperative need of vastly larger funds for our schools, colleges, and universities; the necessity of more liberal support for our ill-paid ministry, especially in view of the increased cost of living; the supreme claim of the retired veterans for an adequate support in their old age; and we commit ourselves with heartiness and devotion to the well-known attitude of the Church on the subjects of Temperance, Social Purity, and Sabbath Observance.

Tenth: To the support and circulation and the faithful reading by ourselves and in our homes of that Christian literature, in book and periodical, created by our Church for the training, instruction, and inspiration of our people.

Eleventh: To a program which shall bring to districts and local Churches the principles, ideals, and methods which have found expression in this Convention. And we ask all our Boards to set aside their secretaries and other officers, as far as possible and necessary, for the service of the districts and area groups in a unified campaign for all these approved causes.

Twelfth: To the utmost co-operation of our Church with all other "Churches which exalt our Christ" in a common and united effort in all lands to bring in Christ's Kingdom.

Supplementary.

In order that the message of this Convention may be carried down to the local Church, we make the following specific recommendations:

That the arrangements for Conference anniversaries and Conference visitation on account of all the causes be so adjusted as to make it possible for the Annual Conference to set aside a sufficient time for the full presentation of these great interests of the Church and for a study of practical methods, under the institute plan, for the solution of these problems.

This plan or some modification of it would seem to be essential if the ministry and laity of the Church are to be fully informed concerning these most important matters.

The conviction has deepened in these days that the Church everywhere needs the vision that has come to the Convention. It would be impossible through any printed word to bring at once the survey of conditions and the inspiration which have come from the living voice. Those who have spoken to us here must speak to the Church. We are convinced that a like uplift of faith and love would follow the presentation of these facts elsewhere as in this great Convention.

So convinced are we of this that we urge upon the Boards and agencies which have been represented the necessity of releasing from the ordinary duties of office those who have addressed us, in order that they may have the opportunity to reach with their quickening message the Churches here represented.

As there is need of a practical plan, which must include many details, there should be a central office to which correspondence with reference to arrangements for follow-up meetings may be addressed. We recommend that the Commission on Finance make all necessary arrangements.

We would especially recommend that before leaving this Convention the delegates should plan for one or more central meetings in each Episcopal area, and that in consultation with the central office the dates of these meetings be so arranged as to make possible a thorough visitation of the Church by the speakers who may be set aside for the purpose.

In order that the laity may be effectually reached with the message of the Convention, we would especially recommend that the Laymen's Missionary Movement be urgently requested to arrange for such sectional and other follow-up convention meetings as the demand of the hour and the wisdom of its Executive Committee may suggest.

II. METHODS FOR ACTUALIZING THE PROGRAM.

The Laymen's Missionary Movement.

FRANK A. HORNE.

THE history of the Laymen's Missionary Movement and its development in our Church marks an evolutionary process that not only has affected this movement, but similar movements and enterprises in our sister denominations. The Laymen's Missionary Movement of our Church was organized under the authority of General Conference in 1908. It then had for its objective the foreign missionary propaganda. That was likewise true of the International Laymen's Missionary Movement. But in 1912, as the result of the experience of the quadrennium, by virtue of the fact of the organization of the Commission on Finance federating all our benevolences, which Commission on Finance was the result of a memorial presented to the General Conference by the Laymen's Missionary Movement, acting in co-operation with other Boards of our Church; our borders have been extended and we now include all the benevolences and activities recognized in our denomination. That has likewise been true, by virtue as I believe of the providence of God, in the interdenominational movement, and this year we witness a united missionary campaign on the part of Foreign and Home Boards in the United States and Canada.

Lest the buzzer interrupts my full speech, I want to give you the five points of my address, which constitute the policy of our Laymen's Missionary Movement as we address ourselves to the outlook and the plan of the Church in the light of the opportunity presented:

First, we strive to stress and emphasize and promote lay activity, initiative, and service.

Second, the Laymen's Missionary Movement desires and expects to heartily co-operate with the Commission on Finance in the proclamation and extension of the new financial plan in all its aspects to every congregation.

Third, the Laymen's Missionary Movement proposes, as far as may be, to carry the message of this Convention to a maximum number of laymen of our Church.

Fourth, we desire in every possible way to promote unity and efficiency in the various agencies and organizations of our Church.

Fifth, we propose to affiliate heartily and enthusiastically with the work and with the program of the Interdenominational Laymen's Missionary Movement and in the proposed campaign of united forces.

Now, first, with regard to lay initiative and activity, let it be said that the laymen of our Church in no sense desire or look for leadership. The leadership of our forces belongs to the minister. We are willing to follow, but we want to be led. We have under God and by reason of the legislation of the last General Conference, a form of organization which provides, as we believe, the very best opportunity for leadership. With the bishops over their areas responsible for the development of the area. Under them the District Superintendents, and may I say that it seems to me and to others that, using a business phrase, it is up to the Bishops to put in the type of District Superintendents that will carry the plan we have heard here into effect. Mr. John R. Mott, in a recent meeting of a committee in referring to his foreign visitation and the wonderful conferences, said that one of the convictions that had come to him as a result of that visit was that more than ever there was needed the activity of the laymen in bringing things to pass, both on the foreign field and here on the home base.

The Laymen's Missionary Movement is asked to go down

to the local Church to stimulate the man in the pew with those latent possibilities, and we want to co-operate with the fine program of the committee in their plans for increasing their membership ten per cent net each year. We want to work with the idea of Church service and we want to work with the pastor, but we believe the time has come for the layman in the pew to lift his vision beyond the mere local interests to the big work of the Church in the extension of the Kingdom of God throughout all the earth.

The Laymen's Missionary Movement also desires to impress upon our laymen the spiritual side of this business. We desire to enforce and promote on the part of the laymen the exercise of those fine qualities of business leadership—energy—force, initiative, organizing ability. We want to somehow enlist these abilities for the spread of the gospel. We want big men with a big purpose for a big job.

Furthermore, this program of the Laymen's Movement includes also the adequacy of Christian stewardship interpreted in measures of sacrifice. I, for one, believe that as a result of the meeting last night—I mean the closing meeting of prayer and devotion—the Spirit of the Lord is here so that laymen are ready here and now to give expression to the spirit of Christian stewardship sacrificially expressed. Why should not the laity be moved by the Spirit of God expressed, as, for instance, in the student volunteers who come up and sacrifice their all and place their lives upon the altar of the Church.

We further believe that as respects Secretaries it is not a question of quantity so much as a question of quality. What we want with all due respect to any economic purpose, is men who do things. We believe it is impossible to adequately present, inaugurate, and execute this new financial plan without trained men to lead and show us the way. In conclusion this job is too big for the Methodist Episcopal Church. Let us broaden our horizon. Let us work in unity and full co-operation with the Christians of all names and all places.

The Book Concern As Related to the General Work of the Church.

H. C. JENNINGS.

I AM to speak of The Methodist Book Concern in its relation to the general work of the Church, and concerning the way in which it may prove of efficient help in carrying out the present united program of Church work and Church life.

There is no more question of the providential organization of the publishing interests of our Church than there is concerning the organization of the Church itself.

Other denominations of Christians have greatly admired our publishing plan and have greatly desired that they might have something like it. It is not too much to say that this arm of usefulness which I represent has had a value which we can not measure in the propagation of the truths in which our Church believes, and in holding the Church closely to its task of evangelism.

Only five years later than the organization of the Church came the organization of The Methodist Book Concern, and that institution has been running now for one hundred and twenty-four years. It is the oldest publishing house in America. It has outlived all such as were in existence at its beginning. It has lived through wars and panics, through changes in polity, through the development of the Church, always the loyal steady servant of the Church. Its growth has been an indication of the growth of the Church, and its present standing is secure because of the present greatness of the Church to which it belongs.

From John Dickins, in Philadelphia, one man only, working alone, in 1789, and from Martin Ruter, in Cincinnati, one man only, working alone, in 1820, the two together having a salary bill of some eighteen hundred dollars per annum, its growth has continued through the years to the present time, until we now have eleven hundred people on our pay-roll with an annual salary account of more than a million dollars. It is the story of a business activity grown from one man with a few tracts as his stock in trade to all this army of employees and to our many places of business, working at the manufacture and distribution of the largest quantity of religious literature published by any firm in the world. We are using more than fifty thousand pounds of printing paper for every working day in the year, covering both sides with the best literature which it is possible to procure and to produce for the Christian culture of all the ages and all the classes to which Methodism owes its obligation.

It is of importance that The Book Concern has as staple a business, as certain of increase as the Church has of increase, and that with the application of all improvements in the practical machinery by which the work is done, a good profit showing is made, and the profits go to the care of the needy among us representing not a great benevolence but a great justice. In all, from the beginning to the present year, $3,548,000 has been distributed to this cause from our profits, two-thirds of which has been given in the last eighteen years.

We speak of the work of the Church beginning with childhood, creating character, inspiring good citizenship, and as the result of such work proving to be one of the great saving factors in the life of the Nation. The Book Concern has come to the front in the production of the best material for teachers and pupils in the Sunday school to be found anywhere in the world. The largest of all the interests of the Church to-day is the Sunday school interest. The soul of education is the education of the soul. It is not often considered that the Book Concern has done a great pioneer work in this matter, that there has never been a periodical or a lesson leaf of any kind issued that has not been published at a considerable loss at the first, that the deficiencies on these things have, in the aggregate, amounted to a very large sum; but the spirit of those who have been in the management of our publishing business has always been that anything that ought to be done, should be done, so from the first leaflet to the present magnificent array of periodical literature, the new things embodying new ideas have been put upon the market and carried by the House until they could carry themselves. The Book Concern has never failed to heartily co-operate in the production, though at a present loss, of everything that will help us better to fulfill the high obligations of the Church in this great matter, and the Book Concern has, by its policy, come into its reward, for the Sunday school to-day is not only the largest customer of the Book Concern, but the most profitable one, and that is because we have the best plan, the best executed Sunday school system in the world. The Sunday school authorities of Methodism have the assurance that their publishing house will not be found wanting when there is any occasion to make an investment, though of large initial cost, which shall the better educate and save the young people in our charge.

It is not to be forgotten that the pioneer circuit-rider carried in his saddle-bags a supply of the books produced by his own Book Concern, not only as a matter of duty required by his Church, but in great joy as an assistant in his work. Largely by means of this "preacher agency," our books have reached a sale of many millions of volumes. With the increase of intelligence and the spread of population, the weekly *Christian Advocate* family was founded—first on the Atlantic seaboard, then following the pioneers in their conquest of the wilderness, and it has come to pass that from one ocean to the other our people find a *Christian Advocate* published within easy reach of their homes, representing the territory in which they live, standing for the highest and best things. There is such a thing as the "*Advocate* Habit" in Methodism. Most of us here to-day were born with it and can remember one of the *Advocates* in our homes as far back as we can remember anything. There is no way of measuring the influence of these silent messengers full of hope and tidings and sound teachings, which are woven into the fiber of our early life. The Church has during all these years, through the medium of the Book Concern, published as many *Advocates* as it could afford to publish, and there is a goodly family. And these *Advocates* are published now in the English, German, Swedish, Norwegian, Italian, and Bohemian languages in this country.

One of the developments of the present time is the enormous mass of periodical literature which is published in this country. Most of us can remember when a half-dozen monthly magazines completed the list, but now monthlies and weeklies in extraordinary number, running into the hundreds, are sent broadcast and sold by millions each month. Most of them are of respectable and many of them of great merit. As men are specializing more and more in their work, there is more and more demand for the specialized magazine, and our Methodist homes are full of magazines attractive and useful in character, but they have been crowding out the *Advocates* that have in other years occupied so high a place and almost the only place in the periodical reading of the average family. I do not inveigh against the present order. I speak of it as a sign of the times.

Within recent years there has been, I am sorry to say, a decrease in the circulation of the *Advocate* family among our own people, while in the same years the number of families in the Church has very largely increased. However, one of the things which should cause us great rejoicing at this time is the fact that, as the result of much thinking and much planning, a new order of campaign, and for other reasons, the tide has turned. As a result of the renewed effort during a year in which there has been a large decline of circulation in almost the entire magazine world, there has been the most notable increase in the subscription list of the family of *Advocates* of any period during their entire history. Not quite, but nearly one hundred thousand families are each reading a Methodist *Advocate* that did not do so one year ago. This makes about two hundred thousand circulation with one million readers. The entire list of subscribers has a little more than doubled in that time. There has been a really genuine revival of interest in the things of our common Methodism, a much wider and more general inquiry concerning matters in which the entire Church is interested. There is a great inquiry throughout the Church concerning the methods by which our theories may be translated into service. The *Advocates* have put out a distinct note concerning the great thing, and more than ever before we have come to value men by what they do for men and not because of any amount of abstract talent they may possess. A man is rated as he should be, not by the money he possesses, but by the money and the work he gives. Power is no longer reckoned as belonging to the man who can grasp the most of it and hold on, but the *great man* is he who can do without things and let his neighbor have what belongs to him. Let the Methodist Episcopal Church take notice and understand that her *Advocates* are not only loyal to the truth of revelation and to the interpretations of the Church, but they are the best exponents steadily, every week, all the year round, of the things we want our people to know and to believe and to do for their souls' health. Presently we shall have another hundred thousand families learning the "*Advocate* Habit," and then other thousands, and it is safe to say that there will not be very much forward work among the activities of the Church where the *Advocates* will not lead the way.

And this leads me to say that the Book Concern, with all its facilities for putting truth on the market, for publishing and pushing periodical literature of the highest class, is, as it should be, the real mouthpiece for every organization and activity of the Church. With hundreds of thousands of dollars invested in the equipment of the best printing shops in the land, able to produce any kind and grade of work, equal in quality and equal in speed to any possible rival, such an institution has the right to expect to be the printing office of the Church in every one of its activities. Our single relation to periodical literature is not as large as it should be; it is vastly larger than it was; but for the Book Concern and its facilities not to be used by all the benevolent organizations and all the educational organizations of the Church as the medium of carrying the tidings they wish to convey to the people presents a strange contradiction.

My Book Concern creed is about like this: It is the business of the General Conference to see to it that the right men are placed in charge of all its publication work, that as they are given responsibility they should be given power, that if they do not measure up in Christian statesmanship to their opportunities, other men should be substituted for them at the first opportunity. We humbly believe that the Book Concern is organized now in about the right fashion, and we announce ourselves as candidates for all the printing business and all the exploiting in a mechanical way which the Church needs. The Missionary Boards, the Freedmen's Aid, Educational, and the Sunday school interests can all reach a larger constituency through the official publications of the Book Concern than they can in any other way, and they can do it vastly cheaper. We are not now pleading that the Book Concern shall be in that way helped to make more money. The emergency that is upon us makes that a small matter. It is a question of how we shall tell the story soonest, best, and get it to the most people. I would like to see the Book Concern, the Missionary Boards, and all the other official organizations of the Church in a kind of partnership which would result in keeping our presses busy all the time, make the necessity for multiplying their number greater, and even give the Boards a share of the profits. Let us do something, anything, with all this mighty machinery which shall bring us closer together in the management and execution of the tasks to which we are consecrated.

MILITANT METHODISM.

The Methodist Federation for Social Service.

HARRY F. WARD.

THE Social Service Movement proposes that every Church shall become an effective missionary force in the organized life of its own community. And the methods to that end are being worked out not in the study, but in the field. Last week I was in three types of communties, and in each one a Methodist preacher was the outstanding community leader. In the open countryside, in the Church at the four corners, through mud and rain came the Farmers' Club and their wives, organized by the Methodist preacher, to consider how they might minister more effectively to the intellectual and recreational needs of that countryside. In the village of five hundred people the leaders of every organization in the village life, with all the people, gathered in the Methodist church at the call of the recognized leader of their community, the preacher of that Church, to see how more effectively they might apply religion to the health and morals in their village. In the industrial town of fifteen thousand, at the call of the one outstanding community leader, the Methodist preacher, all the Churches and all the organizations interested in the community life gathered to find how they might meet the dire illiteracy and bitter vice and the oppressive industrial conditions of their community. The work of such pastors as that is the constructive statesmanship of the Kingdom of God. It is more than that: it is the practical working out of social salvation. It is weaving the life of God into the very fabric of the community. And that is the last expression of the missionary impulse. When it seemed that we could go no farther outward, then the grip of God, taking the wavering enthusiasm of the halting line, drove it back into the very heart of our civilization. How long will the thin, heroic line of the missionary frontier hold their posts if you expose them to the rear fire of an unregenerate Christendom? Men of Methodism, look at a part of your

238

job that lies at your own door. Does the absolutely hideous
vice of pagan cults call for more heroic work than the utter
bestiality of our own commercialized prostitution? Does
the misery of the plague-stricken East call for better Christian intelligence than the death rate of our own communities
from preventable disease? Does the ignorance of Africa
demand a better type of leadership than the illiteracy of
that forty per cent of our own industrial cities that never
finish the eighth grade? Does the misery of famine-stricken
China and India call for a stronger type of Christian
statesmanship than the rotting destitution of our submerged
tenth and the cruel poverty, in the face of rising standards of life, of that sixty per cent of the industrial population that does not get a living wage? Does the hate and
hell of threatened race antagonism call more powerfully upon
the cohesive properties of the Christian religion than the
fires that are boiling underneath the class antagonisms of
our own Christian Nation? The last battle in the conflict
of Christianity and other religions, the last battle in that
deeper, deadlier conflict of Christianity with agnosticism
and materialism is to be fought on the field of social efficiency.

The social service movement proposes also an evangelism
which shall be adequate to reach the industrial group in our
population. It is not a question of getting the workingman
to Church. It is not a question of establishing fraternal
relation with the organizations of labor and other agencies
for improving industrial conditions. It is a bigger task
than that. It is the task of spiritualizing the mind and program of the awakening working class of the world. The
greatest significant movement outside of the organized Christian Church in our modern life is the coming to intellectual
consciousness and political power of the working class. They
are being cemented into a common mind, a common program,
the world around, and the great question for the future of
our civilization is whether that mind and that program shall
be material or spiritual. And behind that working class

movement there is gathering the finest feeling and deepest thought of our modern life. It is the great world movement toward industrial and social democracy, and at the head of it there stands the Carpenter who has the form of the Son of God. The Church that opposes that movement will be trampled into dust beneath the tramping feet of marching millions, and the Church that fails to understand that movement will be left forgotten in the rear. But the Church that has the intelligence to understand, the sympathy to cooperate, and the leadership to bring into spiritual consciousness that great movement will be the Church that will realize the Kingdom of God upon this earth. For our Methodism I crave that place of leadership, a Methodism which has a democratic theology, a Methodism which has a democratic spirit, a Methodism which has a history of contact with the awakening of the working class of England. It is time for us to set apart in our industrial territories men who are particularly qualified to take the gospel to the working class— men who know its history and philosophy and have worked and suffered with these men. That is our particular job. We want men who can do this work in a new way. We must not be afraid that these men will turn the world upside down. God's men have always been doing that, for we have not yet got it right side up.

Men are coming out of our seminaries who are going to preach the simple gospel with power as great as ever it has been preached. But it is the simple gospel that opened with a proclamation as wide as the needs of life. Sometimes the men in the labor halls ask us what will happen if that gospel leads us, as it led the Master, to the seats of the money-changers in the temple. I am not worrying about the pulpit. Men tell me sometimes that the laymen are in advance of the preachers on social and industrial questions. In spots, perhaps, but the spots are not yet sufficiently numerous to constitute any alarming symptom. If your respective communities next Monday should find you men practicing the same kind of gospel that was preached in your pulpits on Sunday, I think the social service department might take a vacation for at least a week. Some of you men may have heard the phrase, "full salvation." Do you want to test it? If you would stand by your pastor, and thank God for it after he has been the instrument of convicting you of sin in your social and industrial relations, then you have got a full salvation.

This social service movement is creating new tides of spiritual energy in the Church to-day. As of old, the Spirit of God is moving among the people, convicting men of sin. As they face the utter misery, the monstrous treacheries of our organized social life, they look God in the face with anguish of soul, and ask how they can absolve themselves even of any indirect participation in these sins; convincing men of righteousness as with a new ethical sense, they are striving to adjust themselves to their brother men in all relations, convicting men of the judgment to come as if the hour of impending doom was at hand, as they see our social ills. If preachers and laymen will work together with the Master, each one showing the redemptive power of the redeemed life, then they will help to lead all their brother men to that great eternal city built without hands, whose Maker and Builder is the Eternal God.

The Commission on Evangelism.

J. O. RANDALL.

THE program of the Commission on Evangelism calls first for an increase in the product of the Church of at least ten per cent. The only subtlety in that call is in the phrase, "per cent." If you place on this chart behind me three columns of figures and put after them as the membership of the Church ten per cent, you will discover this, that the figures in the first column will relate themselves to the figures in the third column in different figures as there are different numbers in the

241

first column. But the center column will not change. Ten per cent increase in a Church of twenty members is the same per cent as ten per cent increase in a Church of two thousand members, or any other number you may like. The subtlety of that simply lies in this, that the ten per cent appeals to every man, no matter what the membership may be. The man who gets ten per cent increase in a Church of twenty-five is just as much entitled to a place in the front row of leaders in the Church as the man who gets ten per cent in a Church of thirty-five hundred members. This gives every man his chance, so that no man needs to be discouraged because of the smallness of the charge he serves. The second feature that is attempted is that we shall have a perfectly definite program. You can not reach a ten per cent increase—and you know we have not been reaching quite two per cent of an increase—you can not reach a ten per cent increase without a definite program, and a program that will not simply relate itself to the mind and hope of the pastor, but one that will relate itself to the Quarterly Conference of the local Church so that every man and woman in the Church will need to know the number of men on the Church roll, and what it really means to increase ten per cent. This will produce accuracy of aim and effort and a deep and consecrated devotion in prayer and service on the part of every man who seriously wants to see the Church of Jesus Christ triumph throughout the world.

The second thing in the program is a constituency roll. This is merely the list of names of men and women and children in any local Church who look to the pastor of the Methodist Episcopal Church for spiritual ministration. When that list is made and men and women know who and where the people are, then we have opened before us a challenge to a mighty and definite effort on our own part. I say what is perfectly familiar to many of you, if you place this list of names before your Quarterly Conference you will find that there are many men and women in the Church who have been longing through the years for the opportunity to do this particular thing, but did not do it because they did not know which man or woman to speak to.

The next thing to which I want to call your attention is the matter of your being entitled to know the experience of leading a man to Christ. There are three million five hundred thousand Methodists that could not this day do anything that would bring them such spiritual vision, such a holy thrill as would come to them by leading a man to Christ. There is no other thing, no other blessing or multiples of blessings that would put the Church of Jesus Christ in such a state of grace as that every man and woman in it would lead another to Christ. Now, if you want twenty-five million dollars, there is no better way to get twenty-five million dollars than to put the three million five hundred thousand men and women of our Church out of the Church, across our threshold, and into the street, where the unsaved men and women are, with the thing with which we have been capitalized and endowed in our own experience.

The Epworth League.

WILBUR F. SHERIDAN.

IT was not a prophet nor an apostle nor a priest who said, "Where there is no vision the people perish," but the author of the business men's book of proverbs. We have been receiving the vision here during these days. It remains now for us to carry it down to the people who are not with us upon the mount. The constituency that I have the honor of representing here this morning of six thousand young people of the Epworth League are not here. We propose to see to it that they, too, shall catch the vision that you have seen. In the Greek Orthodox Church on Easter morning long before dawn the people fill the great cathedrals, and the archpriest at the altar lights the single taper and that light is communicated to the man next to him and so down the aisle and out into the streets and all through the city, where they are waiting with their unlit tapers, until in a few moments the whole city blazes with the lights of those tapers, all communicated from the central altar fire. We propose that these young people of Methodism shall with their as yet perhaps unlit tapers catch the light from this Convention, and all through the city and over this land they shall reproduce the light of the devotion and the enthusiasm and the consecration that is being manifested here. I am, therefore, this morning to pledge to Methodism the loyal support in the campaign here outlined of the young people of the Epworth League and, just as Mr. Lincoln and his Cabinet, when they sent forth their proclamation for recruits, declared that the Confederacy must fall and gave to the Nation the battle cry, "On to Richmond," so we this day, receiving from the leaders of our Church the command that this world is to be won for Jesus Christ, will answer to that battle cry as the boys in blue, two million six hundred and seventy-nine thousand of whom back there in the sixties were under twenty-five years of age, we will answer to these leaders of the Church, "We are coming, Father Abraham, six hundred thousand strong."

We propose to carry this into effect by doing five different things. *First* of all, we propose that the *Epworth Herald,* the paper for the youth of our Methodism, shall continue to be the organ of this world-wide propaganda. Four times this past year it has given its entire edition to missions, home and foreign, and that kind of work will be kept up. In the *second* place, one department of the four of the Epworth League of our Church is devoted and shall continue to be devoted to world evangelization. In the *third* place, on one Sunday evening of every month all of the young people of Methodism will be set to studying this program of world conquest. It may be it is only a small thing for a group of young people here and there, inconspicuous and obscure, to be gathered together in the study of these problems; there is nothing spectacular or striking about it, but, as Burns declares in "The Cotter's Saturday Night,"

> "From scenes like these
> Old Scotia's grandeur springs,"

So I believe it will be from study groups such as I have described that the future grandeur of our Methodist Church will spring. I promise, in the *fourth* place, that we will project lines of study in the local chapters of the Epworth League for the study of Christian stewardship and foreign and home missions. We have that program on foot. *Fifth,* in our institutes we shall carry forward this study of world evangelism. The fact is, that what you have been having here these two days past, and what we are in the midst of now, is only an Epworth League institute greatly enlarged; it has the same ideals and convictions, and absolutely the same methods that are being presented from the manifold different standpoints. Our program is on no narrow lines. You have heard of the preacher who had only two gestures, one up and one down, and he said, "When the roll is called up yonder" (pointing up) "I'll be there" (pointing down). Our program is particularly broad. In the coming Epworth League Convention at Buffalo, New York, next July, from the 1st to the 5th, we plan to have the same type of program that you have been carrying on here; it will be extended, and we hope to have fifteen thousand Epworth Leaguers from all over this land.

Our Brother in Black.

I. GARLAND PENN.

JOHN WESLEY was a seer, a prophet, a statesman. When I say that, I think of the Scriptural statement, "There was a man sent from God, whose name was John"—Wesley. John Wesley uttered many things which we have in reality in Methodism to-day, for John Wesley as a man of vision saw the end from the beginning, and when he said, "I desire a league offensive and defensive," he put the emphasis upon what we stand for to-day in this Convention—organization. When he said, "We must be at it, and always at it," he put the emphasis upon business. So we are here upon the threshold in this program of the greatest day in the history of Methodism, putting the emphasis upon what will get results, namely, organization and business. Organization and business together in this greatest business the world knows anything about will bring results greater than we have ever had before.

I understand I am to speak this morning upon how we are going to put this program into the local Church. If we let this Convention soak in on us—and I use the expression of the chairman of the morning, whom I heard say on one occasion, addressing a colored Conference, "Brethren, let this Conference soak in, like a sponge, that you may be like fountains giving out to your local Churches when you go home."

Now, as to what we are doing as a part of the Church, with the inspiration of this program, let me say that I caught some of the inspiration of the General Conference in its legislation, and I went to the colored people of the South and I said, "This is the day of getting larger results, the day of organization." And I have been preaching that to the colored Conferences of the South—organization, organization, organization. While we are just upon the threshold of things, we are just beginning, yet the Freedmen's Aid Society in its report this year from the colored Conferences shows that the colored people, organized as they have never been before, have given this year forty-eight thousand dollars for the Freedmen's Aid Society, an increase of fifteen thousand dollars over anything they had ever done before. And we are just beginning.

This program represents a get-together Methodism, and if there is any race who knows how to get together it is the

Anglo-Saxon. When Grover Cleveland was nominated several years ago for the Presidency, a noted Democrat—the "Watch-dog of the Treasury," they called him—went through the country saying, "Democrats, get together." They got together, and Grover Cleveland was elected. When we get together as this program means, we are going to give the devil a chase as never before and bring in the Kingdom of our Lord and Savior.

The Methodist Brotherhood.

W. S. BOVARD.

I HAVE been asked to state briefly how the Brotherhood is related to this program of the whole Church. I may say that it is related to that program as the recruiting and drilling force of an army is related to battlefields, to the great challenging conflicts. I am sure that after these days of looking out upon the sublime tasks that challenge the Church, we must all feel that there is a great fundamental fact, the need of more available men for the accomplishment of these great tasks upon which we have been looking. The Methodist Brotherhood is engaged in that field, the development of the manhood resources of the Church, the furnishing to the leaders in the local Church men of power through whom the purposes of the Convention may be achieved. Naturally enough, we find the field of our endeavor in the local Church. And we find there that the pastor is the key man. We come to him with the methods of the Brotherhood as methods by which we seek to develop and organize and train groups of men who shall not withdraw from the Church any energy, but shall contribute to the Church the largest possible energy that shall be available for the achievement of his purpose. These men are to act under the leadership of the pastor. We have all sorts of challenging activities for the development of these unenlisted men. We recognize the fact that men like the fellowship of men, and they like to be appealed to by their fellows in man-fashion with respect to the claim of Jesus Christ upon their lives and consciences. So we gather them in social relations, not as an end in itself, but as an evangelistic opportunity, when men that have the life and spirit of Jesus Christ may touch these other men in a natural, unconventional fashion and lead them to a sane, rich, Christian life. We also recognize the fact that men are appealed to when religion is interpreted to them in the terms of practical, everyday life. And the methods of the Brotherhood stand for preserving a fine balance between all these activities which have for their end the development and enrichment of personal life, such as Bible study and prayer and worship, and those other activities which have for their end the application of this spiritual power to the problems of science in this new day. We believe in applied Christianity through the agency of thoroughly spiritualized men, and we hope to furnish groups of this sort of men for the leadership in the activities in the local Church. It certainly stands to reason that the men connected with the Methodist Church could not be content to merely form themselves in efficient groups for local service, but they should likewise seek to band themselves into a mighty national and world brotherhood, so as to speak with the flexibility of the individual and with the multiplied powers of a great aggregate upon National questions, upon the great world questions, and make sharp, quick work of the evangelizing of the non-Christian nations of the world. You have here the phrase, "get together,"

"GET TOGETHER; 'tis the slogan of the hour,
GET TOGETHER; greatly multiply your power;
GET TOGETHER; 'tis the Master's clarion call,
GET TOGETHER; interlock your hands, your hearts, your all,
GET TOGETHER; mighty tasks now call for action,
GET TOGETHER; flagrant faults still need correction,
GET TOGETHER now, and fight to win the world!"

ACTUALIZING THE PROGRAM.

One Fixed Purpose.

W. E. DOUGHTY.

IF I am correct in the feeling that runs through my molten heart at this hour, if I have my fingers on the heart-beat of this crowd of men, I know how I feel, and I think you feel as I do, for we are all men together. The biographer of one of the English queens said, "She lived in a great, moment in English history, but had no greatness of character with which to meet its challenging periods." Some periods in Christian history are like windowless rooms, and others are like wide-open spaces of a kingly palace. We are living to-day in the palace age of the history of the world. And any man who has his finger-tips on the heart-beat of the world can not but feel that we are living in the greatest age the Lord God Almighty ever made.

The supreme summons at this hour is that we shall have a fitness of character sufficient to meet and victoriously conquer this greatest age of the world's history. I think a telegram and its story is about the only kind of message that is brief and incisive enough to penetrate to the center of our hearts after such a morning as we have had. It is the story of the telegram sent by the great Admiral Togo two days before the battle of the Sea of Japan. He had received a command to find and destroy the Russian fleet; for two or three days that great admiral was tossed about in a great tumult trying to understand how he could find that Russian fleet, and if he did find it, how he could destroy it. After trying various plans, he finally laid out his plans of campaign. He sent this wire to a friend of his: "After a thousand different thoughts, now one fixed purpose." There have been coming to us during these great hours the challenging call. There are ringing through our ears these great calls of Christ and His Church. There have been tramping once again across the throbbing hearts of these men these priceless millions who have no chance to know the living Christ.

249

MILITANT METHODISM.

We have had a thousand different challenges here, a thousand challenging and thronging thoughts have come to us in this last hour of this session. I want to fling out this cry to this company of Methodist men, "Now one fixed purpose." I think the greatest words that were written about David Livingstone, who opened a million square miles of Africa to the gospel, were the words written about him by a man who stood in the crowd and saw that great surging multitude with its face turned toward Westminster Abbey, where Livingstone was to be laid away with the great men of England about him. That man wrote this:

> "It was the last mile of many thousand trod,
>   With failing strength, but never failing will,
> That man is now at rest with God
>   Who never rested in his fight with ill."

Did you get that thrilling verse and that quotation? "With never-failing will?" That is the challenge that I bring to the manhood of Methodism in this hour. No words that I have read of Edmund Burke have gripped my heart down where the rich red blood flows as these words have, "The nerve that never relaxes, the thought that never wanders, the eye that never blanches, these are the masters of destiny." I am sure that the men here are seeking some invincible method to apply these great principles and methods that we have been listening to for these days, a method which is not simply invincible in itself, but if thoroughly applied will make invincible these other methods we have been speaking about. There is such an invincible method. It is this: Prayer is the pivot of power on which victory turns. The story of every Christian achievement is the history of answered prayer.

Why do I feel that prayer is the pivot of power upon which victory will turn, and that the length of reach and power of this Convention will be measured by the depth and purity of your life of prayer and of mine? There are many reasons. I will come at once to the greatest of them all—because of the attitude which my Lord took toward prayer. He considered it more important than healing or teaching. For when the multitudes were surging about Him for healing and teaching, Jesus went apart into a desert place to pray. He thought it of more importance than preaching, for His disciples, when they desired to know the central thought of the heart of Christ, said, "Lord, teach us how to pray." Jesus considered it of more importance than miracles, for when He might have performed a miracle to save Peter, He only said, "Peter, I have prayed for thee that thy faith fail not." Jesus Christ considered prayer of more importance than any other agency in getting men into the work of the Kingdom, for He said, "Pray the Lord of the harvest that He send more laborers into the harvest. The thing that has impressed me most deeply in relation to prayer is this, that the only thing the New Testament says Jesus Christ has been doing for two thousand years is to pray. That is the only ministry to which Jesus Christ has given Himself for two thousand years. And I summon you in the name of the Master Himself to the life of prayer.

Ten years ago, when I was a senior in Syracuse University, there was laid on my heart the burden of organizing a missionary convention and trying to lift the missionary life of Central New York Conference. And out of nine months of spiritual passion and struggle, I wrote down six propositions and these six propositions I have tried to test during these years by this threefold test: First, the test of the Scripture; second, the test of history; third, the test of actual experience. Now, I want here to reaffirm my confidence in these six propositions about prayer and just let the Lord God Himself speak the matter in your heart. The first one of these propositions is this: Prayer opens doors and removes obstacles from the ongoing of the Kingdom. Prayer is as real a force as muscular energy. It is as vital as electricity; it is the only human power that can take history out of its deep-worn bed and lift it and put it down where it belongs, in the Kingdom of Christ. Prayer is the only human power that is powerful enough, that is gigantic enough to break open doors and remove obstacles from the ongoing of the Kingdom. This is a perfectly practical message to every man here to-day. The way to get these doors open in the home Church and the way to remedy those obstacles in the great body of our denomination is to begin to apply God's lever that has pried continents and civilization apart from their beginning.

The second proposition I put down was this: Prayer puts men in the thin red line. Prayer flings workers out into this needy field here and the needy field beyond. The only possible way in which we can fill up the gaps in the thin red line is by prayer. I do not know whether it has dragged across your heart like it has mine, but when I think of Latin America, Mexico, Central America, South America, Cuba, Porto Rico, ninety million square miles with seventy millions of people and only one thousand four hundred and thirty-two missionaries in that vast area, my heart swells with pain. And when I think of Africa, in which this hour there are seventy millions of people who have no written language or even an alphabet of their own, or when I think of Central Asia—great Central Asia, beginning way up here—Turkistan, Mongolia and Manchuria, Afghanistan and Bohkra, a city running up into hundreds of thousands, with three hundred and sixty-four mosques and not a Christian Church in the whole city— that great Central Asia, which is so big you could carve out fifty-two countries as big as England or thirteen countries as big as Germany, and in all that throbbing heart of Asia only three mission stations. The one method that will fill up the gaps in that thin red line is for the men of the Church to take this great principle of our Master to them, and I challenge them to do it.

The third proposition I put down is this: Prayer is the only power that can release sufficient money for the evangelization of the world. The statement made by Mr. Corey is all I need to-night. It was said that no man had ever given as much as a thousand pounds for any Christian Church in Great Britain until Dwight L. Moody with his message of the world redemption went to Great Britain.

The fourth proposition is this: That prayer is the only thing that adequately qualifies men for leadership in the world's evangelization. I think again of David Livingstone, about how he wrote in his diary at Christmas time this sentence, that is like a sword in every man's heart who reads it; he said on that Christmas time, "I have this morning pulled up my belt two holes to stop the pangs of hunger." And then David Livingstone, a little while later, wrote in his diary, "My Jesus, my King, my Life, my All, I again dedicate my whole self to Thee." That is the kind of leadership we must have for Methodism if Methodism is to conquer the planet.

The next proposition I put down was this: Prayer will meet hours of crisis victoriously. We are facing in this Convention this hour a supreme crisis, and that crisis will be met victoriously if the men on this floor will begin now with a new passionate devotion to be men of prayer.

The last proposition I put down was this: Prayer is the only force that can make possible the presentation of the Christian message with compelling power. What we need now is something that can quicken information into inspiration, that can transmit interest into passion, and that can coin enthusiasm into dollars and lives. That is what we need now. After a thousand thronging and challenging thoughts, we need to make one fixed purpose to put this program through with prayer. It can not be put through in any other way.

All these six propositions were summed up in the most marvelous way in the Chattanooga Convention of the Southern Presbyterian Church, where it was my privilege to speak. Out in Africa there was a crisis: they needed more men and money. A little group of those African preachers and native Christians got together for prayer, and they sent a summons through all the Presbyterian Congo, and some of the native preachers walked six hundred miles to get to that prayer-meeting. They set aside a whole day for prayer. After they prayed that day, some of the native Christians were not satisfied and, without eating or drinking, some of them prayed for two days and two nights that the Southern Presbyterian Church might be split open from center to circumference with a mighty passion; and then one of those missionaries came home and went around to the seminaries and the colleges to talk about this, and they planned for the great convention, and some one who was interested in the planning said, "Would it not be great if we could bring up to this convention the men and women who want to go, and challenge the business men to send them out?" At the summons of the leader of the meeting of the last night they flocked up to the platform until there were ranged in front of the platform twenty-nine young men and women who said they would go to Africa if God would send them out. After a few minutes of prayer, there was nothing to do but to challenge the laymen to furnish the sinews of war, and they laid down thirty-nine thousand dollars, and that was increased to fifty-six thousand dollars the next day, to send out that company of young people. One incident more, which I think will summarize all I had planned to say this morning. It is a story illustrating the devotion of a Hindu mother. I have had two experiences in telling this story; one was out at Oklahoma City, with Dr. Trimble, at a Union Convention of the Northern and Southern Methodists, with Bishop Hendrix in the chair. The next morning, Bishop Hendrix, in the open convention before he announced the hymn, said to that great audience: "The thing that hurt me most yesterday was the story of the Hindu mother and her two little children. I awoke this morning with a sob, thinking about the millions of little children who do not know that the Father's face is turned towards them." I went straight home, arriving there late at night. I always like to sleep next to the white bed where my little boy sleeps. That night he got a little cold and in the middle of the night he reached out his chubby hand and said, "Papa, hold baby's hand." I can remember the thrill of it as I reached my hand out through the bars of the bed and took firm hold of that little chubby hand. Then he put his other hand through the bars and said, "Papa, hold both baby's hands." Then I did not go to sleep. There broke against my heart like the sob of an ocean tide the cry of the millions of this earth who do not know that their Father's face is turned towards them like my face was turned towards that little lad. This is the story: One morning a Hindu mother went out to the banks of the Ganges, leading in either hand her two children. A missionary saw her going to the banks of the river, and he knew what she was going there for. He looked into her eyes with all the pleading of fatherhood and tried to persuade her not to do it, not to give one of these little children. Then he looked at the faces of the two children; one of the children was as perfect a baby as any mother ever held close to her heart in America or anywhere; the other was blind and lame and crippled. The missionary went away to his work because he could not persuade that woman to break from the thought of centuries in a single hour's pleading. He came back to that spot, and saw the Hindu mother standing still by the river bank with breaking heart. One child was missing. As the missionary drew near, he discovered that the perfect child was gone; the mother had kept the little blind and lame one for herself. As he looked into the eyes of that mother, he said to her, "Woman, if you had to give one, why didn't you give this little lame and blind one, and keep the perfect one for yourself?" She said, "O sir, I do not know what kind of God you have in America, but I know that out here in India our god expects us to give him our very best."

> "I heard Him call, 'Go Forward,' that was all,
> My gold grew dim, my heart went after Him,
> I rose and followed, that was all;
> Who would not follow if he heard Him call?"

III. THE NEW DAY AND THE PROGRAM.

The New Day in Social Reform.

HERBERT WELCH.

SOCIAL reform is not a new undertaking, nor is it new in its relation to religion. The Old Testament prophets, who perhaps even better than its lawgivers voiced the highest aspirations of Israel, pictured a divine order for human society. A careful student has summed up their teachings under three heads: First, they taught the existence of a righteous God, who demanded righteousness and could be satisfied with nothing less than righteousness. No amount of sacrifice and ceremony would take the place of conduct with him. *Put away your sacrifices. I want none of them. Wash you, make you clean; cease to do evil; learn to do well. Then come, and let us reason together.* These prophets, as one has put it, turned the hydraulic power of religion from ceremonial worship to daily conduct. In the second place, they dealt not merely with what we have called private morality, but with all the social and political problems of their day. And in the third place, they showed that their sympathies were forever with the poor. Without ignoring the faults of the poor or the virtues of the rich, the natural flow of the prophetic sympathy was toward those who were helpless and especially needed a champion. John the Baptist was the natural culmination of this line of prophecy. Speaking to tax-gatherers and to soldiers and to men of other callings, his prime demand was that they should forsake their evil ways. And when Jesus came, He began where John the Baptist left off. "The Kingdom of God is at hand," the Kingdom which has to do with human relation-

256

ships, not simply with man's relationship to His Heavenly Father.

But it happened after a time that the Church lost its social ideal. If it did not surrender to the world, it at least surrendered the world to itself; its statesmen became ecclesiastics, its saints became monks; instead of conquering the world, they ran away from the world. Then came the Reformation, with its new assertion of man's individual responsibility to God; and after that came John Wesley, carrying the old gospel into a new development, putting side by side with evangelism education and social service, ministry to all sorts and conditions and needs of men. The General Rules of the Methodist Episcopal Church as John Wesley framed them long ago presented a broad conception of Christianity. One of their three divisions relates to the personal religious life, the life of prayer and common worship. One of them relates to things that people who belong to a righteous God must not do, and one of them relates to things that people who belong to Jesus Christ must do. There is the devotional and the negative and the positive, all set forth in remarkable combination in the General Rules. Wesleyanism had very much to do with the social movements of the last century. There were stirrings in England and America. Seventy-five years ago Emerson wrote to Carlyle, "We are all a little wild here with our schemes for making the world over; every reading man has a plan for the new community in his vest-pocket." But it was not until the last twenty-five years that we have seen the social movement as we know it under full headway. There is a new literature, a new philosophy; there is a new social conscience, a revival of political morality, the raising of the standards of business ethics. Truly there is a new day in social reform.

May I very briefly indicate three of the marks of this new age? First, it implies a deeper understanding of social service. The natural impulse upon seeing somebody in trouble is to give him relief. Then comes the second thought, How shall we prevent the recurrence of this disaster? Then comes the third stage, What are the underlying causes of this distressful condition? First aid to the injured gives place to careful diagnosis and to modern therapeutics. Take, for instance, our treatment of the problem of drunkenness. The first temperance movement aimed to help the man who was drunk. Next, we looked behind the individual drunkard to the institution that made him a drunkard, and we wondered, "Why spend our time in mopping up the flood while the tap is still flowing?" And we began the legislative movement for closing the saloon. But there was another step to which we have had to come. We have had to ask ourselves, What are the causes of the saloon itself? What are the family causes? What are the social and the financial reasons that lie behind this deep-seated and strong institution of evil? And we have begun to see that good cooking may have something to do with solving the temperance problem; that the creation of a happy and wholesome home may have much to do with it; that inadequate wages and exhausting toil and financial trickery and the social impulse all lie behind this great institution against which we have declared war to the limit. So with the problem of pauperism. We are no longer satisfied to give a dime to a beggar on the street, or shut him up in jail, or put him in the work-yard to prevent his begging. We have gone back to his history and asked what made this man a pauper, what in his ancestry, what in his physical defects, what in his lack of education, what in evil environment, what in sickness? We are not seeking any longer to treat symptoms, but to treat the disease. So with the problem of vice, so with the problem of insanity, so with the problem of blindness, and a thousand more. In a word, the day when charity was enough has passed. Men are beginning to ask for justice instead of charity. The day when the Institutional Church could meet the problem of the slum district is over. Men demand something that goes deeper than Institutional Church ministries or social settlements. The day when welfare work guaranteed industrial peace is passing away, for many men are saying, "If we had the wages that are due to us as our share of the profit of this industry, we would not need this welfare work." There is a deeper, more searching meaning to social service in this new day than in the generation that has passed on. Once more "the ax is laid to the root of the trees."

In the second place, there is a deeper meaning to personal righteousness. It needs to be continually repeated, lest it be forgotten, that there can be no possibility of any conflict between evangelism and social service. Evangelism claims the loyalty of every last individual to Jesus Christ; social service proposes to put that loyalty into active operation in all of life's relationships. They are only two parts of one continuous process. Nothing can take the place of evangelism. There will never be a Christian State that is not made up of Christian citizens. There will never be a Christian social order except as Christian men bring it about. Nothing can take the place of individual responsibility to God, the cleansing of the heart of man by the power and the grace of God. As one has put it in homely phrase, "You will never get an honest horse-race until you have an honest human race." But we must not stop with the regeneration of the individual. No man is truly righteous except as he is righteous in his relationships. There are such things as pure mathematics and applied mathematics; pure mathematics deals with abstractions, and applied mathematics deals with concrete facts. But in religion there is no such distinction; there is no Christianity but applied Christianity. We must recognize the old sins in their modern clothes. It has been strikingly put that "boodling is the new treason, blackmail the new piracy, embezzlement the new highway robbery, tax-dodging the new larceny, child labor the new slavery, adulteration of foods the new murder;" but these old crimes baptized with more respectable names are just as devilish as in the ruder days. We must readjust our standards of

259

judgment. If Jesus Christ knew anything about the heart of man and the comparative values of various virtues, then the sin of the elder brother was more subtle and deadly than the sin of the prodigal; the sin of the Pharisee—the man who made long prayers and devoured widows' houses by excessive rents and cruel foreclosures—the Pharisee in his sin was more hopeless than the harlot in hers. It was more urgent in the view of Jesus that a man should establish friendly relations with his brother than that he should offer a holy sacrifice to God. "Leave thy gift before the altar," said the Master, "and go." Even benevolence is secondary to right-eousness. There is a very strong emphasis in this Convention on the financial side of our obligation to God; and that is certainly well. It may very likely be true that the most far-reaching action of the last General Conference was the creation of the Finance Commission, with all that that means to the future of the Church; and yet our chief business in this Convention is not financial, but spiritual. Our biggest task is not to give our dollars, but our days. We want money, we want more money, but we want more holy money, money sanctified by toil as well as by prayer. Thank God for the men who can give their dollars and their tens of thou-sands of dollars that have come to them as a result of honest work in the world's service; but do not forget the heroism of some unknown man who might have had his tens of thou-sands if he had chosen, but for the dear sake of Jesus Christ and his brethren, has consented to be a poorer man that he might be a better man. That is heroism of just as fine a type as that of the great, generous giver to our benevolent causes. I appreciate the complexity of these problems, which make men ask, "What is right in business?" I appreciate the helpless feeling that sweeps over good men in the face of these collective evils. Yet somehow the sins of the community involve us; and somehow we must take upon us their shame and their burden. Think of the boys who are going into gambling and thievery when an athletic field would keep them decent; think of the girls who resort to low dance-halls and dives when a playground or a wholesome club would keep them sweet and unstained! Think of Chicago, which is eating up five thousand young girls a year in the jaws of its lust, and spending fifteen million dollars annually to gratify that passion. Think of special privilege still exploiting the poor. Think of fifty thousand deaths and two million injuries every twelve months in industrial accidents. Think of the ninety thousand men in the iron and steel trades, a quarter of them working twelve hours a day, seven days in every week, and half of them receiving less than eighteen cents an hour. Think of the six million working women in this country with wages averaging six dollars per week, and some of them on two or three dollars a week, when nine dollars is necessary for a life in decency. Then, facing these facts, let us ask the duty of those who love righteousness and hate iniquity.

The third mark of the new day is a new alignment of the forces. The Church has never been wholly separated from the forward movement, but now again more definitely and positively it is identified with all that makes for social betterment. It is recognizing that its mission is as comprehensive as that of Jesus Christ Himself—to destroy the works of the devil. It sees that the Kingdom of *righteousness* can not prevail if wages are unrighteous; nor *joy* when so many little children are unhappy; nor *peace* while conflicts between classes and nations still rage. To this disordered world the Church owes not simply a gospel of personal forgiveness and divine assurance of eternal life, but a gospel for all ills; not a fragmentary gospel, but a whole gospel for the whole man through the whole world. This need the Church is frankly facing. By the socialization of its activities, by special organizations within itself, by a declaration of social rights which constitutes the noblest creed of modern times, the Church is taking its rightful place of inspiration and transformation. And in this movement the Methodist Church—its very nature

261

favorable to democracy, its emphasis never on doctrines or forms so much as on experience fruiting in life—is fitted to bear a leading part. It has a unique opportunity to prove worthy of its great traditions and rally to the call of this new crusade. Its bishops have summoned, its General Conferences have spoken, its leaders have appeared. Now, by wise and bold action of its preachers and its laymen, by declaration of its sympathy with all the oppressed and the unprivileged, by intelligent survey of its fields and their needs, by co-operation with all social and political agencies for social uplift, by an inclusive conception of the scope of religion, it may give the leadership in social reform which it gave long ago in evangelism and which is due from the largest Protestant body in our land.

The New Day for Christian Citizenship.

Ira E. Robinson.

TIME by eternal steps has brought us to a period of learning, invention, government, and all that pertains to human happiness never before known. But with that period has come to all those who live and act in the present greater duties and responsibilities than were presented by the more limited growth of preceding times. Entirely different from the work which confronted our fathers is that before us. Theirs the working out of good, ours the same, but with clearer conception, in a wider sphere, and in a greater way. Do we not conceive in this new day, with its wonderful achievements, its manifold material blessings, and its open avenues for attainment, the growth of His eternal plan and the part He has allotted to us in the bringing of it to pass?

Our great American Government was born of devotion to principles of innate justice. It came out of untold sacrifices for right. It was founded for the advancement of God's own law. Government, properly understood, is but an instrumentality for God. It is a great conception for the promotion of His way with His people. If, in government, we depart from the law of righteousness and love, we thwart the true purpose of government. Government may be considered as rule through law, yet there is no true law but that founded on the simple precepts of divine justice, that we should live honestly, should injure no one, and should render to every one his due. Blackstone tells us that these precepts are the Creator's own mandates and that they are the foundation of all law. They are equally binding on the citizen, the ruler, the State. In the Decalogue these simple principles were first codified for man. They have ever since formed the basis of society. They were reiterated by Micah of old: "What doth the Lord require of thee but to do justly, and to love mercy, and to walk humbly with Thy God?" They were taught, amplified, and exemplified by the Master Himself. American liberty, rightly conceived, is but the liberty of righteousness and love. It is the liberty that grows out of a proper conception of the brotherhood of man. It is indeed the nationalizing of the gospel of Christ. Nations as a whole, as well as individuals, need and must recognize the Master's creed. The State that does not rest on the spiritual strength of its people has an insecure foundation. The State which has not a people imbued with a faith to live and achieve on a high spiritual plane will not make history.

The brotherhood that Christ ordained, so long resting in individual lives, in this day is presenting itself to human conception as that which in a larger way than individually must be exemplified in our great democratic Government itself—in all public affairs. Though this new day, with its rapid commercialism, its gross materialism, its growth of class, its tendency to reason rather than to faith, is fraught with the dangers that always accompany commercialism, materialism, caste, and reason apart from faith, yet righteousness and love make open warfare on the tendency of the times as never before, and with clearer recognition than ever in the past. The omens are good. Works of charity and help-

fulness abound. Men give liberally of time and means for
others. Distress is relieved on every side. Innumerable organizations are maintained for the uplift of mankind. Never
on so large a scale has Christianity been practiced. Even
the nations of the earth respond to its sentiments in their
relations with each other. But still there is jar in the world.
Oppression and strife continue. In some quarters brother forgets to love brother, and class is arrayed against class. Problems confront us, the settlement of which must be undertaken
and faced bravely. Christian harmony is not complete. The
simple precepts of justice which we have observed as underlying all law are too often overridden. Too often money and
might prevail over right, selfishness and greed over brotherhood and love. Men in high places continue to forget their
true relation to God and to fellow-men. Individual citizens,
in the face of blight in the community, stand apace though
duty loudly calls. With all our blessings and achievements,
with all our good works, we have not fulfilled.

As is the citizen, so is the State. The stream can not rise
higher than its source. The citizen is the leaven in the loaf.
The ideals that we should have in government can only come
by ideals in citizenship. No government can be great, good,
and useful unless its citizenship is so. The strength of the
whole fabric comes from the material of which it is made.
The State is not merely a name, or a base reality. It is a
community of *men*.

> "What constitutes a State?
>   Not high raised battlement or labored mound,
>   Thick wall or moated gate;
>   Not cities proud, with spires and turrets crowned;
>   Not bays and broad armed ports,
>   Where, laughing at the storm, rich navies ride;
>   Not starred and spangled courts,
>   Where low-browed baseness wafts perfume to pride.
>   No; Men, high-minded Men."

Then, how necessary that men be prepared for true citizenship! How necessary, in order that the State may be the

great administrator of God's divine precepts of man's relation to man, that the citizen be what the State should be! On every hand we have complaint that officials acts, that legislation, that governmental policy are not what they should be. Do we forget that these things so often condemned are upon the whole a reflection of the level of our citizenship? We seek to find a remedy on a large scale, by reforming the government itself. We imagine that the whole may be made good by a stroke, without looking to the foundation of the whole. As Mr. Chesterton says, we think backwards. We continually overlook the fact that mere legislation, that the mere making and enforcing of laws, that fines, penalties, and imprisonment do not put conscience into the mind of man. It is time for us to realize—and to act on the realization— that the public conscience is only the conscience of the individual citizenship, and that its origin is not primarily in the much promulgation and enforcement of constitutions and statutes. The source of that conscience is elsewhere indeed. It lies in the citizen's conception, by a spiritual touch with his Maker, of those simple but divine rules by which his conduct must be governed. If the conscience of the great majority of the citizenship is of high order—if it is nurtured by a touch with its divine source—constitutions and statutes will reflect it and will be obeyed. Without conscience in citizenship constitutions and statutes make only a weak, ill-conceived government. We must begin at the right end in our reforms. Not with the government merely, but in the heart of the citizen. Let us cultivate and foster in every man, in every community, so true a conception and practice of man's duty to his fellow-man that the same shall be reflected in our States and Nation, by executive, legislator, and judge, and thus a sovereignty of love reign supreme, even over the minority that catches not the inspiration. Great questions of capitalism, of corporate control, of the relation of employer and employee take up the time of our statesmen and fill the columns of our newspapers and magazines.

For the solution of these questions what more is necessary than a citizenship imbued with the true spirit of Christian charity? Is capital at all dangerous when lawfully accumulated and expended by Christian men? Is there danger of dishonest, watered stock, of unlawful gains at the expense of the public, of neglect of protection for the lives of the traveling public, when corporate officers are Christian men? Is there danger of continued misunderstanding in labor matters when employer and employee, following the creed of the Carpenter of Nazareth, meet as brothers? But it is said that perfection can not be hoped for and that all men can not be made Christians; all capitalists, corporate officials, employers, and employees imbued with love and righteousness. True, that may be. But the power of might and right are such that when the great majority that control in this Republic have felt the revival and impress of the spirit of Christ, that spirit is sure to be reflected in the working out of every public question.

What, then, can be done for a telling uplift of our citizenship so that high character in it, through an everyday recognition and practice of the simple rules of right, justice, and love, may redound to better and more exalted brotherhood and government? The attainment is easy if men will only cease to live for self and live for others as well—if men everywhere will give the exalting personal touch. The attainment is sure to be achieved when men shall depend for good not solely on the power of money, but on the greater and more lasting power of the spirit within them. Out of the bigness of this new day the call to every citizen is for the best that is in him. Shall we not take advantage of the great and ready opportunities of the age to spread the gospel of love and righteousness? The home, the Church, the school can be fostered to even greater results. The cause will advance now as never before, if we are bent on its advance. The modern lines of communication and touch will spread it swiftly and widely. Shall not the new things of the new day be used for Him that gave them? They have not been given to us for our selfish ends. The railroad, the press, the telephone, the automobile, the speedy and useful things innumerable are at our hands for *service*. It is easier than ever to do good, to make the wide brotherhood of man that exists materially to be equally as wide spiritually. Shall we not use the new day for our spiritual advance rather than to allow the age to make us gross by its comforts and ease? The right-thinking man will make the times bend to his religion, not his religion to bend to the times. The call of the new day is to every man with power for good in whatever way he may possess it. The truth of the story of the talents is more applicable to-day than when it was told more than nineteen hundred years ago. God demands in this enlightened prosperous day that we *personally* do the work He has assigned us. We can not acquit ourselves by farming it out and depending on hired servants wholly to do it. We ourselves are servants. In God's army no substitutes are accepted. We are prone to think it enough to pay the preacher and leave to him alone the lending of encouragement, love, and uplift. The day is too large for that time-worn method. "One act of charity," says Robertson, "will teach men more of the love of God than a thousand sermons." We think of missions across the seas, when many a mission personally for us is calling us to duty if we only open our worldly-blinded eyes. Not alone among the distressed, but in politics, in business, is there missionary work for the Christian citizen.

That the new day may be really glorious and bright, men oan *every hand* need inspiration by good deeds and good words from their fellow-men. The lowly and less fortunate need the strength and confidence that come from the kindly interest and good-will of the more fortunate. The weaker citizen must be spoken to, aided, and inspired by the stronger. Soul is quick to catch strength from soul when the stronger soul is willing to lend its power. Practical Christianity will rapidly upbuild and extend Christian citizenship. Christianity needs no better advertisement than its practice. Though the sphere of most men is limited to a community, yet what may not be expected when the great majority of capable men that compose every community attend daily to the advance of love and righteousness? The maintenance of our citizenship lies in the high personal touch of citizen with citizen. Here we may paraphrase the Scottish bard and say that "Man's humanity to man makes countless thousands glad." The greatest work that a man can do is that which lies nearest. His first duty is to it, from its very situation. There is a fortune in living for others. In this the age is richer than in all else. Too many of us want to be seen of men—to do what we mistake for great things. Better to write our names on the hearts of men than on the pages of history. Why seek so-called greatness anyhow? True manhood overtops all titles. The last shall be first. Not for a moment must I be understood as speaking for a soft-hearted citizenship. The Christian citizen has a big heart of love, but a brave soul to strike down oppression and unrighteousness when the militant method is demanded. No true Christian was ever a coward. History has proved this. Still, how wonderfully does genuine love win its way! What barriers it burns away! When, however, for maintenance of right, courage and fight must come into action, what is more inspiring than the fighting Christian citizen?

There are gentlemen who will say that the thoughts uttered in this address are ethereal and impracticable. Yes, too many there are who have not felt the true meaning of life and its purposes. To them no apology is offered. Let them not retard us in the conception that God gives us of personal duty, but let us by such a tide of power and uplift, starting from our own noble efforts, make them to see what unselfish and truly patriotic work will do for the betterment of the race, and thus cause them to join the procession of a mighty majority.

O Methodist Men, here assembled from every part of our

great land, the new day calls the great Church which we represent to greater achievements in the making of Christian citizenship. Methodism has long been one of the mighty forces for good. In this age of ripest opportunity, we shall surely excel. Our God is marching on!

The New Day in Evangelism.

L. J. BIRNEY.

METHODISM was conceived of the Holy Ghost and born of that virgin Divine Passion, to bring this world to God. She was not brought forth into the world to methodize it, but to vitalize it. And she has just one right to claim the world to be her parish;—not her years, nor her millions, nor the continents she spans, nor the doctrines she believes, nor the stars she has already placed in the diadem of her Lord. Just one thing: the measure in which the passion that gave her birth inspires her still. When she loses that she ought to die. That passion is the very quintessence of the Kingdom and the love of God, and the first requisite it must be of any Church that has a right to be militant or can ever hope to be triumphant. My father once turned an old horse into the best pasture on the farm to work no more, but to receive the tenderest care of that household for the remainder of his days, because on his devoted old back and by his toil the whole family had been reared. And so he ought to have done. But God will not do that for a Church, and God ought not. For the Church of to-day wrought not the glorious past. She simply inherited it. And no Church can claim the future by virtue of a great past, but only by virtue of the great passion that made the past. There is no protection to-morrow because of service rendered yesterday. God is just as mercifully merciless in the Church as He is in nature toward the organ that ceases to perform its real function. It tends to become a mere appendix, and the law of the survival of the fittest seals its doom.

MILITANT METHODISM.

But here is firm ground for great optimism, for not in a generation has there been such a restless hunger, such a prophetic yearning to know how to bring men to God, how to find and lead the great crowd of wandering sheep, how to lift up the heavy eyes of materialism to see the skies, as in this thirteenth year of the century which is to behold the mightiest triumphs for the Kingdom of God this world has ever seen. The inner heart-cry of this transition age is slowly but surely gathering into a great chorus, "Lo! the spiritual morning cometh." Commerce has obliterated our horizons, and set our feet firmly in a great brotherhood, and then by the magic of steam and lightning has contracted the world until every man is in our own door-yard. Science is again bowing her head in reverence; philosophy is again seeking the altar as the only place she can rest, and the question-marks that frightened every traveler on every road a decade since are turning into guide-posts, and religious certainty and intellectual respectability lie down together. We see a new day, a new age, a new world. The battle of scholarship, reverent and irreverent, has been fought about the old land-marks, but the smoke of battle clears away and the old flag is still there, and the great fundamentals upon which Methodism reared her mighty structure have not been moved a single inch. The great Church is swinging back again to her ancient task of bringing men into the Kingdom of God. And there are signs, and this great Convention is one of them, that she is settling down to that gigantic business with a concentration and a determination that will soon challenge the heroism of any one who dares to "follow in His train."

But in this new day we discover that while the old spirit is all-sufficient, the old methods are insufficient for the herculean task that the Son of God has set for us. There are three of four great characteristics that stand out clear and sure against the background of the evangelism of this new day, which give us hope and courage. One of them is the new emphasis upon personality. The man is beginning to stand out from the mass. Julia Ward Howe once said to Charles Sumner in Washington, "Come down to my house and meet a personal friend." Sumner's reply was, "I am losing my interest in individuals and becoming interested in the race." Julia Ward Howe wrote in her diary that night, "By the latest accounts God Almighty has not got as far as this." God Almighty never will. And the more God has His way in this world, the more will the individual come into view. And the Church is at last learning to see Zaccheus instead of the crowd and to go down to his house for his soul's sake.

Methodism has had masterful skill in the art of public appeal, and she should never lose that fine art. She is the mightiest spiritual force on this continent to-day, because she has known how to use that power in the past. But it is the clearest demonstration of history and the surest conclusion of reason and experience that this world will never be brought to God by public appeal alone, for the great multitude of the lost sheep of the House of Israel never hear the public appeal. In every community from which you come —almost every community—there are sections in which it is the ninety and nine that are out instead of the one. But the ninety and nine will be brought back exactly as the one was brought back—by sending not one after the ninety and nine, but ninety and nine after the ninety and nine. There is a far deeper principle at work when Phillip goes out and finds Nathanael and brings him to Christ than when Peter stands up to preach a sermon that brings three thousand to Christ, provided that the Spirit which made possible the latter inspires the former, and that deeper principle rests upon the fact that the final reality in this universe is not any truth that Peter announced or that can be announced in any public appeal. That final reality is personality, and the only evangelism that will ever bring this world to God is the evangelism that personalizes itself as evangelism has never done in the past. Dr. Durbin once said in a great congregation, "No

271

man is ever brought fully and finally to Jesus Christ except through the office of some other person." Dr. Peck being present, arose and called his statement in question, saying, "Was not the Ethiopian brought to Christ by reading the Prophet?" And Dr. Durbin replied, "Understandest thou what thou readest? and the eunuch replied, How can I except some man should guide me?" In that reply Dr. Durbin placed his skillful finger upon one of the great fundamentals of the coming Kingdom of God. There are three factors in that Kingdom: first, a Supreme Person, but by the very law of personality it is forever impossible for that Supreme Person to find His way into humanity except through personality; personality is the only possible revelation of personality. "Go ye" is just as fundamental to the Kingdom as the principle of incarnation. The second factor in the Kingdom is truth. But there is no such thing as truth in the Kingdom aside from personality. The truth of astronomy or of physics is true in a perfectly lifeless and manless world, but the superlative, saving truths of holiness and love and redemption and regeneration and sanctification and atonement, these do not even exist except in personality, and they can find their way into human hearts only through personality. The last factor in the Kingdom is the world of persons, but again, by the very law of truth and the law of personality, the Supreme Person and the supreme truths can never reach the world of persons except through personality. The coming evangelism will not simply depend upon a few preachers and a few missionaries, but upon a multitude of persons; it will use the foolishness of preaching not less, but it will use the high wisdom of redeemed personality immeasurably more. The sermon that won the three thousand to Christ on the day of Pentecost has dominated our ideals and methods all too long. We have too long tried to bring in the Kingdom by addition, and the Kingdom will never come except by arithmetical progression. If Peter had saved three thousand souls every day after Pentecost, and if his so-called apostolic successors had had religion enough to do the same thing, it would have taken a thousand years to bring the world to Christ as the world was in Peter's day, and there would have been thirty new generations unaccounted for; but if each of the three thousand had gone out to save one a year, and each new disciple had done the same, the entire world would have been reached for Jesus Christ a whole generation before the Gospel of John was written. If those blessed feet were lifting from this earth today in ascension, leaving twelve men to save fifteen hundred million, and all the world were pagan beside, and the twelve would go forth each to win one a year, and each new convert would do the same, before the babe born yesterday would reach eight and twenty summers every man and woman in this world would have been brought to God, or at least have had the gospel preached to him. I submit that in the light of that fact, these nineteen hundred years of so-called Christian history are dangerously near to blasphemy when they are held up against the white light of the cross. And in the light of that fact the dream that has been in great souls of the gospel being preached to every creature in this generation is not fanciful at all, but is of easy accomplishment if every nominal discipleship were vitalized into reality.

The second characteristic of the evangelism of this new day is a deeper discernment of the nature of sin and its effect upon human life, and, I state it reverently, the discernment that no atonement God could have made would absolutely wipe out the effects and results of sin in the human life. In the reaction of the older evangelism from the moral horror of a limited election we swept too far and overstated the nature of the atonement and the work of divine grace in the human heart. We made it, at least down in the common thought, to mean not only the power of God to cleanse from all sin and pardon all iniquity, but absolutely to suspend the law of cause and effect, of seed and harvest; and the practical result of that, down in the great crowd, was an easy postponement of the call of God to the soul, expecting a full recovery by the power of the atonement at a more convenient season. That was the secret of the pronouncement by a great evangelist a few years ago to a great company like this, when he leaned over the pulpit and said—he was honest, earnest, sincere, too—"O men, come back to God! No matter how you have sinned nor how long you have sinned, and God will make your life as if you had never sinned." That is not true. God never said that; God never can say that. And the evangelism that presumes thus to juggle with the laws of life, far from lifting the world up from its sin, is blinding the world to the nature of sin and teaching the world to meddle with God's infinite love. The moral government of this universe is not such a flabby affair as that; and the new evangelism with its deeper insight into the needs of humanity and the nature of sin and the purpose of the atonement sees just as clearly as ever the power of pardon and of God's infinite grace, but it also sees and is teaching that the soul that is out of Christ for a single day or year has lost something that Almighty God Himself with all His love and power can never give back again. It is seeing and it is preaching that the prodigal can come back from the swine to his father, but that he has left forever with the swine some of the finest and highest possibilities of his life. It is seeing that there are no crevices in this moral universe through which a soul can slip unnoticed and escape the results of sin. And the new evangelism is translating that fact of the inevitable result of sin in the fiber of man's whole moral and physical and intellectual being into the terms of the infinite, brooding love of God, and putting it down into the consciousness of the great crowd, where it is bearing fruit in a new sense of the unescapable God, and in the conviction that the Christian life is the only life that fits into the moral structure of this universe. And preaching that and teaching that to the rising generation we are to have a new grip upon the conscience of the world, for in spite of anything we may say, whether or not it is right, the great world about us is losing interest in punishment for sin in the future, but science has helped us to convict the world of the irrefutable fact of the effect of sin upon life to-day and forever, and that is to be the note which is to call men everywhere to account for sin until they are able to discern a higher motive for holiness.

And that leads directly to the third great characteristic of the evangelism of to-day which is the most hopeful of them all. One of the greatest things that Ruskin ever said, was in a letter to Alfred Tennyson. One day, after he had taken a walk in London and saw the little children upon the streets wandering without a shepherd, he went back and wrote this to Tennyson: "The more I see of the world, the more do I believe that not the sorrow of the world is the wonder of the world, but the loss of the world is the wonder of the world. I see by every wayside perfect miracles of possibilities in the lives of the boys and girls going to waste forever without a teacher." The Church is waking up to this stupendous fact, that the chief business of the Church is not at all to save the lost, as we have believed for centuries. The chief business of the Church of Jesus Christ is to save loss, which is immeasurably more difficult and more imperative. There is just one way to save loss, the incalculable loss that our Church has sustained all along, and that is by feeding lambs instead of hunting sheep. In God's name, brethren, Methodists, in God's name, if we can not do both (we can), let us keep the lambs and let the few sheep stray rather than to hunt a few sheep and let the lambs scatter never to be found again. We will never, notwithstanding all our conventions and money giving and devotion, accomplish the task until the Church learns to centralize its work around the conservation of life instead of the reclamation of life. And the new day which is ahead of us shows at no point more surely than in the change of attitude toward the child. If Methodism had been as true practically to her doctrine of the child as her doctrine of the child is true to the nature of the child she would have herself held the balance of power for Protestantism in this land against the vast aggression that lifts itself up everywhere and builds its towers upon the hilltop in every city. Why? Because long before Methodism was born she learned the immeasurable value of the child. If all the energy and devotion and the time and service that have been given by the Church universal to converting men into the Kingdom of God had been used in keeping the children from being converted out of the Kingdom we would no longer be praying, "Thy Kingdom come." It would be here. It will never be here until the child is placed in the heart and center of all our prayers and efforts.

One more characteristic of the evangelism of this new day that gives us hope and courage. The Church of to-day sees just as clearly as did our fathers that social reform and uplift will never come except by the regeneration of the individual, but the Church of to-day sees as our fathers could not that to put the regenerate life back into a hopeless moral and social environment and do nothing to change it, is a sin. Science reaches the fever by reinforcing the blood in the veins of the individual, and then it gives itself—in almost a Christian martyrdom—to banish forever from the earth the conditions in which the fever was bred. So in this new day, not only does the ancient passion for souls still burn in the hearts of men as they seek to save the individual, but the same passion,—the passion to save,—is burning hot in the very foundations of our whole social structure, to destroy forever the conditions that have made so long and so sadly ineffective our work for the souls of men.

IV. LAYMEN AND THE PROGRAM.

What Would You Be Worth If You Lost All Your Money?

George Innes.

There is more than one reason why I am glad to be here to-night. The first one and the chief and important one that I shall speak of is the happiness and joy that I have that I may be able to perform some little service for the Methodist Church, because the Methodist Church did a great deal for me. When I was a young boy just out of school and engaged in business for myself, there was no organization of the Church that I was a member of then, and the Methodist Church took care of me and ministered to me richly for years as a member of its body, and I am therefore glad indeed that I can be with you to-night. There is a second reason why I am glad to be here, and it is because in this room about eight years ago I heard the peculiar message which showed me that the thing for a servant of God to do was to consecrate his property as well as his life.

The subject that has been given to me for to-night is one that came to me some few years ago. I was in business at that time. I am a Methodist to-night—I was for seven years —and surely we are not going to apologize for giving personal testimony in a Methodist meeting. I was in business in Southern Minnesota. I had several lines of business in the place where I lived. I was engaged in the retail lumber business and in the grain business, and also in the bank, and in colonization in Northwestern Canada. One night, after we had taken an inventory in our lumber business and an inventory in some of the other lines of work, and found that the profits were very good, and after we had had our annual meeting of the directors of the bank, and had paid a very nice dividend, I said to my wife: "I am going to the bank to-night and I am going to be gone until pretty late. Do not wait for me." She said: "What are you going to do at the bank? Is any one else to be there?" "No, I am going down because I have some work I want to do." I knew the profits that we made in the lumber business, and in the grain business, and in the bank, and I knew after a few minutes I could get at the profits on the land, and I don't know whether any of you men know the real joy of anything like that, but I was going to have a real good old souse in covetousness. I was just going down and figure that out and sit there and have a good old time. So I went down and I wrote, "Here is your profit on lumber, and here is your profit on hardware, and here is your profit on grain, and here is your profit on the bank," and then I figured out the values of land, and I said, "That is startling—I did not think it would be so much, but here it is." I thought again, "No, I did not think it would be so much," and I said, "Now for a good time." But the Lord spoke to me and He said: "You did not figure on this extra. You are going to have a good time from that which you did not earn, and now do you not think you ought to thank Me before you go to enjoy yourself this evening?" So there in my office alone, with the curtains drawn, I got down on my knees and thanked God for giving me a few thousand dollars which I considered that I had not earned. "Now," I said, "I can have a good time because the rest is mine; I got this." But He said: "Who gave you the power to get that? Don't you think you ought to thank Me for that, too?" I said, "That is true, You gave it to me all right; I'll get down and thank You." And so I did. Then to my dismay He asked me another question. He said: "What would you say if I were to take it all away from you? The Lord gives and the Lord takes away; would you say, 'Blessed be the name of the Lord?'" Would I say it? I said, "That is different." Then the thought came to me, and I think the Lord spoke and said: "You have figured up what you are worth with this money. You say you are worth so much. What would you be worth if I took it away? What else would you have?"

The fact was that I did not have anything that I knew of. I had been a member of the Church for nearly twenty years. Often I had said, "Lord, give me the grace and courage to go out and win some one for You." All my life, since at the age of twelve I had joined the Church, I had desired to do this. But the years slipped by and I did not do it. One day I was traveling from Devil's Lake, Dakota, to a town in Montana. As I lay in my berth it seemed to me that the Lord spoke to me and said, "To-morrow you are going to die." It startled me and frightened me, and then I remembered as I looked my Visitor in the face and prayed, that the Lord had said, "I will take care of you." So I said, "It is all right; I can go with You." But He looked at me and said, "But you are going alone." That is a terrifying thing: to go into eternity alone. The Lord said to me: "You know every stick of lumber, every bushel of grain, every acre of land. Why don't you deal with Me in that way? Do you know any lost ones in this town? Why don't you make a list of them?" So I wrote down their names. I thought of a competitor in the grain business who was a good friend of mine and who would believe me. And I thought I would go to him. But then I thought, "He will ask me about the man who has been working for me for twenty years." But I said, "I can not go to him." I could not win my friend until I did go to this man. I saw that, but I said, "I will call the preacher in to-morrow and ask him to go and get my co-worker out of the way, and then I will go to this friend of mine." I actually did that thing. I called the preacher in and said, "Have you ever spoken to Charley about his soul?" "No." "Don't you think you ought to?" And he said, "Yes, I ought to, I know it." Then something came to me and the voice said,

"You know that all the King's horses could not pull that man into the Kingdom over the top of you; why don't you go to him and confess?" I said, "I will go; you need not go." Well, I will not detain you men with the whole story. I went. I met him at the door. He expected that I wanted to talk to him about some business. When I said, "Charlie, don't you want to take Christ as your Savior?" he broke into tears and was saved.

We talk about personal service—the reason we do not do it is because we are cowards. Not long after that I moved to a large city. I canvassed the Churches of that city, one hundred evangelical Churches, and found only two with men who made it their business to go into the streets and alleys and try to win other men to Jesus Christ. I joined one of them. For the years I was in that city there was scarcely a Sunday afternoon passed that I and others were not in the streets of that city trying to win men, and I can remember only two Sundays when men were not brought into the Kingdom. They will come. I came home one Sabbath afternoon and went into the house and told my wife what a great God we had had. She said: "Our oldest boy—he was five years old then—'asked me a strange question last week; he said, 'Why are n't you and papa and I missionaries?' I do n't know what put that into his head." I said, "What did you say to him?" She said, "I did not know what to say." Men, what would you say? If you Christian men of the Methodist Church were asked that question why you could n't be a missionary, what would you say, what legitimate reason could you give for not being? I said, "We will have to answer him, he is our boy; we can not let a thing like that go unanswered." It was midnight that night before we went to sleep, and before we went to sleep there was a plan promised to God that we would go away unto the farthest ends of the earth for Christ's sake, and if He wanted us to stay there we would stay, and if He did not want us we would come home and re-engage in business, because God calls men into business as definitely as into the foreign field, and whatever we made would be for Him. The thing was signed by writing a letter to my mother and a brother. We bought our tickets and started out. I had thought I had known something about stewardship up to that time. This question of stewardship is a mighty problem, and speaking of stewardship, what does it mean? Does it mean tithing? To my mind it means tithing afterwards; after what? After the thirty-third verse of the forty-fourth chapter of Luke, and not until then. What is that verse? "Whosoever he be of you that renounceth not all that he hath, he can not be My disciple." That is the stewardship of property. Jesus Christ was talking to those who were to follow Him in this great conquest of this world, and He said, "Before we start we might as well have this thing understood; whosoever there be of you who renounces not all that he has, he can not go with Me."

You have been discussing here in the last few days the problems of the Church. As a layman not pretending at all to be one who can diagnose all the ills of the Church, let me tell you frankly what I think is the matter. I think down at the root of the whole thing, the trouble lies here. Why do we say, "What is the matter with the Church?" when we know. Do you allow liars and drunkards in the Church? No. Paul said in Colossians, "Mortify the sins within you," and he names the awful sins of lust, passion, and evil desires, and he winds up, as though putting a climax on the whole thing, by saying, "Beware of covetousness, which is idolatry." Why need we ask what is the matter with the Church when we know that the amount of unconsecrated money in the Church of Jesus Christ to-day that has not been laid upon the altar would evangelize the world a thousand times over. You find it mentioned perhaps more than anything else in the Bible. All through the Scripture it lies cheek by jowl with adultery. You hear Billy Sunday and think he uses pretty strong language, but you read the first eight chapters of Jeremiah and you will find language than which Billy Sunday could not

281

use stronger. Jeremiah speaks of the evil of adultery into which Israel has gone, and in the fifth to the eighth chapters he says that this adultery which has consumed Israel is consuming Judah, and they are given over to covetousness. And if that is not a picture of the world that gives more to tipping porters on the train than it does to the Church of Jesus Christ, I do not know what it is. I am condemning myself with you. I remember before this vision came to me that I was sitting one Sunday morning in Church, when the annual plate was passed round for the collection for Foreign Missions. I was sitting there when the plate came down, and I was thinking about some business enterprise I was going to carry out, and I actually put the large sum of twenty-five cents on that plate as my offering to God—the expression of my desire that the world would be brought to Jesus Christ. I did not hear much of the sermon—do not know much what he said, but I knew that I had committed a sin; I had conscience enough left for that. I went to the preacher afterwards and said, "I do not believe I gave enough this morning; here is five dollars," and he was so happy about it that he wanted to put my picture in the paper. When the fact of the matter was, that before that year closed I had been to Indianapolis and sat in this hall and went home and figured out my obligations for Foreign Missions alone and found that it was $500 and I had it to pay. You have heard Mel Trotter tell the story of how he went on some of his dreadful debauches, and how he went home after one of these days and his wife met him at the door and said, "Mel, the baby is dead," and you have heard him say how with that little dead baby in his arms he promised his wife he would never touch whisky again, and you have heard him tell how he went out that very night and took that little dead baby's shoes and pawned them for whisky. That is an awful sin, but I want to confess, men, in shame, that the man who sits as an officer of the Church and is so consumed by the lust of covetousness that he will put twenty-five cents on the plate when on the least basis he owes five hundred; I want to say to you that that man is guilty of worse sin than Mel Trotter.

We heard this afternoon of the thousands laid on the shambles of lust in Chicago, but you go with me to India and I can show you ten or eleven thousand little girls every year who are taken to the temples and married to the stone god, that their lives may be forever spent in shame, worshiping the gods of India. Take a guide and go and see it; let that guide be the Holy Spirit and none other. Let Him take you to these regions, and if you have eyes to see and ears to hear you will come back with a soul scarred with scars never to be erased. But that is just sin—just sin. What did our Savior say when He stood on that high mountain of privilege, the Mount of Olives; what did my Savior say when He looked down? Did He condemn them for those things I spoke of in India? "No," He said, "Because of your unbelief," and, friends, your unbelief and that sin of covetousness. We say we are better than the people of India. I remember when I came back from that trip I went into the bank where I had been banking as a business man. Before I went away they were willing to give me anything in reason, but I noticed when I came back from that trip that when I went into that bank they did not see me. I knew what was the matter, of course. I had announced that I was to be some kind of a missionary. Finally, one day, just more in a joke than anything else, I spoke to the vice-president of the bank. I said: "What is the matter? Before I went away you were always kind. There seems to be something different. Have I done anything to offend you?" Well, he turned to me and he told me very courteously and yet very plainly that he just simply thought there was something wrong; that was all. Now, men, you would not like to be considered dippy, would you? I didn't like that; and I walked out of the bank and said: "Lord, maybe I am wrong. Maybe this is simply a fantastic thing. Maybe You don't want me to do it at all." But I prayed on the steps of the bank and said, "Father, give me

MILITANT METHODISM.

something that I can get hold of that will show me that I am right or that I am wrong." I looked back to a morning in Allahabad. A friend of mine, Sam Higginbottam, who was in charge of a leper asylum, said to me, "Won't you come and see the leper asylum?" I said, "No, I don't care to go and see that." Then I saw that he, who had to go among these people every day, was disappointed that I would not go this once. So I said I would go. As we went along he told me how it used to be a mud house with thatched roof and a filthy place. But he said: "Now it is different. The appointments are good." He told me about little Frances, who was brought up in an orphanage of the Church Missionary Society of England. She was taken sick and the doctor said she was a leper. They sent her to Allahabad, accompanied by her brother. She did not know what was the matter with her until she arrived. When she saw the asylum, she said to my friend, "Am I a leper?" She fell on her brother's neck and cried until they were afraid she would take her life. Finally one day my friend said to her: "Frances, you have had a chance in life. There are millions in this land who have not had one chance. Can't you teach these other women here?" And she heard his word and took interest and heart and taught, and in a short time she had won these women to Christ, and she thanked God that He had sent her there. And so I began to understand a little of how our Savior was willing that the leprosy of our sin should touch His pure life that He might win us to Him. On the steps of the bank I thought of little Frances and of the multitudes in all lands to whom Christ wishes to come and incarnate Himself in them. I said: "No, the man inside is wrong. It is no mistake to give your life for them."

I wish that every man within my hearing could have been where I was awhile ago. I wish I could tell you how much you ought to appreciate the God-given leaders that you have. Your heart would have been touched as mine has been touched. I wish you could see the missionaries on the fields as I have

284

seen them. I have been in your stations in China, and I
want to say to you, humanly speaking, the reason I am here
to-night is because of the unanswerable challenge of the missionary. I recall the day when I was taken to a place in
Jerusalem that they called Calvary, and the guide pointed to
a mark in the black pavement, to a piece of marble, and said,
"There is where they say the cross of our Lord stood," and
he pointed to another and another and said, "There is where
they say the other crosses were." And as I think of the
lonely graves of the missionaries in foreign fields I am con-
strained to say, "This too is Calvary." I am supposed to
speak something of money. I agree with all the program
you have for money, but I want to say that when you and I
win this world for Jesus Christ we will do it when we go to
Calvary, and not until then. There has never been a generation since the Lord went to glory when those who profess
to love Him, if they had really fellowshipped with Him, could
not have brought the world to our God. "Except a corn of
wheat fall into the ground and die it abideth alone," and
that is all there is to it. To my mind that word "alone,"
that awful word "alone," is one of the saddest things I can
think of. To spend eternity alone is a dreadful thought, and
yet the fact is that there are to-day among our Christians
many who are willing to spend eternity alone.

Now I must close; I did not realize that I was taking so
much of your time. I go from place to place; but men, do not
think me guilty of coming here from Philadelphia that I might
speak to you some easy words. I have come to you, men of
Methodism, for I have been one of you, and I am still one of
you; and I say, let us go to the altar and give it all. Use the
same earnestness in giving testimony in reference to stewardship as you do when you ask the Lord to take away your sin.
About three hundred years ago, a mystic said that to his mind
the bees left their most excellent honey in the wounds of
the Lion of the tribe of Judah. Let us drink long and eat
long of the sweetness of that honey of the rock. My last

word to you is, let us believe that the Kingdom of Heaven is at hand, for I want to say to you that when the men of the Methodist Church and the men of my Church and the men of other Churches will give on the altar all they have to witness for Jesus Christ, God will give us the Kingdom.

The Laymen's Witness to a Supernatural Gospel.

FRED B. SMITH.

WE are here to-night, answering what I believe is the greatest call that has ever been announced to organized Christianity. We are Christian men, we are brave men, and therefore it seems to me it is not at all out of place that in the midst of the sweep of this mighty spirit we should pause a moment to remind ourselves that these are serious days in Christian work. We are in the midst of a crisis the full measure of which no man in this room can understand. Now, when I make use of that over-worked word "crisis" I am reminded that there has always been a crisis in Christian work, that there always will be a crisis. God pity that man who calls himself a Christian, who does not every day feel that he is meeting a crisis. We are in a desperate crisis. This is no hour to be optimistic. There is a crisis on to-day in the labor world. I wish every one of you, for thirty minutes, could have been with me the other day when the United Plumbers of two great cities met on a Sunday morning to discuss whether they would go on strike, and I wish you could have heard a wild-eyed man as he raced up and down the platform like a demon. He said, "If we ever get our rights in the world, we must smash the Church; the Church is against us," and the crowd applauded him. O yes, there was a man tried to answer him, but he was hissed down; while that wild-eyed man, who said the only way the laboring man would get his rights was to crush the Church, was cheered to the echo. Don't belittle that. If you go out with one of those stock-made sermons of how the men are swinging

286

into the Church, you only prove that you have not been outside of a spiritual hothouse for a long time.

There is a crisis on in the commercial world. The other day twenty-one men sat down with their host, who was a Christian man, and launched an eight-million-dollar enterprise. After that their host, an earnest and devoted Churchman—seven-tenths of you would know him if I called his name—said: "We have launched eight million dollars' worth of commerce in forty-five minutes. I want to know how you stand in relation to the Church." He went around to each of the twenty-one, and seventeen of them said they were Church members. Then he said: "If we would go at the Church like we do at business, we ought to turn this town upside down in a year. Of you seventeen men who are members of the Church, what are you doing?" He went round the table again and asked them that question. Fourteen of the seventeen said that they had "cut it out," "nothing to it." Out of the whole room only three of those men said they were vitally in the Church.

That crisis has struck the educational world. The other day I spoke on a Sunday afternoon to two thousand men in a university where there were four thousand registered. The president of the university honored us that afternoon by his most cordial words, but on Monday when I took dinner in his home he said, "I was conscious that you lost that crowd at one place; there was a moment when they got away from you." I said, "When was that?" He said, "Near the close you plead with those two thousand university men to be related to the Church, and I was conscious that they sagged away from you when you said that." He is a member of the Church. I said, "What is your inference?" He said, "My inference is this: the university men with whom I am dealing may be interested in welfare work and social reform and political reconstruction, but my impression is that the next generation of university men are not going to be churchmen." I do not agree with him any more than I agreed with that labor agitator. But the sad thing was that that university president said it and thinks that way. I told him later that the trouble with him was that he was hobnobbing with the wrong crowd. Notwithstanding he is saying it, and his attitude is reflecting itself in the university.

That crisis is on, a crisis or a paralysis. Before we leave this never-to-be-forgotten hall, let us get down on our faces and call to the eternal God to help us realize the seriousness of this hour. Let me tell you to-day the insidious tides of the heathen world are sending their neutralizing messages in upon us. The other day I met a Buddhist priest, who told me he was sorry to miss me while I was in his country. I said, "What are you doing here?" He said, "What you were doing in my country, I am evangelizing." I said, "You are not going to have as good a time as I had." He said, "All we need is one conference and we will put our brand on every Christian Science Church in this country; that is our doctrine."

Notwithstanding all this, I believe that we are at the beginning of a tremendous revival of religion. There is an upheaval, there is an under-swelling that is somehow pushing great moral ideals to the front. The question that confronts us to-night is whether much of this is going to clear itself from the Church, whether it is going to inhere in a new cult outside the Church. But I am bound to say to you this, I have come to that place where I am willing to say that if the Church is so conservative that she can not revise her curriculum enough to include some things that are now being announced in the moral world, I will say, O God, send on that great moral wave, even although it has to come outside of the Church! We have this condition to-day, that every hall of legislation is turned into a prayer-meeting. There is not a State Legislature that is not discussing great moral topics, and now we have in the man at the White House and in the Premier of the Cabinet men who are prayer-meeting leaders, who are on their knees asking God to lead them on.

There is one great wave that is around us in our country, a sort of altruistic wave that is filling everything. The last time I was in Tokio one of their leading statesmen, who is himself a graduate of Harvard and a Buddhist, said to me: "You Westerners owe us a lot in Japan. You came in with your Western civilizations and ideas and it has weakened our old faith until we can not see anything in it, but you did not give us anything else, and you owe it to us to stand with us until we find a new and better faith for Japan." And, by the authority of the Imperial Government, Japan is now on a search for a religion. Cross to China. A few weeks ago four hundred million Chinese said their prayers with their hearts turned toward the throne. The throne is gone, the emperor is gone, and four hundred million Chinese do not know how to say their prayers—the very center to which they prayed has been removed, but I can not help but think that somehow in the next ten years there is a chance to put Jesus Christ on the throne in China as perhaps we will not have for one hundred years more if we miss this present opportunity.

The psychological hour for the achievement of Christian ideals throughout the world is upon us to-day. What is the world asking us to-night? One thing is necessary, and I hasten to it. If we are going to put Christianity into the heart of our own country, if we are going to make Christianity the battle cry of sociology, if we are going to make Christianity the religion of the world, we must step into the clear with one explicit statement, namely, that ours is the *supreme* religion.

I am asked to speak to-night upon the witness of the laymen to a supernatural religion. And I am bound to pause here a moment to say that I am afraid that we Christians ourselves have been almost apologizing in such a tone of voice that we have dulled tremendously the sharp edge of conviction that our religion is a supernatural religion. Certain insidious influences have been at work until it is amazing to find how many Christian men lower their voices almost to a whisper when they speak about the miraculous birth, the miraculous resurrection, the miraculous ascension. We have pretty nearly in many circles lost the ring of our voice when we talk about the supernatural elements of our religion. First of all, we have juggled with the Bible until it is amazing how cautiously some men have to select anything from the Bible. I do not want to be classified with the man who objects to any critical study of the Bible, but I do want the critical, scientific man, if he is a Christian, when he finishes to say, "That is the Word of God and no other book is." And I want him to finish by saying that it is an absolutely impossible Book to understand, for in the hour when you fully understand that Book, I turn to some other. I believe that Christ is not *a* Savior, but *the* Savior. I believe that Book is not *one* of the text-books of religion, but *the* Text-book of religion. We want a new declaration that this Christianity is a supernatural religion emanating from the heart of the loving God.

What are our evidences of the supernatural in the world? How are you going to know our faith is supernatural as is no other faith? We are not bereft of knowledge; we are not bereft of argument. I can take a man who tells we that rationalism is the order of the day and I will say to him, "Will you please explain to me by rationalism the existence of the Bible?" I will tell him that the two Bible Societies, the British and the American, last year published two million copies of it, and that for seventeen centuries practically unchanged that Book has been standing. I will say to him, "Please explain that to me." Well, that is a partial evidence. It is not full evidence. I could not take the case to a jury on that alone. It would satisfy me, but not all men. We are not bereft of evidence. Some men tell me that Christianity is only a rational evolution, only a little higher development of certain ethical ideas, and that Jesus Christ was only a man born like other men and who died like other men. I say, "Very well, but explain to me the Church." Any man who talks about the Church dying out permanently is intellectually in the same school with the man who stands at the ocean where the tide has been running in until the banks are full and then, by the laws of the tides, starts receding; this ignoramus, not knowing the law of the tides, stands there and says, "Ah, ha! this creek is going dry!" The Church is going to live until Jesus Christ has finished His work of redeeming this world. I have seen Africa, India, Burma, and Ceylon. Metaphorically, let me tell you what the newest building is in every town; the newest building in every city we visited was a church or a hospital built in the name of Jesus Christ. Again I ask the man who says that our religion is only rational, "Answer me, where did we get our moral standards?" There are some evidences of the supernatural in the Bible after seventeen centuries of an unbroken career; there is evidence of the supernatural in the presence of the Church; there is evidence of the supernatural in the moral ideas of Christianity, but the supreme witness of the supernatural is nothing but a redeemed individual, a soul born out of sin into the light and liberty of Jesus Christ. I wish to-night to accent every method I have heard, and they have been great. What has been programmed to-day in this hall, whether you call it militant Christianity or some other word, you have heard a program that if you work for seriously will make Methodism militant. Do you want to know the method that will push it clear through to the front? It is the method that looks squarely after the redemption of the individual soul. In other words, the program of the salvation of the individual man is that thing which finally nails down tight Christianity as a supernatural religion. I say it because no other religion has it. I rode north from Calcutta with Professor Boesch, who in 1893 was at the World's Parliament of Religions at Chicago. We discussed Hinduism for two days. I was ashamed to find that that Hindu professor was vastly more familiar with the Bible than I was. He got me again and again by references to our Bible, and he insisted that I should read those great passages from the hymns of the Vedas, and he would say, "Have you anything more beautiful in your Bible?" I read to him the Sermon on the Mount, and when I went through the Beatitudes he did confess that he did not think they had anything in their literature that could match them, but he believed that somehow they must have been dug up in ancient Hinduism, and I was at my wits' end. I said to him, "Suppose some man in Hinduism is taken in sin and goes down in awful passion to the bottom— what has Hinduism got for him?" He said, "O, Mr. Smith, Hinduism does not pretend to cure sin." I said to him, "Professor, you have not any religion at all: Christianity proposes to cure sin." Why do I emphasize that? First, because it makes Christianity supreme; secondly, because it is the basis of this whole social reconstruction. The sociologist says that now. Every man says that the social reconstruction must be based upon individual regeneration. Let me tell you that any method of social welfare which does not reckon with individual regeneration is just as wise as whitewashing a fence—it will wash off in the next storm.

There is a problem that confronts us to-night in fulfilling your program. Is it money? No. It is life we need. And how are you going to get life? We need a supernatural action on the man's life. We need more men converted— soul, mind, and body—to God. Then we will get money. I tell you, my friends, if you ever dull the edge of the individual relation to God in conversion and just smooth it out in a freak sociological appeal, our Missionary Boards are going to go hungrier yet for men. It is life we need.

Again, this needed evangelism is going to be very largely propagated, sustained, and extended around the life of the laymen. This is going to be a laymen's contest. I say to you ministers, "Do not be afraid of the layman; push him out into the arena and let him be a fool for Christ's sake if he must." A minister said to me the other day, "I do not dare to trust my laymen to lead the mid-week prayer-meeting, for once in a while a man makes a terrible break." Let him make the break; what he says is not the thing—it is the fact that he is there; he is the new apologetic. Men are asking this question: "Can a man be a Christian on a day like this; can a laboring man, who has to feel the injustice of his life, be a Christian? And can the employer, who has done everything in his power for his men for years and knows they are going to strike at him, be a Christian?" Who can answer that? The preacher? No; he may help a little; no, but essentially the layman.

This is what I close with: have we got the power to do the proposed work? Let me turn you away from programs and scientific statements and problems, and let us cry out for that supernatural power that will carry through this thing without defeat.

PART V.
The Larger Outlook.

A Plea for Prayer.

WE have come to the last day of this great Convention. It has been manifest, I am sure, to every one who has been present that the Lord has been with us each day and hour of our session. I pray that this last day we may all be instant in prayer, that our hearts may go up before our Lord and bespeak His Divine presence in our gathering to-day. This has been a holy place. The Lord has been peculiarly manifest in all our sessions. Let us continue to wait upon Him.

This Convention was conceived in the minds of a few, and in their thought it grew from two days to three days, and finally to a Convention of four days' duration. To some it seemed as if we were undertaking too much, but the Lord was leading us, and He has approved our doing with His presence. And now, men, as we begin this last day, let us pray for eyes to see, hearts to understand, and wills ready to realize the larger opportunities that are surely ours in the near coming Kingdom of our Lord and Christ.

J. EDGAR LEAYCRAFT.

The Larger Outlook.

VITAL Christianity has an ever-broadening vision. Growth in spiritual life necessitates a widening horizon. The relationship to Jesus Christ which is first personal, in forgiveness of sin and a life based upon new ideals and stimulated by a new power, rapidly widens to take into its fellowship others of like life and purpose. Nor may the circle of interest remain fixed. A growing understanding of the Master reveals far-reaching claims. God is the universal Father, Christ is the world-Savior. All kingdoms are yet to be permeated with the ideals of His Kingdom and move onward and upward through its inherent and indwelling power.

It was fitting that the final sessions of the Convention should be given over to a consideration of the larger outlook for the coming of the Kingdom. The program swept wide horizons—education, literature, benevolence, world influence, and world conquest through the accepted ownership, leadership, and lordship of the Christ. The hours were surcharged with firm purpose, vital faith, and radiant hope. The ultimate regnancy of Christ in all the affairs and institutions of the race-life was the confident note of the closing day.

I. THE LARGER OUTLOOK FOR EDUCATION, LITERATURE, AND BENEVOLENCE.

For Education.

WILLIAM H. CRAWFORD.

THERE is substantial agreement that Methodism did wisely in founding schools. There is not substantial agreement as to the wisdom of continuing to maintain them all. The theological schools are a necessity. If men are to give their lives to preaching and expounding the Word and to defending the faith, they must be trained for it, just as men are trained for medicine and law. The most economical method and the best method of furnishing such training is the theological school.

The academy is another matter. Here there is wide difference of opinion. I shall perhaps fairly represent the sentiment of our educational leaders if I say that, in a region where there are no adequate high school facilities, the Church does wisely in maintaining academies. And I may say this, too, that for the sake of those of high school age who do not and can not have proper home surroundings, and for those past high school age suddenly awakened to the need of an education, the Church would do well to make provision by maintaining academies. The academy has done much for Methodism. To my thinking, it is still an exceedingly important factor in the life of the Church. It will be a long time before we can well do without it.

But what about our colleges? If there are wide differences of opinion as to the academies, there are still wider differences of opinion as to the colleges. Many there are who say that it is no part of Methodism's task to maintain institutions of higher learning. They admit there may have been need for these institutions in an earlier day, but not now. We might as well face the fact that only a small proportion of our people take higher education seriously. I mean higher education as represented in the schools of the Church. There are scores interested in missions to one who cares anything about education. Perhaps this is not nice talk. But what is this gathering of Methodist men for? Are we not here to see things as they are? Shall we not have a square look at the worst as well as the best? Can we hope to gain anything by smooth sayings which cover up the truth? I am here this morning to tell you that *in the matter of her schools Methodism to-day faces a crisis*—a crisis which is staggering some of our strongest men. I know men, princely men, connected with our educational work who do not know which way to turn. It is bad enough to face the blinding storm of criticism and opposition from outside the Church. We expect that. But to be struck at as we are by so many within the Church! That is hard to bear; but that is our lot.

Let me tell you what some of the critics are saying about us just now. One group says, The State will take care of education. If we accept the common schools at the hands of the State, why not the college and the university? We pay our taxes for the support of these institutions. Why should not our sons and daughters have the advantage of them? The annual income of State universities is from a quarter of a million, to a half-million, to three-quarters of a million, to a million, and two at least just about touch the two-million mark. So the State universities and colleges ought to be good enough for anybody.

A second group of critics says: Our money, the money of the Church, is needed for missions and other benevolences. Africa is calling; so are China and India, Korea and South America; the festering sores of our great cities are crying; the indemnity for the wrongs done to the black man must be satisfied; hospitals should be built; homes and asylums and sanitariums ought to be multiplied.

A third group of critics says: The schools ought to take care of themselves. For more than a century the Church has been pouring her money into the colleges and universities. They have been given buildings and equipment and endowments up into the millions. The time has come to call a halt. If the colleges do not have enough money after all the begging they have been doing, let them raise the tuition fee. People who want a college education for their children should pay for it. No, sir. Not another dollar for the colleges. They must take care of themselves.

I might mention other groups of critics, but the three named are enough to serve my purpose. You see without further argument that my subject has its ugly aspects. Our cause is not by any means a lost cause, but in the case of many of our institutions it is a losing cause. If we do not bring the Church to a larger appreciation of the worth and need of our schools, and that right speedily, many of them will have to go out of business.

My own conviction is, and it is a very earnest conviction, that *if Methodism shall continue to grow and prosper and do her full share in the work of redeeming this old world for our Christ, she must foster and maintain her colleges on a much larger scale than heretofore.* I say a much larger scale because of the greater need and the greater opportunity. In support of this proposition, I bring a threefold argument. I maintain that Methodism should maintain her colleges on a much larger scale, first, *for the sake of the home and social life of our people.* There are hundreds of boys and girls every year who make up their minds for college because the appeal comes from the Church—the Church in which they were born, the Church in which they were converted, the Church in which they have been reared. It adds much that the institutions to which they are pointed and invited are under the patronage of the Church. There are large numbers of parents who are willing to entrust their sons and daughters to such institutions who would otherwise decide against the higher educational program altogether. This also ought to be taken into account, that no home is complete nor is the social atmosphere of a community complete unless it includes appreciation of scholarly achievement, a taste for good books and high standards of culture. The college as a part of the program of the Church in an immensely potent influence in bringing about such conditions. The scholarly men in the Faculties of our colleges become known in Methodist communities and Methodist homes. Our people take pride in the part they play in the educational life of the Nation. In some such way the culture of the college influences the life of the home, of the Church, and of the community.

The second part of my argument for larger maintenance for our colleges is that we ought to do it *for the sake of an efficient leadership in the Church.* If you will read the history of Methodist triumphs, you will find that in almost every instance the leadership has been vested in men trained in our own schools. Look at the men who are leaders to-day. Who are they? Take our chief pastors, for instance. Who are the foremost intellectual and spiritual leaders among them? They are the graduates of our Methodist colleges. Take the men filling our most important pastorates. Who are they? Nearly all are graduates of Methodist colleges. Take the men who are making our Church literature. Who are they? Graduates of our Methodist colleges, every one of them. What about our foreign missionary secretaries? What about the men who are leaders in the work of home missions? What about our Freedmen's Aid secretaries? What about the leaders in the Sunday school work, the Epworth League, the Brotherhood movement, the Federation for Social Service? Who are the outstanding men in evangelistic work? Who are grappling with the down-town problem, striving to redeem the waste places of our great cities? Almost without exception they are the graduates of our Methodist colleges.

For her positions of greatest responsibility, when leadership of the highest type is required, Methodism is almost wholly dependent upon the men who have been trained in her own schools. Is there any prospect that it will be otherwise in the future? I see no sign of it. On the contrary, it looks to me that the Methodism of the future will be even more dependent upon the men whose training has been in the colleges founded and maintained by Methodism. Only the other day I read a report of some studies which have been made under the direction of the Board of Education of the Presbyterian Church. It was found that of the recruits for the ministry and for home and foreign missions, less than seven per cent came from State universities, while an average of over eighty-three per cent came from Church colleges. I believe in the State universities, and I hope you do. But is it not perfectly clear that these are not the institutions to which we must look for our future preachers, our missionaries, and our Church leaders?

The third part of my argument for doing more in the way of maintaining our colleges is that we ought to do it *for the sake of the cause of education.* When the Martyrs' Memorial at Oberlin College was dedicated, President Stryker, of Hamilton College, said that the great need of education in our time is moral revival at the very heart of it. I believe that to be true. Education in this country sadly lacks in moral dynamic. I am gratified that several of our strongest Methodist educators have gone to the presidency of State universities. I hope to live to see the day when there shall be no State university in all this land which does not have at its head a man of strong Christian character and influence. I want the superintendents of education in our large cities to be men of the same type. I want the same thing for the principals of our high schools and all the schools. If this shall come to pass, it must be brought to pass. I desire, and you do, that Methodist colleges with their ozone of moral earnestness shall help and help largely in the training of men for these positions. We can do it if the Church will give us the men and the money.

I have come now to the point where I want to say a word about the position of our critics. The critics say, The State will take care of education. I say it is absolutely impossible for the State to furnish the sort of education we must have. The education we need is the kind that is in sympathy with the ideals and aims and work of the Church, an education surcharged with the teaching and spirit of Jesus Christ. This the State university is prohibited from doing by the very terms of its charter. The critics say, The money of the Church is needed for missions and other benevolences. I say there is no hope for any missions in the future to give money for— home missions or foreign missions—unless we maintain our colleges. Where are the greatest centers of missionary sentiment? In our colleges. Where must we look for missionaries

THE LARGER OUTLOOK.

to carry on the work we have begun in foreign fields? Where only can we look? To our colleges. Bishop Bashford was right in sending his money to Ohio Wesleyan University and saying that he could do more for China in this way than by giving the money directly to China. The critics say, The colleges ought to take care of themselves. I say that if we keep our colleges within the reach of the poor boy and the boy of average means, the boy from the farm and the boy from the home of the mechanic, there is no hope for us but to have help and large help from the Church.

On behalf of the educational institutions of our Church, I ask for three things; and I want you, the men of Methodism, to stand by us and see that we get them. The things I ask for are: First, that the next General Conference shall so legislate in the interest of the financial support of our schools as to make effective what we thought we had accomplished at the last General Conference. We want one, and only one, collection for education from every local Church in Methodism. Second, I ask that throughout the Church the cause of education be put side by side with the cause of foreign missions and the cause of home missions as equally great and equally deserving. Third, I ask that those who bear rule among us shall use all means in their power to encourage Methodist people everywhere to pray for our schools and talk for them, to defend them and support them. If these things be done, I have faith to believe that in the future even more than in the past the schools of Methodism will constitute a vital part of her greatest strength.

Brothers, the best has not been reached. We could not be Methodists and believe that. If I seem to prophesy too much, it is because I find warrant in the way mighty men of the past, trained in the schools of the Church, have under God "turned the stream of centuries out of its channel," overturned governments and transformed communities and nations. If John Wyclif could go forth from a college in Oxford to be the morning star of the Reformation, if Martin

303

Luther could go from Wittenberg to be the mightiest religious reformer in all the Christian centuries, if John Wesley could go from Christ Church College to lead in the greatest spiritual awakening since Pentecost, if James M. Thoburn could go from Allegheny College to be the peerless and apostolic missionary for India, if John R. Mott could go from Upper Iowa University to be the most potent leader of Christian men in nineteen centuries, influencing the college men of the world as no one else has ever done; if these and many others, trained in the Christian college of yesterday, have so wrought righteousness, subdued kingdoms, and turned to flight the alien armies of ignorance, atheism, and superstition, is it too great a stretch of faith to believe that the college of to-morrow will do as much? It is our high privilege to build more secure the foundation of the college in deep learning and to beautify its superstructure in all the graces which grow out of fervent piety.

For Christian Literature.

David G. Downey.

Christian literature may be defined as that form of literature which, in utter loyalty to the moral, ethical, and spiritual principles of Christ, influences, molds, and controls life. The question for our consideration this morning concerns the larger outlook for such literature. That the age is thrillingly and throbbingly alive is not open to question. On every side and in every realm we see the evidences of an intense and tremendously energetic life. It is indeed true that much of the force of life is expended objectively. The tendency of the time is toward action rather than thought, and because of this we sometimes question the present place and the future power of Christian literature. It is worth remembering, however, that next to fiction, books dealing with some phase of religion are the best sellers. And it should further be remembered that not a few works of fiction or of the imagination are themselves religious or semi-religious—dealing with the ideals and principles of Christ and Christianity. While there is much magazine and book literature that is crude, bizarre, non-moral and positively immoral, it must not be forgotten that the ethical, social, and spiritual ideals of Christianity have achieved a standing and secured a hearing in these very types of literature such as they have never had heretofore. The world, the reading world, is interested in the things that concern religion in general and the Christian religion in particular. Nor must we forget the brilliant galaxy of younger men—essayists, editors, and poets—who in our own day are thoroughly loyal to the essentials of Christianity. As one reads the essays of Benson and Brierly, of Van Dyke and Mabie, of Chesterton and Crothers, he knows full well that "no dead mechanism moves the stars or lifts the tides or calls the flowers from their sleep. Truly this is the garment of the Deity and here is the awful splendor of the perpetual Presence." And what shall be said of the modern poets—of Richard Watson Gilder and Edward Rowland Sill, of Sidney Lanier and Henry Van Dyke, of Vaughn Moody, Edwin Markham and Frederic Lawrence Knowles? This much at least—they are not singing of bonnets and bodices, of the amours and intrigues of illicit love, of the fashions and foibles of an inane social world. No; they have tuned their lyres to high themes, and the message of each and all is the message so sturdily sounded by Gilder when he says:

> Keep pure thy soul!
> Then shalt thou take the whole
> Of delight;
> Then, without a pang,
> Thine shall be all of beauty whereof the poet sang—
> The perfume, and the pageant, the melody, the mirth
> Of the golden day, and the starry night;
> Of heaven, and of earth.
> Oh, keep pure thy soul!

At the present hour, as we survey the field there is every reason for encouragement. Christian literature is not retiring from the field defeated or discouraged. Many opponents are struggling for the mastery. There is the call and cry of eager contestants, but our historians and theologians, our singers and our essayists are still heard and felt. What of the future? The future is with us and the children whom God hath given us. The realm of literature is a realm to be not only claimed, but actually conquered for Christ. Christianity must make literature a means of grace, a channel through which the power of the Spirit shall freely flow.

Every fresh and vital movement of humanity creates its own literature. Such a movement was primitive Christianity. And we have the literature of that movement. That is the incomparable literature simply because the movement itself was incomparable and unrepeatable. The power of Christianity's impact upon human thought and feeling is evident in the abiding influence and power of the literature that it created. How bare and poor the world would be bereft of the four Gospels, the letters of Paul, John and Peter, and all that great body of literature that clusters about these masterpieces! The Christian life created a new literature, and the literature and the life combined created a new world. With a slight change, Van Dyke's word about Christ is true of that early Christian literature of which Christ was preeminently the source: "Where it came a new efflorescence of faith and hope and love flowed over the landscape of the inner life. Flowers appeared in the earth and the time for the singing of birds was come." Such a movement we find again in the period generally known as the Renaissance. Humanity drank from newly discovered springs of knowledge and the refreshed and illumined intellect of the race went forth to the intellectual conquest of the world. The Troubadours began to sing, the artists to paint, the sculptors to carve, and the poets, philosophers, theologians and historians to write. It was the revival of learning because it was the revival of life, and out of life came the letters and the literature. Another such fresh and vigorous hour struck when the sound of Luther's hammer reverberated round the world. It was largely an era of theological discussion. Christianity was fighting for the right to live and to be free. Luther and Melanchthon, Erasmus and Zwingli, Calvin and Cranmer stand pre-eminent. Out of that vital movement came the Reformation literature with all that it implied for civil and religious freedom in Europe and in the America just then looming large upon the horizon of the world. Methodism is another illustration. The most vital and humanizing event in the history of the eighteenth century was the speaking and writing of the Wesleys, Whitefield, Fletcher and their colleagues. As always, so then the new life shaped for itself a fit medium for its expression. We find this new expression in John Wesley's sermons and journals, in Charles Wesley's hymns, in Fletcher's Checks, and in Adam Clarke's Commentaries. These men were heretics in their day because they were abreast and more than abreast of their age. They are the standards of orthoxody for our day. Nor has Methodism on this side the sea been unmindful of her duty and opportunity. She has had her historians and theologians, her expositors and controversialists, her essayists and singers— all voicing in their own way the superabundant and many-sided spiritual life of their age. This age of ours is a new day. Its characteristics are mastery of natural forces, intellectual grasp, humanitarian feeling, spiritual yearning and search. Christianity must produce a literature that fits the hour. The old elemental and fundamental truths must be expressed in the thought forms and language of the new day. The old coin needs to be thrown into the crucible to come forth new-minted with the stamp and superscription of a Christianity living and reigning, not in the first or the tenth, but in the twentieth century. Methodism must do her part in this great work. How shall this literature be created, and what are some of its characteristics?

We must prepare leaders in literature. Our secondary schools, our colleges and our theological seminaries have no more important task than the training of young men and women who in their turn shall be the creators of a Christian literature that will meet the need of our modern day. We need theologians and historians, expositors and essayists, poets and mystics—men who will touch the whole circle of life and interpret it in terms of moral and spiritual value. What are our schools for but to train Christian leaders in this as in every other department of life? We need trained Christian scholars who will dominate in the newspaper and magazine world and make that realm an influential power in upbuilding the Kingdom of righteousness. The ancient glory of the Church, as a creator of literature, is in danger of slipping away because we are so busy acting and doing that we do not have time to think and brood and then record in permanent and worthy form the ripe fruitage of our thinking and brooding.

Christian literature of to-day and to-morrow will be constructively progressive. The late Dr. Charles J. Little has said: "The movement of the gospel is the miracle of history; its progressive conquest of its environment is the mightiest victory recorded in the annals of mankind: here are displays of heroism that Alexander might have envied and Cæsar would have listened to, amazed. The Tenth Legion of Jesus Christ, His glorious company of martyrs recruited from all countries and from all ages, marches across the centuries, trampling triumphantly upon the slaveries and barbarisms, the organized unrighteousness and the disorganizing brutality of the ancient and mediæval world. Yet the splendor and variety of this historic miracle, of this unfolding power of an endless life, is too little known or scarcely known at all. The splendor of it and the inspiration of it both are lost." Who will recover for us the splendor and the inspiration of this abiding miracle? Who will write for us in this humanitarian age the story of the Church's humanizing influence on society and State? We have many who tell the story of the Church's sociological failures, but who will write for us the story of her sociological successes through her own activities or through the individuals and organizations whom she inspires and supports? The Christians of the early days wrote the creeds according to the measure of their philosophical, scientific, and spiritual lights, but who will re-write them in the light of the truer philosophy, the saner science, and the deeper spirituality of to-day? The gift of the Holy Spirit, who guides into all truth, is not for the scholar of the first century alone. I believe in the Holy Ghost, living, reigning, guiding, and inspiring the hearts and minds of men, and in the councils of the Church, to-day!

Christian literature will be spacious and broad as Christianity itself. When Keats after his first reading of Chapman's Homer wrote:

> Then felt I like some watcher of the skies
> When a new planet swims into his ken,

he was indicating for all time one of the high qualities of Christian literature. It at once puts one in a broad and spacious world. And religion needs just such a setting. Too frequently Christianity, or the expression of it, has degenerated into erraticism or fanaticism. Men have mistaken their own narrow and limited notions of the faith for the faith itself, and have sought, not always in vain, to impose meager and limited ideas and ideals upon the Church of God. Even as in Paul's day we have with us well-meaning and righteous men who have no comprehensive conception of the length and breadth, the height and depth of Christianity. It is worth remembering that Paul did not give place to such, by way of subjection, not even for an hour. He stood faithfully and fearlessly for a broad and liberal interpretation of the sweep and place and power of Christianity. We still need men with the deep spirituality, the ample intellectual outlook and the strong grip upon the fundamentals of the faith that were characteristic of the great apostle to the Gentiles. Such literature as we have in mind will not think it necessary to steady the ark—God always sees to that. It will make for balance, sanity and breadth, and will give to the adherents of Christianity the spiritual vitality, the intellectual spaciousness, and the broad tolerance of the Son of man, who is also the Son of God.

Such a literature will surely dispel the idea that culture and piety are inconsistent or mutually exclusive virtues. The Christian literature of to-morrow will unite these virtues, too long separated, in holy and indissoluble bonds. There is no greater crime against the inner life, and the outer expansion of our Methodism, than is committed by those who speak and write as though intellectuality were antagonistic to spirituality, and who imply that ignorance is the best tool for the Holy Spirit's use. Note the addresses and articles in which the assumption is made that the scholarly man can not be deeply or thoroughly evangelistic; listen to the appeals which practically suggest that the only need is the Holy Spirit and which by implication disparage the training and the culture of the schools. The Holy Spirit is absolutely *sine qua non*. But are the operations and influences and gifts of the Holy Spirit given chiefly to the superficial and untrained thinker? Other things being equal, is it not true that the Holy Spirit can make best use of the carefully trained and well furnished mind? In these days when we are admitting into our ministry men who have not even had a high school education it is no time for Methodism to disparage the need of intellectual training. Intellectual virility and Spirit baptism are not antagonistic, they are complementary. Lacking either, the Christian is weak. Possessing both, he is strong—a workman that needeth not to be ashamed. The most efficient Christian workers of the ages have been men of the highest culture; culture that received its inspiration from and was under the control and the guidance of God's Holy Spirit. One has only to think of Paul, chosen of God because he had the necessary intellectual, moral and spiritual furnishing; of Augustine, Luther, Wesley, Brooks, and hosts of others; to see how shallow is the thought and how hurtful the speech that would antagonize these complementary and essential qualities. Christianity is as deep as life, as charitable as God, as lasting as eternity. The Christian literature of to-morrow will be kin to Christianity. Methodism, thank God, is not a small, meager, narrow segment of Christianity. It partakes the essential nature of the Faith. To create a literature that shall be worthy of Christianity as expressed through Methodism is no light task. It is, however, a task to which God calls our beloved Church, and with His help the Church will meet the Divine expectancy.

With leaders trained in our schools and coming forth to their tasks with the understanding that the literary realm is to be claimed, captured and conquered for Christ; inspired with the purpose to make the periodical and permanent literature of the world an arm of power for the Church; translating the essential and eternal principles of the Faith into the language of to-day; interpreting Christianity after the fashion and speech of the Christ, and in His spirit, rather than in terms of narrow dogma; holding ever the highest possible human culture under the illumination, guidance and control of the Holy Spirit, who still guides the Christian scholar in the pathway of truth, there can be no possible question as to the outcome! Watchman, What of the night? Answer—The Morning Cometh!

The Larger Outlook for the Retired Ministry.

J. B. HINGELEY.

THE reason why this question, which has been before the Church for more than a century, is still a live question was illustrated by the meeting this morning. Conquering Methodism always has a program of conquest and woe to the wounded, the aged, and the fatherless when a campaign is on or a battle is pending. Programs and speeches, and appeals for them must give way to the cry for action. The whole task

311

of the Church will not be accomplished until the retired ministers and the widows and dependent orphans of deceased ministers have been accounted for. I will present to you the size and character of the problem and the conditions under which it is to be met, while a great-hearted layman, Mr. Marvin Campbell, the treasurer of the Board of Conference Claimants, will speak of the laymen's duty to those who brought Methodism to them.

The proposition of properly providing for the Conference Claimants of the Methodist Episcopal Church is one which, not only because of its great importance, but because of the size of the problem, may well demand the most earnest consideration, and if it is ever solved all the forces available for its solution must be utilized. In round numbers there are 3,000 retired preachers and 3,000 widows of deceased preachers and 600 dependent orphan children of deceased ministers. All these are Conference Claimants according to the Discipline of the Methodist Episcopal Church, and even a modest, reasonable provision for their care demands an annual distribution of no less than a million and a half dollars. The problem of the Church is to secure this million and a half dollars.

Full reports as to what is being done in the several Conferences are published annually by the Board of Conference Claimants. I think you will recognize the limitations of the present provisions for the support of Conference Claimants when you realize that out of the 6,600 Claimants there is only *one* who receives $700, and but four who receive more than $500, and in all there are less than 300 who receive as much as $300, one in every fifteen. On the other hand, there are 4,400 Claimants, more than two-thirds of the total, who receive less than $200. One-third of the total number receive less than $100. One hundred who receive less than $50. Hence while we felicitate ourselves on the fact that the amount distributed has almost doubled during the last five years, yet we are very far from a reasonable solution of the problem.

THE LARGER OUTLOOK.

But the atmosphere is good. Ten years ago it seemed necessary to explain the duty of providing for or pensioning Retired Ministers. To-day the world challenges the Church because of its indifference in this matter and the Church is placed on the defensive. The question it must answer is not why should we pension veteran ministers, but why don't we more liberally pension them? Last month's report of Rock Island Railroad employees' pensions shows retired engineers receiving more than $700, a larger amount than is received by any retired minister of the Methodist Episcopal Church; and shows railroad conductors and firemen receiving $400, while there are not one hundred retired preachers receiving as much; and shows retired helpers, laborers, hostlers, section men, crossing men, etc., receiving $240, while there are not five hundred retired Methodist preachers who receive so large an amount. In all the Pennsylvania Railroad has distributed more than nine million dollars to its aged, sick, and disabled employees.

The sources of our receipts are as follows:

(1) Our largest asset is the amount directly contributed by the Churches for annual distribution, which amounts to almost a half a million dollars. The Church is increasing its apportionment for this purpose at the rate of about $30,000 a year. But there must be an apportionment of one million dollars to be raised directly by the Churches each year for annual distribution. Annual Conferences must assert themselves here. They accept largely increased apportionments made for them by others for benevolences and for the Episcopal Fund. They must themselves increase the apportionment for their brethren until there is sufficient to meet every claim.

(2) The second large asset is the Dividend of the Book Concern, now $250,000 a year, but which easily can be increased $100,000 next year.

(3) The income from Annual Conference Investments— that is, moneys held by Annual Conferences under different

organizations, the interest of which is annually applied to Conference Claimants, increasing each year. The amount so invested is now about $4,000,000, and the General Conference has asked for an increase of $5,000,000 before 1916.

(4) The Chartered Fund is the oldest institution of the Church and has been paying a small dividend to Annual Conferences within the United States for one hundred and twenty-five years.

(5) The Board of Conference Claimants, organized in 1908, whose highest usefulness has been indirectly exerted on the Annual Conferences and by spreading information and in exalting the standard of support set by the Discipline has had a brief but eventful history. Since its organization the annual distribution throughout the Church from all sources has increased from $600,000 to $1,100,000, an increase of more than $100,000 each year, and last year in round numbers was one million one hundred thousand dollars. Thank God! During the last four years our Conference Claimants have received $800,000 more than during any previous half decade. Incidental to its larger inspirational work, the Board has paid its own way and has returned to the Annual Conferences for necessitous cases $115,000, and now has in its treasury $25,000 awaiting distribution during 1914, making a total of $140,000 added to the distribution given in every instance to necessitous cases—that is, to those in any Conference whose needs are in excess of the amount that can be provided by the Annual Conference itself.

But the greatest task set before the Board of Conference Claimants to-day is that of leading the Church toward the completion of the Sesqui-Centennial Jubilee Gift of Five Million Dollars for Conference Claimants, asked by the General Conference. This Five Million Dollars includes not only amounts placed at the disposal of the Board, but also funds in Annual Conferences and Preachers' Aid Societies. These are funds for perpetual *investment*, the income only to be used from year to year. Of this Five Million Dollars, One Million

Dollars is asked for the Connectional or General Permanent Fund of the Board of Conference Claimants, the income together with its other resources to be distributed to the Annual Conferences to help needy cases. The Board already has $200,000 so invested and is seeking from all who love the old preachers gifts for this holy purpose. God gird the Church for this task!

MARVIN CAMPBELL.

As a layman I approach the most important interest of the organic Church, its preachers. For every five effectives there is one superannuate and about the same number of widows. The interest of the five effectives is so closely allied to the two claimants as to be almost inseparable. I shall devote my time wholly to the claimants and to you. I want you convinced that the superannuate should and can have full Disciplinary allowance. But you say you are convinced. Permit me to say that if you, this body of men, were convinced that he should, and can have, the full allowance, then he would have it. Not about sixty per cent as now. I trust you catch the logic as well as the compliment to your ability to do and to have done.

A very few facts, if not forgotten or neglected, will give the superannuate his full allowance. Responsibility rests almost wholly with or within the Annual Conferences. In providing for claimants, each Annual Conference is a little dominion of its own with autocratic power. Each Annual Conference determines who are its claimants. It fixes its own rules or conditions as to retirement. It may assess upon its Churches any amount it deems necessary. These are powers that apply to no other interest or ward of the Church. If the claimant is not fully paid, responsibility rests almost wholly with his Annual Conference. Take that one fact home with you, and he will be paid. Another compliment to your ability to do and to have done. The one superannuate and the one widow are as surely entitled to payment as are the five effectives. There is no higher duty than the honest payment of honest debts. The disciplinary allotment to the claimant is a debt, a debt for ministerial support. We have no religious right, no honest right, to refuse payment unless from absolute inability. We have the ability both as to wealth and liberality. We have not yet demonstrated ability as to organized and systemized method. It is, however, both fair and gratifying to say that we are in better, much better condition than four years ago.

The law gives the superannuate more consideration than the effective, but he does not get more consideration. The Annual Conference can assess upon its Churches whatever amount it will for the superannuate; it can not fix or suggest any amount for the effective. He must take his chances with his Quarterly Conference. Our Discipline does not well define conditions that entitle to annuity. It should. Until then each Annual Conference should establish clean-cut rules. The option to distribute, based upon service or necessity, could not be justified if all were entitled to years-of-service-annuity, for to take from those who have met annuity conditions would be unjust. It would create deplorable uncertainty as to annuity, no matter how faithful or how long the service. I repeat there should be well-defined conditions as to annuity and then rigidly observed. Each necessitous case must be passed upon as an individual, but it should not be met by taking from the entitled annuitant. Annuities paid are for ministerial support. Necessitous payments are in spirit and fact benevolences, commendable, but nevertheless in spirit benevolences. The annuitant should not be taxed for benevolences; they should be met from other sources. The spirit of annuity is not reward for having been a preacher, but for having continued a preacher until unfitted for the itinerant service.

Can the annuitant be paid in full? Well, can we do what others have done, what others are doing? The Methodist Church of Canada, the United Methodist Church of England, the Wesleyan Methodist Church of England, the Australian Methodist Church, all do pay their Conference Claimants full annuity, and have paid for many years. There is absolutely no failure. If we are so loyal to our Church, if we are so just, if we are so capable in administrative ability as are the Methodists of Canada, of England, of Australia, then full annuity can be paid, for by them it is done. We must admit indifference or imbecility, or we must grant that it can be done. Will you take this home to your Annual Conference and meet the responsibility? The Churches to which I have referred have well defined conditions as to annuity. They also have a necessitous fund, but it is not created by taking from the annuitant. The 314 superannuates of the Methodist Church of Canada average thirty-four years of service. Some, perhaps many of our Annual Conferences average twenty-four years. With them no man retires upon an annuity with less than forty years' service unless unfitted for itinerant work. Let me repeat, payment can not be made to the one not entitled except to take from those who are entitled. What stronger call for systematic method?

Indiana Methodists will illustrate the average. They are listed as paying annual grand total, $400,000, for various benevolences. Shortage due claimants. $23,000, about 35 per cent deficit. A membership that pays $400,000 in various and some of the remote benevolences can and will pay the $23,000 debt if brought to their notice with anything like the insistence or system of the secular world. I question the religious right to pay the $400,000 until the $23,000 debt is paid, but all can be paid.

Let me make one practical, concrete suggestion which is by far the most important thing I have to say; i. e., Have a Laymen's Aid Society or, what is more practicable, broaden the scope of your Preachers' Aid Society, and especially of its Field Agent. Give him not only the power to solicit endowments, but to raise a current budget to meet the entire claimants' deficit that is not met by assessment. He will easily find ways to prevent any annual deficit and yet be more efficient as to endowments. A single example will illustrate what I mean. I am told of a Methodist much interested in claimants, who pays for various benevolences more than $1,000 per year and for claimants $5.30 per year. He pays more than $5.30 to the Humane Society. He pays the various benevolences because brought to his notice by earnest field agents. He pays the $5.30 for claimants as his ratio share to the budget of his Church. Nobody asks him to pay more. He would undoubtedly pay liberally if asked. There are hundreds of such cases, men able to give, ready to give. In some degree the Church is full of such examples. Place upon your Field Agent the double power, the double duty, of securing a present budget for the deficit as well as securing endowment, and your problem is solved. In every Quarterly Conference there should be a claimants' steward to co-operate with the field agent. A claimants' steward is even more logical than a district steward. The records show thirteen times as many claimants as district superintendents. Why not a steward to look after the thirteen decrepit, as well as a steward to look after the one effective? All are in the same class, all upon the same payroll, ministerial support.

Endowment is needed, but don't depend upon endowment's income; it will be many, very many years before this will be sufficient. The claimant must be provided for by the budget plan as surely as must the effective, and a part of it at least must be upon the ability-to-pay plan, just as the effectives' salary is raised upon the ability-to-give plan. A flat assessment upon all the Churches of the Conference is in part right, but the whole amount can not be had in this way, some poor Churches can not give any more. Wills and after death bonds are desirable, very desirable, but don't neglect your righteous poor while waiting for the death of your godly rich.

In conclusion: We do not lack money, we do not lack loyalty to the Church, we do not lack solicitude for the superannuate, but we do lack method. I repeat it, we lack method. Will you take that fact home to your Annual Conference with its autocratic power and establish method?

The Larger Outlook for Deaconess Work.

D. W. HOWELL.

THE work of the Deaconess I will present to you in the form of a story. While one person tells the tale, it must be remembered that the details have been gathered from many parts and recounts the service of many workers.

In the doorway of her home a young lady stood and watched the setting sun and meditated upon her own future. Deep down in the secret chamber there was a desire to make her life worth while, and to her such a life must be religious. The June previous she had graduated from college, and now she must plan for her future. In response to inquiry her pastor presented nearly every field for woman's service, but she could not decide. It must be confessed that in her senior year she had read a booklet on "A Deaconess and Her Work," and she could not get away from its insistent call. Almost against her will she consented to go to a training school. She was as much interested in learning about the Deaconess Movement as in preparing her lessons in the Courses of Study. She found that it was nearly two thousand years since the Deaconess was recognized as a part of the organized body of Christ's followers. With the founding of the Apostolic Church these consecrated women began their work of ministry to the lowly and the needy. It was the keen eye of the Galilean Peasant that discerned the undeveloped possibilities of womanhood, and it was the Master who strove to bring her service into the Kingdom He came to establish.

She followed its history and use and disuse through the centuries. She marked its beginnings in our Church in the early eighties. She watched it grow until every part of the nation felt its power. She beheld its material achievements until in one city alone she saw property valued at $1,500,000. Beyond all these she felt that the movement magnified genuine womanhood. It seemed to offer an opportunity to do a woman's work, in a woman's way, through a woman's affection. In it, as a woman, she could glorify God. Two years quickly passed. With her diploma in her hand she stood aghast before the many open doors. She never dreamed the Deaconess Movement had so many different fields of service: Parish Workers, Settlements, Slums, Baby Folds, Industrial Schools, Hospitals, Travelers' Aid, and many more. It was the end of the year; prepared with all proper credentials, she attended the Annual Conference. There she was consecrated a Deaconess of the Methodist Episcopal Church. Then it was that her real life service began. Here is her story:

"My first appointment was to a Baby Fold. I was given charge of children between two and three years old. I had five to wash and dress and amuse. After awhile a sixth was brought to me, a boy just past two. He was so thin that I pitied him. When I heard of the inhuman treatment he had received I loved him. I remember one day I took him for a ride. He ran from the house with me but stopped at the curb, and looking up at the driver of the automobile said, 'Will you bring me back?' He must have recalled his old home. How that boy got into my heart and how I longed that he might grow up to love my Christ!

"From that home I was moved to another part of the country and given charge of an Italian Mission for girls. One day as I was walking along one of the streets near my Mission, a dirty face looked up at me and I recognized one of my girls; her every-day dress not a bit like the one she wore on Sunday. She put her arm around me and smiled. We walked arm in arm for some distance and discovered that the child of an Italian loved just like other children. I worked with and for those girls. I wanted them to know my Savior. Some of them became Christians. Again I changed and went almost across the continent. I became a parish worker. A small class of boys was given me. Soon we had ten, and then twenty. In my first year in that Church ninety different names were on my roll. At the end of the year seventy was the record. Then I was glad that I had studied psychology and pedagogy. Those boys were at that age when they know everything. How I studied them! I won them. When the year closed every boy of the ninety save fifteen had given his heart and his life to my Lord, and the Church had seventy-five new members. I desired to remain in that Church, but like the Israelites I was commanded to journey through the wilderness. My new work was in an Italian Mission. In that building came men and women, boys and girls. Among other lines of work I organized a club of boys. I found a man to help me. The club had a name, secret to all but members. The letters of that cabalistic name were blazoned upon a banner. One meeting was held, when I realized that the boys were more than both of us could manage. Instead of psychological and pedagogical methods, I had to call in a policeman. This gentleman with a uniform awed them. Gradually they changed, and in a little more than one year from the day of organization five of the nine stood before the altar of the Church, were given the right hand of fellowship and welcomed into the Church militant. I trusted the boys so completely that when I attended the Annual Conference I left them in charge of the Mission. It was hard to leave my Christian boys, but another change found me working as matron of a Home for working girls. Twenty-one girls were in my care, and I felt the responsibility of guiding them through the delicate and dangerous years of their youth. If I ever prayed it was at that time. Soon I grew fond of them, and our home was so much a true home that they called me mother. One night I noticed one of the girls looked worried, but I could not make her tell me her troubles. It was but a few days when she came to me and threw her arms about my neck and with her head on my shoulder cried, 'I can't stand it.' It was some time before I could get her to tell her story. Hesitatingly she told the tale of her temptation and her victory. I called the president of our Deaconess Board. He went right to the head of the corporation. When the facts were proven a man was without a place. When I heard that the man had been discharged I was troubled. I was only a woman and I wondered if he had a wife and children. I found that his wife was heartbroken. I went right to the man who had discharged him. He was surprised to see and hear me plead for the sinner. He said to me, 'Come here to-morrow at ten.' I was there, as was also the man who was discharged. This hard-hearted head of a corporation had secured a job for him in a factory where only men where employed.

"My next move found me a Superintendent of a Bee-hive of Industry. Nearly every type of work was in operation. Hard and unusual names continually came to my ears. In this metropolis I taught in an Industrial Class at one time eighteen different nationalities. While here a new phase of service came into my life. Here is a picture of my weekly Bible class of criminals. They meet in this room, and about this long table you see in the picture. Do you know that every man has his bad record? This man served a term in a penitentiary; yonder man with a good face was a wife beater. I would not have believed it myself. When he was drinking he was a demon. Do you know that at one time he had turned his wife out of doors in the winter time. He seemed to enjoy the sufferings of his children. But do n't be too hard in your judgment. When he was sober he was gentle as a woman and as kind as any Christian. It was my joy, week after week, to trace that company of Christian men. I forgot all their past lives. They were God's children and co-workers with me in bringing other men to the saving power of Christ.

"The big field in a great city so drew on my strength that I was compelled to leave. It was a sad day for me when I bade good-bye to slums and haunts of sin and shame. I was sent to a small hospital among the mountains. Everywhere

I heard talk of 'The Hills,' the lofty peaks lifted their crested head toward the sky and I began to find out what was meant by the lure of the mountains. One day there came for treatment a man from 'The Hills;' we all looked at him with his rugged frame, bushy hair, and shaggy beard. He looked so much like a bear that we all called him the 'Bear.' One day a boy brought in a basket full of flowers called anemone. I arranged a dish for our Bear; the nurse took it to his room. She was busy about her work and forgot all about the flowers. She heard an unusual sound and, turning around, saw the man's face bedded in the flowers. I was called, and I stood in the doorway for several minutes. When he lifted his head, tears were running down his face. He looked at me and said, 'No one has been kind to me in years.' I went to his bedside, took his hand in mine, and stroked it gently. He cried as I had never heard a man cry before that time. I was frightened lest it might injure him. From that day we talked more about the kind Christ. My 'Bear' became as gentle as a child. He would sit and spell out the words in a Bible with big type. When he went back to 'The Hills' he went singing of the Redeemer.

"The years fairly chased each other, and one day it dawned on me that my hair was snowy white and that the years were beginning to work their furrows in my face. I was assigned to a small training school to guide young girls and help them by my experience."

Before I leave you, let me say that the outlook for the Deaconess Movement will be brighter if three things are brought to use.

First—The best young women for our training schools.

The day is past when a girl can go from the shop immediately to slum work. Too frequently it has been tried and too frequently disaster has been the result. We want our training schools filled, but with the best young women of Methodism.

Second—More women for city redemption.

I believe in the social regeneration of society as firmly as any man, but I also believe that the permanent upbuilding of our great cities must be through the transformation of the individual into the child.

Third—Recognize the power of womanhood in the evangelization of the world.

You know that the mightiest power making for righteousness is a genuine woman. Every one will bear me witness that the persuasive love of a woman's heart awakens more holy and Christlike impulses than any other human influence in all the world. Tell me, men of the Convention, your plans. Do not, I pray you, forget to use the mightiest power God has given you—God-filled, consecrated womanhood.

The Larger Outlook for the Church.

W. O. SHEPARD.

WHAT I originally had in mind to say will not suit this hour. We have risen to such heights during these great days while we have been sitting together and thinking of world problems. We have been looking into the millennium, have been thinking of the work necessary to make our Church a world force, an army, a providential movement or agency for the solution of millennial problems, and a hush has come over us and we have felt these days that the Spirit was brooding over us and coming nearer and nearer to us and settling down upon us, and the King has been in our midst. And if I interpret aright the impressions of these men, they have come to a conviction that we are in the midst of a new epoch, that an apocalypse is just beyond, and that it behooves us to prepare for that which awaits us in the near future years. We have heard a great deal about the newness of Asia, Japan, Africa, South America and the Islands of the Sea, and we have heard much about the new spirit in our institutions, but perhaps we have not quite realized how new everything is in our own land. These are the latter days for us.

THE LARGER OUTLOOK.

Now, I make this proposition, that the Church of Jesus Christ must have a part in this new age, must keep up with this newness, must get the mighty stride of these mighty times in which we live. Three million strong, the Methodist Church, the sun glinting upon its power twenty-four hours of every day, its bells calling to never ceasing congregations,— it is too large to be left out in the cold. The Church of Jesus Christ is too big to be ignored in this new day. It must be accounted for and must give an account of itself. It must do so for its own sake. A stone is a stone in itself, of itself, by itself, for itself, in its relation to other stones, in the relation of distance and direction, but a spirit can not be a spirit in itself, of itself, by itself, for itself. By its very nature it must have interrelations. It must go out in love; it must go out in sympathy. Is the Church of Jesus Christ a thing or is it a spirit or a spiritual organism to have relation with other spirits and other spiritual organizations? If it confines itself to living a selfish life, it tends to thin itself; loving its life it shall lose it; loving statistics it will soon be ashamed of statistics; loving its life it will soon have only a name to love; but if it is unselfish and grasps these great problems, gets into the midst of them, it becomes a mighty force, and gives an account of itself in this startling age. It must have a part in this, because the only civilization which this new movement in human society will be satisfied with must be a Christian civilization. We must have the Christian solution of our problems or no one will be satisfied. The world seems to be tending toward brotherhood. We hear about brotherhood everywhere, and are thankful for it. But there can be no brotherhood which is not based upon fatherhood. Whether we hear the word "Brotherhood" in capitalistic circles or Church circles, unless there is Fatherhood of God, brotherhood is as unsubstantial as a castle in the clouds. So the Christian solution of our problem is the only one. When Jesus said, "Our Father," when He said, "When you pray, say, 'Our Father'" He gave the Magna Charta to the unfortunate, the oppressed, the poor, and bridged all chasms and inaugurated that civilization which is to be when men are brothers the round world over.

And then again, there can be no solution of these problems without the Church. Dr. Birney was right when he said that this whole matter must be a matter of life, the personal element must enter in. If we are to accomplish these matters with so much upon our hearts these days, there must be two factors. There must be the ability to do the work. That is one factor, of course! That goes without saying. But there must be another factor. There must be, "Woe is me if I do not do the work." There must be the personal work. I am perfectly willing that science should try the solution of the problem in Africa. Perhaps if those in the heart of Africa knew about the parallaxes of the stars it would do them a lot of good; if they knew the distance of the stars and that the stars are composed of the same elements that we find upon the earth, perhaps it would do them much good. I think it would. And if so, where is the man who says, "Woe is me if I do not do the work?" I find no fault, but that personal element is absolutely necessary. It becomes therefore a matter for the gospel of Jesus Christ. A matter for the missionary spirit of Jesus Christ, the first Missionary. I am perfectly willing that any one who loves his philosophy shall go down to the Ganges and tell that poor woman kneeling on its bank that her soul is the latent potentiality of matter, that she is the result of concurrent forces. It might do her a lot of good. Where is the wise man, where is the scribe, where is the disputer, who has said, "I am willing to go to India with such a purpose?" I am perfectly willing that one shall tell the theory of evolution to the islands of the sea. Perhaps it would do them a lot of good if they knew it. It might indeed do them much good to know it. But if so, where is the wise man, where is the scribe, where is the disputer of this world, where is the one who says, "I am willing as much as in me lies to teach

326

my theory to them that are in the United States and in the islands of the sea also?''

Now Methodism must have a part in this. The history of Methodism from the beginning has been that the world is its parish. The genius of Methodism indicates that it must have a great part in this if it is to be Christianity in earnest. And the fact that it has made promises indicates its responsibility. Nothing is more despicable than for a regiment to desert in the midst of battle. And others have gone into the midst of this great contest against the forces of evil with the expectation that this division of God's Church would do its part; and therefore we are under the obligation of our strength, of our numbers, of our definite promise. And if God is to continue speaking in history and the other denominations are to do their part in this great matter, we can not well see how they can succeed without this numerically largest, most enthusiastic, and most widely flung branch of the Christian army.

I stand before you with great joy to say this afternoon that our Church has a part in these great movements, that we are catching this stride, that we are coming to this vision. Something new has come to pass in recent years. There are perhaps some who can not see it because of the details, like those who can not see the town for the houses, or the woods for the trees, but there is a movement. Among our missionaries, for example, they have the vision. May I, to illustrate what I have in my mind now, tell of some experiences that came to me when a member of a committee having to examine candidates for the missionary field through all this Western country? We wanted a man to go to a certain town in India, fifty miles from a railroad. There were just three Americans in the town. It is under a tropic sky, and one almost takes his life in his hands who goes there. We wanted a physician. A young fellow came and could not stand the test; so with another. Finally a young man stood before us; he had had a college training, a medical school training, and one year of interneship in the hospital. He modestly said that his income the first year out of school was three thousand dollars. After he had stood every test and answered satisfactorily every question that could be put to him, I looked him in the eye and said, "Doctor, if you knew this was the very worst place the Methodist Episcopal Church had to send any man, would you still want to go?" I wanted to make him uncomfortable if I could. If he could be turned back from going there, I wanted to do it. No man is fit to hold the plow if he can be turned back. I thought I would make him uncomfortable, but he made me uncomfortable. He looked at me for fully thirty seconds and seemed to ponder the question in every way, and then he answered me as calmly as one man can speak to another, "Yes, sir." And he went. I told this story in the chapel of a university, and Bishop Warren was on the platform; he said, "Tell the students that since that young man went to India he has been the means of the conversion of two thousand people."

And our ministers are getting the stride just as the missionaries. Where is higher criticism in this Convention? I believe I am the first man who has spoken of it. Ten or fifteen years ago, if you saw a dozen ministers together the chances were that they were talking about some phase of higher criticism; now the chances are, nine out of ten, that they are talking about the work of the Kingdom of God. And our men are not asking for easy places in these days. I appointed a man to travel over the burning sands of Arizona a year ago. The year before, he traveled, not by automobile or pullman, but afoot, three thousand miles. After I gave him that appointment I said to him, "You have a hard task," and he said to me, O, so modestly, "I will do better this year." Soon after I heard from him, and he wrote me, "Yesterday I traveled thirty-eight miles, and the day before thirty miles." Mr. Atkinson, the superintendent of that mission, wrote me some months later, asking me to send a man to take the place of Trevor Orton, for the zeal of the

Lord's house had consumed him. I went into a town where there was a young fellow broken down with typhoid fever. He had a Church in a neighborhood where it is a curse to be born and a boon to die, where men and women were steeped in a worse than a witches' stew, and he had broken down under it. I looked at him and said, "You must not work too hard; you have a hard job." With tears in his eyes, he said: "I like a hard job. Do n't think of ever giving me anything but a hard job." Dr. Jefferson it is—is it not?—who says, "Seest thou a man who desires an easy place? There is more hope for the fool than for him." On that I have several observations to make: in the first place, he won't get it. There is no easy place; and in the second place, he would be a fool in days like these. The only difference in places is that in some places a man will be submerged, and in other places he can work.

We surely want to have a part in this matter. I would like to dwell upon the fact that the laymen are waking up. Witness the Men and Religion Forward Movement! Two little fellows were talking about it and one of them said, "What is it?" Said the other, "It is some kind of gambling." "Nonsense! Why do you say that?" The reply was, "I heard them say they were going to win the world." I would like to dwell upon the fact that the Brotherhood Movement is a mighty movement. It is magnificent that men are willing to wear upon their bosoms, not the sign of a little ritualistic knowledge, but the badge of their fealty and loyalty to Jesus Christ. Witness the Adult Bible Class movement! I was in a city in Illinois of sixty-six thousand people, and twenty-six thousand and forty men walked the streets of that city with bands playing and flags flying, and everywhere the banner of the cross and on it the words, "By this sign conquer." With these movements on, we want to have a part, we must have a part. As we go down to our Churches let us get down under our loads and lift the Church, and present it without spot, without wrinkle, without shame, to our Christ.

II. THE LARGER OUTLOOK FOR WORLD CONQUEST.

A United Church a Conquering Church.

GEORGE P. ECKMAN.

LORD MACAULAY has presented a very graphic picture of the allied forces of the Duke of Marlborough and Prince Eugene on the eve of the battle of Blenheim, in 1704. Then two captains, equal in authority but differing in creed, prepared for a battle, on the event of which would depend the liberties of Europe. The Duke of Marlborough had passed the greater part of the night in prayer, and just at daybreak received the sacrament of the Lord's Supper according to the rites of the Church of England. He then hastened to join Prince Eugene, who had probably just confessed to a popish priest. The generals consulted together, forming their plans of action, and then repaired each to his own post. Marlborough gave orders for public prayers. Then might have been witnessed a strange spectacle. The English chaplains read the service at the head of the British regiments. The Dutch troops listened to their Calvinistic chaplains, upon whose heads no hand of bishop had been laid in consecration. The Danes heard the supplications of their Lutheran ministers, while Capuchin monks encouraged the Austrian squadrons and prayed for the blessing of the Virgin upon the arms of the Holy Roman Empire. Then these forces, utterly diverse in opinions, but animated by a single purpose, went bravely forth to the field, and before nightfall had achieved a victory which changed the political complexion of Europe.

Here is the Church of the twentieth century split into a bewildering diversity of sects, many of which are engaged in fortifying systems instead of proclaiming a life, or striving to bind fetters of dogma upon men rather than to relieve them from bondage. Every one can see that if these divergent forces can be cemented into an harmonious whole, the probability of their conquering the world will be vastly magnified. How shall they be unified? "It is a simple matter," responds the red-hatted hierarch of Baltimore; "it is only necessary that all Christian people shall acknowledge the sole lordship of the Roman pontiff, and that every knee shall bend to the authority that sits upon the shore of the Tiber." "A very simple matter," cries the Anglican communion, through its representative denomination in the United States; "let all Christians acknowledge the historic episcopate, the apostolic succession; let us visé your ordination parchments, and the rest will be easy." "A very simple matter," cry those little sects which exalt system above soul, and creed above conduct; "simply acknowledge these principles for which we have been contending for many years, and the rest will be easy."

"He that sitteth in the heavens shall laugh, the Lord shall hold them in derision." The very angels of the celestial world must be amused, when they are not annoyed, by our petty trifling.

> 'See how we grovel here below,
> Fond of these earthly toys."

"Go ye into all the world and preach the gospel to every creature." It is the command of Jesus Christ. "Your marching orders," says the Duke of Wellington, "obey them." "Lo! I am with you alway, even unto the end of the world." "It is the word of a Gentleman of the strictest honor," says David Livingstone, "and there is an end of it."

The unifying principle of Christendom is the single purpose to redeem society according to the plans and specifications of Jesus Christ our Lord. And if the scattered regiments of the Christian Church will but sink their differences and obscure their prejudices, if with unbroken front they will move up to the citadel of the world's sin we shall not be waiting long until we see the watch-towers toppling and the triumphant army, as in the days of Joshua, marching over the prostrate walls of the city and taking the land of promise in the name of God.

It must, of course, be a conquering Church if it is to lay claim to being a Christian Church. What a slander upon the body of Christ it is to designate any institution as Christian that does not know how to overcome the world! No feeble and ineffective organism can honestly wear that sublime title. The Son of God was manifested to destroy the works of the devil, and they who propose to follow Him must exercise the same dynamic and produce corresponding results.

For the works of the devil are not wholly driven from the face of the world; many of them are deeply entrenched in the life of our modern nations. It is written that some-time men will "beat their swords into plowshares and their spears into pruning-hooks, and that nation shall not lift up arms against nation, neither shall they learn war any more," but to-day Christendom is armed with engines of destruction of which the fervid imagination of John Milton never conceived when he attempted to portray the awful strife raised by Lucifer in Heaven; and they plow all our seas and menace the peace of the world. The diabolic folly that sends millions of men to death in order that a strip of narrow territory may be given to a people or a new bauble to a monarch is foredoomed by the sentiment of the Christian Church. It is written, "Thou shalt love thy neighbor as thyself," but in Christian nations to-day mammon rears his haughty crest and into the hungry maw of corporate greed you are pouring thousands of little children who are condemned to toil at tasks too severe for their tender years. You are compelling women to bear burdens under which they faint, which make it impossible for them to perform the noblest functions they owe to the human race, and which make them incapable of resisting the temptation to surrender womanly honor for the purchase of ease. In order that there may be larger stock-holders' dividends, or that you may provide more comforts for those who are already comfortable enough, you subject hundreds and thousands of men to occupations which are hazardous to life. You stand by and observe the appalling sacrifice of human strength and try to salve your consciences by declaring that the expanding civilization of the twentieth century requires such tremendous expenditure, while the devil smirks over your acquiescence in his nefarious work. It is said that no drunkard can enter the Kingdom of Heaven, but the liquor plutocracy is as arrogant as ever. Like a loath-some serpent it trails its scaly length over the platforms of political parties. It lays its shiny folds upon the desks of legislators. It hisses its hateful threat even in the temples of religion. It spews its deadly venom upon our streets, poisoning our children, debauching public sentiment, and paralyzing political integrity. Some day an aroused public conscience armed with a goodly cudgel will beat the life out of this monster, and this work of the devil will be destroyed by order of the Son of God.

These are but illustrations of the many complex problems now confronting the Christian Church. If the Church is to be invincible it must first of all recognize the supremacy which belongs to her among the moral forces of society, and must insistently proclaim that primacy in the face of men and devils. I can not believe that Jesus Christ was merely throwing off a rhetorical flourish when He said, "On this rock I will build My Church and the gates of hell shall not prevail against it." He intended that this Church should be the earthly expression of divine authority in the world. The Christian Church has not been compacted by centuries of history and developed by ages of Christian thought and service without a divine predestination to a sublime purpose. The Christian Church is to fill the whole earth and exercise authority over universal society in the name of the Lord.

But with a strange fatuity the Church of our times seems

disposed to list itself among many competitive agencies seeking to elevate mankind. It permits itself to be catalogued on a parity with the press, the drama, the school, the political institutions of our day. You will hear people say that the press preaches to a wider constituency than the pulpit, that the theater will sometimes give a better sermon than does the Church, that fraternal, mutual benefit societies show larger humanity than does the Church, that literature and art and music are spiritual forces more beneficial than public worship, and that our organized charities are more Christlike than the missionary movement projected by Jesus Christ our Lord. To state these declarations before such an audience is to refute them. The Church has no reason for existence if it does not rise superior to all other agencies seeking the redemption of society. Unless the Church affirms its primacy and defends it against all who seek its overthrow, it will not be able to command the respect of the people who live in this age.

If the Church is to be invincible she must also summon to her standard all who are in agreement with her main proposition, which is the redemption of society from iniquity. There are two sermons of John Wesley which are not frequently enough perused by our people. One is called "The Catholic Spirit," and the other, "A Caution Against Bigotry." "Is thine heart right as my heart with thy heart? If it be, give me thine hand." You speak of Christianity as a universal religion, but you treat it as if it were a kind of a partisan affair. You draw a picture of God and say to me, "Bow down and reverence or you are no true worshiper." You crowd the poetic speech of Jesus into hard, metallic molds and say, "Accept these narrow dogmas or you can not have fellowship with us." You expand the Sermon on the Mount into minute particulars for the regulation of every detail of human life, and you say, "Obey these or you have not the spirit of Christ." Everywhere we are turning men away from fellowship with the Christian Church by requirements which are not based upon Scripture or founded upon reason. I am no latitudinarian. I hold fixed convictions and I am proposing to proclaim them, but I find nothing in the New Testament which requires me to condemn men who can not pronounce my theological shibboleths and who can not without intellectual dishonesty agree to many of the minor non-essentials of Christian doctrine. All over the world to-day there are men who love mercy, deal justly, and walk humbly with God, but can not accept all that the Church of to-day requires of them without sacrificing the principle of truth in their lives, and we say to them: "We put you on our waiting list. When you have been fully qualified we shall admit you." O, stupid and ineffective policy! The next revival should be one of clarified common sense. No man need be asked to bow down before any other man's theological caricature of God. We know the law of eternal life: "Thou shalt love God. Thou shalt love thy neighbor as thyself." To love God is not merely to adore a picture some other brain has drawn. It is to love goodness objectified in a Person of infinite holiness. Do you love eternal righteousness? There is my hand. After a while we shall have the judgment to say: "Do you want to lead a clean life? Do you believe that Jesus Christ has the secret of that life? Will you enter into His sublime ambition to make a clean world? Will you follow Him to the death? Here is my hand." And over these clasped palms the pierced hands of Jesus will be laid to cement the bargain.

Then, take up those great questions in which the whole world is concerned to-day. Justin McCarthy has said that the progress of English reforms has usually pursued this course: First of all, the writers bring it before the public mind and prove that the thing they are trying to advocate is justified, but Parliament pays no attention to that. Then it gets out among the people. An agitation ensues, but still Parliament does nothing of a practical nature. Then the people are no longer to be suppressed, violence breaks forth,

335

and finally, just before revolution has actually come upon the nation, the English Parliament takes up the matter and gives it adjustment. Is not that a picture of the Christian Church? Is it not true that everywhere the air is fairly vibrant with enthusiasm for social reform. If we believe in Divine Providence we must be convinced that the temper of the times is no accident. The finger-print of the Eternal is here. The Socialist is abroad in the land; violence, threatening, and cursing are everywhere. The Church dimly sees her peril. She rubs her eyes and finds that she has the charter of human freedom in her possession, that it is her business to abolish oppression, and with hesitating feet she joins the procession of liberators. O, Church of the living God, get in front! Sound the charge, lead the hosts over the ramparts.

But finally, if the Church is to be successful, she must place her main reliance upon supernatural power. Christianity is a supernatural religion, and must be propagated by a supernatural agency if it is to accomplish a supernatural work. I will not quibble about the word supernatural. We know it is used to differentiate material from the spiritual. If the Church is to be successful it must depend not upon man, but upon God. The early apostolic Church realized that. The primitive Christian conducted the whole business of life in an atmosphere of devotion and under the dominance of a spiritual purpose. Every meal was a sacrament, and every house a temple. Every social custom was inter-penetrated with a spiritual intention. The whole destiny of the Christian movement was pitched upon the power of God to express Himself in the life of man and bring the world to a knowledge of the truth in Jesus Christ.

That early Church saw the wisdom of this when on the day of Pentecost the Judean capital was swept by an influence supernal which shook it from temple to wall, from palace to hut. They saw it again when Peter the fisherman, without a touch of science or philosophy, and with a sermon composed chiefly of quotations from the Old Testament, so preached the gospel that three thousand souls were brought into the rapture of conscious salvation. They saw it again at Cæsarea, when an enlightened pagan, having heard the gospel, he and the multitude about him broke forth into songs of rejoicing. They saw it again on the Damascus road when the most liberally educated Jew of his day was stricken by light which first blinded him and then blazed glory into his soul and led him to swing his talents and accomplishments over to Jesus Christ. They saw it again when sallying forth into a civilization brutal but elegant, these humble Christians drove everything before them and buried philosophic heathenism and Roman imperialism into an eternal grave. When persecution poured upon them like a pack of wolves, they took to their knees and besought God to give them relief, and the power of the Holy Spirit shattered prison walls, filled their bosoms with enthusiasm, and enabled them to carry the gospel through the whole Roman Empire.

Do you not believe that the world is waiting for a re-enactment of scenes like these wherever in the world Christians pursue their activities? Do you not feel as you read the pages of current history that the Church will rise with undaunted spirit, with unconquerable faith, and with divinely inspired wisdom to meet the issues of our day and carry the glad tidings around the world? When the publishers of Peary's book descriptive of his discoveries at the North Pole offered him the largest sum ever given for a work of that nature, their explanation was that his was the last of the earth's great stories. The latest it may be, but not the last. That is in process of writing, and every faithful Christian disciple has his finger on the page and is seeking to make the narrative full of power for succeeding generations. An old prophet saw its culmination and broke forth in ecstatic song: "The wilderness and the solitary place shall be glad, and the desert shall blossom and rejoice, and the eyes of the blind shall be opened and the ears of the deaf shall be unstopped; the lame man shall leap as a hart and the tongue of the dumb

shall sing; for out of the wilderness waters shall break forth
and streams in the desert, . . . and the ransomed of the
Lord shall return and come to Zion with songs and everlasting joy upon their heads; they shall obtain joy and gladness, and sighing and sorrow shall flee away." O, to be a
participant in the great enterprise by which Jesus Christ
proposes to conquer this world is sublime enough to trans-
figure the humblest personality! O, to share in the ultimate
conquest of our Lord is glorious enough to make the proudest
monument of the world cheap and tawdry! "Awake! Awake!
Put on thy strength, O Zion!"

The Ownership and Lordship of Jesus Christ.

George Sherwood Eddy.

As we come towards the close of this Convention we are
brought face to face with this question of the ownership and
lordship of Jesus Christ. The facts will fade in our memories,
feeling will pass, and in the end our personal relationship
to Jesus Christ will determine what we are to do about the
things we have heard in this Convention. A year or ten
years hence, will you and I be able to say, "I was not dis-
obedient to the heavenly vision?" Dull must he be of soul
to whom God has not spoken in these great calls that have
come from the home and foreign fields. Now, as we go home,
what are you and I going to do and what are we going to be?
Life is a stewardship, a trust from God, and every breath
we breathe makes us a new debtor to Him and dependent upon
Him; every pulse-beat is the life of God within us; this body
is a temple; all these possessions we call our own, whose are
they? "The silver and the gold are Mine; the earth is the
Lord's, and the fullness thereof." It is all a trust from
Him. Have you recognized that ownership and lordship of
Jesus Christ? Think of the difference that would make in
your life and mine! Think of the difference it made in the
life of Paul. Think of Saul of Tarsus coming down that

THE LARGER OUTLOOK.

Damascus road; then think of the ownership and lordship recognized by Paul. He had been working for God, but now God was working through him: is He working through us, and are the rivers of living water flowing full and free like a mighty flood? Does God dare to trust us with much power or full power? Think of the difference it made in the life of that blundering, honest-hearted Peter, blinded with self-wisdom, with self-love, with self-glory, and at last cursing and swearing that he did not know his Lord. There was the end of himself. Then, broken, humbled, that man standing that morning by the little Lake of Galilee, face to face with his Master, Jesus Christ. His work on earth was done, He had lived, He had died, He had paid the price once for all. He had risen, He had given the last commission, and all heaven was waiting to receive Him and crown Him King of kings and Lord of lords. And Jesus, risen, with heaven waiting, tarries for an interview with one man. I can see Him standing there, the King of glory, waiting for Simon to finish his breakfast. Then, longing to get possession of that blundering heart, He says wistfully, "Simon, son of Jonas, lovest thou Me?" That question searched his soul. And with all his heart he could look his Master in the face and say, "Thou knowest that I love Thee." "Feed My sheep." But it was not ended. Deeper probed that question of love. "Simon, do you really love Me?" Again he honestly answered, "Thou knowest that I love Thee." And then once again, "Simon, lovest thou Me?" And Simon—I think there were tears in his eyes and grief in his heart—but he answered, "Thou knowest that I love Thee." Then He said, "Feed My sheep." And then He went back to heaven and knew that the work would be done and that one heart down in this world recognized the Lordship of his Master, Jesus Christ, and that he would live and die for Him. The cause was safe and He went back to glory.

We come to the end of this Convention, but is it not true that One stands here to-day in the hush of these closing hours

339

with all power given Him in heaven and earth, yet helpless
before you, knocking with His pierced hands, asking that
one question, "You know the fact, you have heard the addresses, you have the feelings, but what are you going to do
and what are you going to be? Will the rivers flow? Will
the dead be raised? Will the world be won? Will you be
true?" He presses that question home to-day to every heart
in this room. He asks us this question to-day, "Lovest thou
Me?" It is a threefold challenge of love: "Lovest thou
Me enough to give thyself? How much dost thou love Me,
weighed in the balance of love?" What is the ultimate purpose of your life and mine? Is it to get or to give? Is it
for selfishness or sacrifice? Is it for silver or for soul? For
mankind or for God? For self or Christ? "Lovest thou Me
enough to give thyself?" There are waiting fields over there
in that other half that have never heard. I see young men
here, some under forty, some under thirty-five—young pastors and laymen with life before them. There are places
out there that can be filled even in the English language.
Never mind the age. Brother, would you go if the way were
opened? Would you go to-day? Many a heart answers, "I
love Thee and I long to go." Yes, we do. Some have to
stand beside little open graves out there. A letter just received from a brother says: "My litle boy died from tropical
dysentery. Three months later my little girl sickened with
the same disease. My wife had to be carried from the hospital to the bedside of that little one, who soon died. My
wife is ordered home on account of sickness. Pray that
we may not have to go home." "Lovest thou Me? Enough
to give thyself in the person of that daughter or son or little
one?"

"Lovest thou Me enough to give thyself in prayer?"
Prayer moves the Power of the world. Do we know how
to pray? I will tell you of a man who knows how to pray.
How did he learn it? A young, self-confident, Peter-like
pastor out in China. But a woman was praying for him.

340

She could not preach. She did not know the language very well. There was a series of special meetings to be held. The one who was to preach one night failed to appear. She called the young pastor and said, "Pastor, you will have to take the meeting to-night in the church." He lost his temper and said, "You knew he was not coming; you are trying to make me take the meeting." Broken-hearted, she got down on her face to pray. In tears she prayed. That night the young pastor got up to take the meeting. Somehow, before the meeting ended the power of God fell on the audience and on that pastor. Men were convicted of sin. He came in and said, "Pray for me, a sinful soul, for I have seen God this night." I saw that man in a Student Conference there in China. His name is Dingley May. I saw him in that Conference and watched him, for I had heard about him. I had heard that he prayed two or three hours a day. When the last night came we were really very tired, but until near morning that man was praying for every delegate by name, sending those boys back to evangelize their country and to save it. When I asked him to pray for me, I saw him put my name on his list No. 1, those for whom he prays every day, and I saw that my number was 1,142. That man is raising an army of ministers for Japan. I said, "What is your method?" He said, "I have no method but prayer." No eloquence, no great learning, but that power of prayer—do we have it?

"Lovest thou Me" enough to give thyself? The second time he asks that question, "Lovest thou Me" enough to give thy substance? How much have I given? How much have I kept? I sat beside a young couple the other night at table. I said, "What are you going to do?" They said, "We are going out this fall." I said, "Where?" They told me of a great land up in the north of India, a closed land where no man has ever entered. I looked at that brilliant scholar and at that young girl, and I said: "The first convert he gets, they will put a bullet through him. The first we know, that

girl will fill an open grave out there." I said, "Do you
know what it means to go to that land?" "O yes," she said,
"we know." Tears filled my eyes and I said: "Splendid!
Go ahead!" And then I thought, "Do I want them to go
ahead and lay down their lives, and then am I afraid to ask
a man to give up his substance to back such precious lives
at the front?" You can not go, many of you; the time has
passed when you could go, and God wants you here. But
would you send a substitute? Why not? I saw a man yesterday, and the last time I saw that man he did not believe in
foreign missions. We were crossing the water ten years ago.
This man said, "When they come to me for foreign missions,
I tell them I only believe in home missions; and when they
come to me for home missions, I say I believe in something
else." But he has been growing since then, and he said
yesterday: "My wife and I sat down this week and said,
'Let us agree that we will lay nothing by; we will run the
business and cut down our own expenses to the limit of sim-
plicity, and give all the rest to the Kingdom—not lay it up
here. It is so restful to have just handed it over to the
Master.'" Brother, have you found that rest and that joy?

"Lovest thou Me" enough to give thyself, thy substance,
and thy time? Some will give money who have no time.
But out in Korea I sat in a little church seventeen years ago,
when I started in out there, when there were seven men baptized in a little room ten feet square, which they dared to
call a church. I have been there since and seen fifteen hundred people at the Church service, eight hundred at the
Wednesday night prayer-meeting, all wanting to pray. From
that Church of seventeen years ago they have sent off forty-
two branch Churches and congregations, and one thousand
five hundred are left in the mother Church. How do they
do it? Because every Christian is a witness, and the gospel
is still good news in Korea. Is it not still good news here?
How many of us laymen won a soul this year? How many
of us spoke to a man this month? I found the gospel the

same good news to open a man's heart the other night on the train, the barber on the train—just as powerful and just as new. Christ asks our time. I saw a laymen leave a convention like this in this State. He went back home and gave a little of his time. He saw twenty men and they gave fourteen thousand dollars in that Church that year. It was better than if he had given the amount himself. They take up a collection of days in Korea. They took up a collection of three thousand days. Do you wonder that they increased their gifts in that Church that year? O for a collection of days of service! Are we going back to witness, are we going back to work in our Church? "Lovest thou Me" enough to give thy time?

In closing, it is not only a threefold challenge of love, it is the threefold call of service. It is a call to heroism. O, those men out at the front know what heroism means! Here is one of them (showing a photograph). Who is he? An M. A. of Harvard, Ph. D. of Princeton—he is out there in Korea. He was at Minneapolis and some of you saw him and heard him there. As a little boy he came to the little Christian school a proud Confucianist, braced against Christianity as the hated foreign doctrine, but he heard the words "liberty" and "government," and he went out with those men and organized an independent party; they captured the Cabinet; they were introducing reforms. Suddenly the old emperor turned against them, the guards rushed from the palace and they were seized and thrown into prison. Some of them were beheaded. This man's turn was to come next; he was to be beheaded, and after that—what? "Where am I going?" Confucianism did not tell him. He remembered then that back in the mission school he had heard of the Heavenly Father, of His Son who had died, and of the heaven beyond. He told me that he did not know how to pray. He was chained in the stocks and covered with vermin, with his limbs twisted in torture. He bent his head and cried with broken heart, "O God! save my country, save my soul!" It was a good prayer for a man who did not know how to pray. He sent out word to his own Confucian father in the city to get a Bible to him, and that father smuggled a Testament to him through the bars of the jail. I hold in my hand that precious little book (exhibiting) that fed that prison for seven years, that saved that man, and that started a revival in that jail. It is a little English Testament. He could not hold it in his hands, for they were chained; another held it in front of him and turned the pages while he drank in the message and told his fellow prisoners. When the jailer came in he boldly witnessed, and the jailer at last believed and was baptized, with all his house. Paul was in prison at Philippi one night; this man was in the prison in Korea seven years, and in such a prison for filth and cruelty as probably even the Roman Empire never saw. He started a Bible class, and forty men joined, the jailer joined, and a revival broke out. At last, fortified by the Spirit of God, that litle group of men came out to win Korea for Christ. O, the heroism of some of your men at the front! It is a call to the heroic, to us as well as them. Will we respond?

It is the call again of that waiting world. That world has never heard of Christ because we have never told them, but that world is ready. Dr. Mott and I crossed Asia, and the last city was Mukden, in Manchuria. In 1900, in that center of the Boxer persecution, there stood a poor, humble preacher; the swords were raised above his head. "Are you going to preach that Jesus doctrine?" He replied, "As long as I live I will preach it." They cut off his ears, and they gave him one more chance, and they said, "Are you going to preach it?" He said, "I will." They cut off his lips, and with strength ebbing from him he said, "I may not be able to speak much longer, but I can believe and I witness for Christ." With a terrible cross thrust they cut out his heart and he fell. His little girl fled into the cornfield, clasping a Testament in her hand. The Boxers caught her and they said, "Aren't you afraid to die?" Smiling, she said,

"Afraid or not, it is all one." And as she smiled the sword cut her down. I wish you could have seen that great crowd in that great hall built by the Government—five thousand Government students at an evangelistic meeting in that hall built by a Confucian Government; the Minister of Education, a Confucianist, and thirty-six of the officials, professors and teachers in that Government institution, where thirteen years ago these men were falling in the Boxer uprising.

And lastly, as we close, it is the call not only to the heroic, not only the call of that waiting world, it is the call of Jesus Himself, who says, "I was a hungered, I was athirst, I was naked, a stranger, sick, and in prison." "Simon, son of Jonas, lovest thou Me?" Enough to give thyself, enough to give thy substance, enough to give thy time? How many hearts can answer back, "Thou knowest that I love Thee," and go from this Convention with His commission, "Feed My sheep," recognizing in that unbroken fellowship with Jesus the ownership and Lordship of Jesus Christ?

III. THE LARGER OUTLOOK FOR THE OC-CIDENT AND THE ORIENT.

The American Republic a World Influence.

WILLIAM A. QUAYLE.

I AM told, with what degree of veracity I can not say, that there was once a man who said that the American Republic had blemishes. He is now dead and his name is not worth inquiring after. But I am not here to-night to find the freckles on the face of the Republic; there are plenty of dermatologists who can do that. There are blemishes in the Republic, there are fatuities in the Republic; there are shames in the Republic; but thanks be to the great, strong God, the Republic in spite of them is magnificent. And I greatly deprecate that on state occasions, on 4th of July and Memorial Day, men of attempted sagacity discover an opportunity to slur the Republic and tell what it is not. But, citizens, might it not be lovely once in a while just to give way to a hallelujah? might it not be good once in a while just to shut our eyes for a minute and say there never was such a country as we are in? But I would not brag to-night. There is one thing about our Republic that I greatly delight in, and that is that you can not lie about its excellencies. Because its excellencies are so superb that even Jack Falstaff could not lie about them. But you know there are so many folks that pay a great deal of heed to the fly in the ointment; they do, not pay much attention to the ointment except as it is an incarceration process for the fly. Then they repeat, ''There is a fly in the ointment.'' It is not necessary to talk very much about that, but it is rather necessary to remark that in spite of its weaknesses, its fallacies, its frailties, its

346

failures, the Republic has gotten on so that her voice reaches the ears of the earth. That is worth while remembering. And the Republic, after all omissions and subtractions, is a world majesty and has a world demeanor and has influence. Now, one time a gentleman by the name of Columbus, Mr. Columbus, was walking out westward to get eastward, and he sternly intended to visit the coast of China, and all of a sudden and unawares he stubbed his toe against the American continent and found it here. Which is another way of saying that the United States is on the road to everywhere. Which is another way of saying that if you want to get East in a jiffy, you must go West in a hurry; just a way of saying that the United States is a half-way house for the planet on the road to anywhere, on the road to everywhere, and can not be omitted. On the road for every high design, on the road to every noble destiny, on the road to every supreme surprise, on the road to every divine enterprise is the United States of America. In other words, America has come out into the open. It can no more be obscured than the sea. It can no more be forgotten than the sun. America has rather arrived and to stay, and is well and getting along in spite of what has happened to it, thank God!

But what I say is this, we listen to so many people who with chapped lips eternally prate about what we are not. It is worth while to pause a minute and say what we are. Lots of people have talked about graft so much that if they had nightmares they would see grafters. A little grafter goes a long way, and there are not many of them; and a little less talk about them would make them less numerous. That is the truth of the matter. They get more publicity than they demand! The Republic is not a grafter. The great ninety million are not grafters. The great millions of the Republic are working away at their job. What is their job? O, working is their job, and getting tired is their job. And sleeping to rest up is their job. In other words, the United States is a world influence not because of magnitude, but because of behavior. A little land! Why, America could take Greece in the palm of its hand and not notice anything in it, and Montana could take the Holy Land in its hand and think the hand was a little dirty and wash it out. But is that anything against Palestine? No, Christ came from Palestine. O, Palestine is so vast that the only continent of heaven will be named Palestine because of the Holy Land Christ trod. He was there and made that place significant through the eternities. And Greece was little, but ah me! it spake with the eloquence that moved the world. America is big and don't deny it. It is a big continent, but not by breadth of the shoulders, not by riches of money, not by many marts, not by profits of all sorts that can be told—not by that, but because America has something to say that the world needs to hear. A while ago when I was a lad people might argue about the influence of America, but they can not do that any more. That matter is not up for disputation. We have touched the world and the world has felt the thrill of it, and we are here and our voice needs no megaphone to be heard to the uttermost parts of the planet. Now, what is the reason? That is what I am here to answer. Would to God that I knew the eloquence that would flame before men's vision this powerful truth, that our influence is felt in all parts of the planet. We have no individual dialect; we are talking in the language of the earth, so that men everywhere hear it. We do not talk Chinese, but the Chinese hear us. We do not talk Japanese, but Japan hears us. There is not a man forlorn and overburdened on the planet but when he hears "America," does not begin to look up to the sky and say, "I belong to the sky; would God I were there!"

Now America's influence rests first because it has made labor aristocratical. You know work was thought to be democratical; it was thought to be the function of underlings. America has made labor the work of upperlings. And if a man came on this platform and said, with great politeness, and with his trousers turned up to the top of his shoes and a collar up to his ears, "I am a laborless individual; I have never labored and never will," we would call him a hobo and put him in the police-patrol, and that is where he belongs. America has made labor aristocrat. We are a brood of laboring folks. I say here to-night that the American Republic, being a race of working people and only working people and ever working people and magnifying labor, has made labor unridiculous, magnificent, and glorious. Do not misunderstand me; I do not say that we are the only folks that work; I do not say that we invented work; I do not say that we are the only diligent people on the earth: I say that the American Republic set to work with a race of people that had nothing to make everything, and we have made so much that the dukes pass their hats to us and say, "Give us a collection." It is not a small matter, my friends, to make work aristocratical. You can not get a man of self-respect on this continent to say that he is unemployed. In other words, one of the influences of American civilization is to make work magnificent. Everywhere an American goes he says he has got a business. Of others, if you ask, "What is your business?" they will say, "We are of the leisure classes." Are there any leisure classes in America? No. We all work or get worked—that is all there is to it. O men, I incline to the opinion that we have not largely enough estimated the nobility of this achievement, that we are a race of shopkeepers; they used to laugh at us, but we built the shop and we keep it, and nobody can get it away from us. Amen.

Then, the American Republic's influence on the world is the influence of a new occupation for riches. I am not rich, but I am saying here to-night that it is one of the leanest of lean things to eternally harass riches: It is not the part of the Church nor of sagacity to do it. It is a pretty good thing that some people have more brains than most of us. The whole question of riches is coming by it honestly and distributing it liberally. American riches have set an absolutely undreamed-of standard of riches for the planet. Over in

England if you get rich, you found a family. In America you found an institution, which is better—that is the difference. O, do you take any care to read year by year of the munificent beneficence of American riches poured into the coffers of God Almighty. O, me! the world has got to give. Why? Because America shows the world how. Here you see a man going around and won't even let the hook-worms hook without putting brakes on them; won't even let education educate without endowing it—colleges, universities, hospitals, infirmaries, every good thing that God Almighty has hinted at, people have endowed in America. But you can't have riches stingy any more. And why? Because America won't let them. I say here to-night, not being apt in figures but being pretty good in judgment—I say here to-night, that America has done more giving in its brief lifetime than the whole history of the world has known. O, if we get money, we give money; if we earn much, we give much!

Again, American influence is that it has believed and proceeded on the belief that Christianity could stand on its own feet. I used to think that Christianity had to be bolstered up by governments and in order to have a Church you had to have a State to hold the Church up. We have learned that you have got to have a Church to hold the State up. We have learned that the Church is not a pensioner of the Government, but the Government is a pensioner on the Church. We have found out that Christianity can stand out in the wind and the weather, and the winds blow and the storms descend and the thunder crash, and the storm goes by and the Church roof is washed by the calamity. It is a great matter that the Church does not have to be held, and I will say here to-night that nothing seems to be more sublimely eloquent than that the American people have not any foundation of government for the Church. Why? Why, because the Church sprang not out of the kings, but out of the heart of Christ. When they tore away there to the heart, the Church leaked out and began to sing a hallelujah chorus. Trust the Church to keep alive and well, and don't hold its hands and talk pathetically to it. Say, "O, Church of God, God loves thee!" Then all the Church bells will begin to ring. We need less fussing about the Church and diagnosing of it, but more loving of it and going to it. I don't take much stock in telling what classes of people don't go to Church. No good in saying a lot of people don't go to Church. More go to Church now than ever. Who pay the bills of the Church? The people do. Why? Because the soul is higher than the roof of a schoolhouse and the dome of the Washington Capitol, and higher than the groined roof of the sky littered with stars. And the Church in America has stood alone. Here stands a fact: the Church of God belongs to mortality and so long as men stay mortal the Church of God will be here and self-supporting, and America says that. That is a great message.

Then, America's influence is to the effect that it makes people dream. Most people do not dream unless they go to bed, but the worst thing about that is, you can not sit up with your dreams and you do not know what they are, and if they wake you up they are not things you want to sit up with. In other words, America's influence is to make dreaming an occupation to be desired. To dream by day is to dream for good. The other day I came over from the village of Washington with Bishop Cranston, and went back to break my fast in the diner in the rear of the train, and I waded through three cars full of people, not a single person of whom—man, woman, or child—could talk American speech. And as I walked through the car and looked at them, I believe my heart was like the brooding heart of God. I wanted to take them up in my arms and kiss their faces. Three carloads of people who need a thousand things, and what brought them here? America brought them here. They had been told a dream, and I looked into their eyes and I wondered if my eyes could say what my heart could tell them, which was, "O men, O women, O children, America, my America, made you dream." Whenever I see people like that I think of my own father and mother—my mother, a girl in her early teens with golden hair that caught the rays of the sun, and eyes as blue as the sea of the islands on which she was born, with a heart as sweet as the lilies of God on resurrection morning—my sweet mother, a girl dreamed away to America. Why? She thought it was a better place for a woman to live—the Quayles always were smart. And my father—a lad, a fisherman's son with a father in the vaults of the great sea for a burial-house—my father, a lad, came to America in steerage! What a good passage that is! What made my mother, a girl, come to America? America made her dream. What made my father, a lad, come to America? America made him dream, and America is making the world dream. I beg of you, when you fisticuff that foreign immigration and scoff at people that do not speak our speech, to think that if God were here He would meet them at the wharf and say, "Welcome!" Let them dream. America has made the world dream, and will forever.

America's influence for the world has been to get it to be big. This continent is so big that by the time you get used to turning around in it you have to be a globe-trotter. You have to go so far to get anywhere it takes a long time to do it. What is the trouble with the people? They are bad—yes, I know they are bad. But what is the trouble with the good people? They are little—little. Little, Littler, Littlest. You say that is not the way to compare it, but that is the way folks are, that is all. What do they need? They need expansion. They need God to get His two hands inside of their sky and push it out. O God, push our sky out to-night. They need that, and by the time people have been in America a while, big things seem normal and accurate and commensurate and feasible. And I charge this company to remember that it is not a happening that the United States of America and Canada are the largest contributors to foreign missions.

THE LARGER OUTLOOK.

Why? Because we got used to big places, and the world seems little to us now. O America! you have made us familiar of the planet. It is a great matter to get on speaking terms with the planet; to think in world dimensions and love in world dimensions. When people do not want to give to missions, what is the trouble? They are little; they are not bad, they are just little. They ought to get out into the street so they will be bigger; they ought to get out under the sky. It is pretty hard to stay little in America. It is magnificent to be in a country where the world floods in on you and you take it as a matter of course.

America influences the world because it has caught that men can be kings—not a man, not a king settled down on you, but a king coming up from you. If you know a sublimer thing than this you speak of it when I am through, namely, an election day, when the Nation goes out, saying, "We are pretty busy ourselves, and we will take some unoccupied brother and make a President of him." That is the reason we elect a President—because we are too busy to take the little job ourselves: that is all there is to it. Lots of us could do that business, and we acknowledge it. Dare you trust men to rule themselves? Mexico can not. Are we angry at Mexico? We are not! Would we speak hastily to Mexico? We would not. But we have a race of people that have shown that a democracy may trust itself to rule.

I call your attention to this, that all the things that I have named that are magnificent in our Republic, and more that I might have mentioned—all of them we learned of God. We learned them of Christ. We are retailers of second-hand material. Christ told them all to us. He has given them all to us. O America, live forever! O, my America, keep God's Sabbaths. O, my America, read God's Word! O, my America, love God's character! O, my America, hear God's voice! O, my America, fall prone on your face at the feet of God's Christ! And then a thousand, thousand years you shall live to see the sun of an eventful morning.

The Chinese Republic and Its Future.

GEORGE SHERWOOD EDDY.

A FEW months ago landing in China, at an opening banquet, the young China arrayed in full dress, we saw in that banquet the signs of the new Republic. Within a year of absence China had suddenly passed into constitutional government and four hundred millions had stepped out of the past four thousand years of history into a modern Republic. On either side of the room were draped the flags of our Republic and the flag of the Chinese Republic. There were signs in that room that showed the great awakening that has been sweeping over that Chinese nation and the continent of Asia. This Republic has seen the rise and fall of Nineveh and Babylon, of Assyria and Persia, and of Rome, and the mushroom growth of mediæval Europe. This Republic has four thousand years of past, with a great future still before her. She will not be deserted by Almighty God as she enters on this stage of constitutional government. Do we forget in our pride and giant strength to-day that we were once thirteen feeble, divided Colonies, in debt, unable to develop our vast resources, without a friend among the nations, and God did not desert us in the hour of our weakness and need? He will not desert the Chinese. As Lincoln said of the common people, so we may say of the Chinese, that God must love them because He made so many of them.

There were signs in that room not only of a political awakening, but of a great intellectual awakening. There were returned students from Yale and Harvard and Oxford and Cambridge and Berlin and Paris and Japan and the mission schools of China leading in every department of the national life. In city after city we found deserted temples handed over to house modern colleges, the ancient examination halls being torn down to build the new Parliament buildings and a modern university. Within a month of the treaty of Portsmouth that marked Japan's victory over Russia, with one stroke of that vermilion pencil the emperor swept away that obsolete system of education that had been in use for two thousand years, and adopted the modern principle of education.

Not only signs of a great political and intellectual awakening, but signs of a great economic awakening. At my side sat that night a man who might be called the Andrew Carnegie of China, a Christian business man, running those great steel mills with five thousand Chinese laborers. A decade or so ago they were picking up old horseshoes in London and shipping them out to China to make third-rate plows for those farmers in Central China. To-day, underneath those hills have been discovered the greatest coal fields in the world. In Shangsi Province alone a German authority estimates that there is coal enough to supply the world for a thousand years. The greatest supply of cheap labor, and perhaps in time potentially of skilled labor, in the world! There I saw skilled Chinese laborers handling thirteen thousand horse power machinery under electric control, turning out the great white-hot steel rails that will thread their way from north to south and east to west, all over the country.

But there were signs that night, not so much of a great awakening that was merely political or economic or intellectual; there were signs of a great religious awakening in that Chinese Republic. We began up in Tientsin, the first place in North China. There about the walls of that city, where for one hundred years they fought to keep out the foreign devils, we saw gathered that night two thousand Government students in that great Guild Hall. Who were those men? Remember, literati were the brains of China, had stood like the great Gibraltar of this world. My friend in China said that if he could have had one man from that class of literati as the result of his life work he would have been glad to give his life to attain that end, and especially so if he could get twelve leaders from among them. There they were, two thousand men, a fire in every eye. These men are concerned about something, about the question, "What will save China?" What is to be our point of contact with those men? If we say, "Jesus Christ will save your soul," they are not concerned at the beginning whether they have any soul or not, but about the great question, What will save China? Some one asked me, "How do you begin to approach that class, prejudiced as they are?" That night, as we faced those men, I said: "I hold in my hand a fivefold problem and a fivefold prophecy. It is the hope of China, it is the glory of China." They began to wonder what was in my hand. Then I unfolded the new flag of the Chinese Republic. It moved us to-night to see "Old Glory" here; but those men, burning with a new patriotism, some of whom had cut off a finger to write their petition for liberty in their own blood, men that would die for China, as they saw the new flag, rose and burst into cheers. It touched their hearts. The fivefold problem had to do with Tibet, with the question whether Mongolia was to be divided between Russia and Japan, whether the nation was to fall asunder and be partitioned among the nations, etc.; it was a fivefold prophecy. The blue on that flag denoted justice and honest officials; the yellow, the pure gold of character; the red, the blood of sacrifice that had already been shed in the land to make China free; and so on. That led to the further thought of the great sacrifice. That flag was a fivefold call to national unity, to practical patriotism, to social service, to moral earnestness, and to reality in religion. Those men, deeply concerned over the national problem, came back the next night to hear about the "Need of China." If I had begun to talk about sin they would not care whether they were sinners or not. But I said: "As I came across the Yellow River I found some dykes built by a grafting official. He had made the dykes so that they would fall and he could build them again. Down came a flood, and thousands of lives and multitudes of property were destroyed, and famine followed in the wake. One man sold China, one man robbed his country.

THE LARGER OUTLOOK.

How are you going to save that province? Money won't do it. He will steal it as fast as you make foreign loans. Machinery won't do it. Education won't do it. Nothing will save the province but that man's moral character. And how are you going to reach that without religion?'' They began to see that there is a connection between what will save China and moral character. For an hour we pounded away on dishonesty and the impurity that is ruining the officials and students of China, until these men with growing conviction are now ready to admit that only living a pure life and breaking from the bondage of sin can save their country. The next night we spoke on the Hope of China. I remember as I went down that night in that bitter, blinding winter storm, I said, "Nobody can come out tonight." But to my surprise two thousand men were back again, crowding the aisles, crowding the platform. I asked them what was the hope of China? Did they have any hope of solving her crushing problems? Stand up and tell us. But not a man stood up. I said: "I believe I have found what is the hope of China. Jesus Christ is the only hope of China; Jesus Christ is the only hope of America, and the only hope of the world." For an hour not a man left the room. You could have heard a pin drop as we told them of Jesus Christ and how He could save the individual and the nation. Fifteen hundred stayed for the after-meeting, and then we asked how many men would rise to promise that they would study those four Gospels with open minds and honest hearts, attending the Bible classes; that they would pray to God for guidance and help, and would follow Jesus Christ with honest conscience. In the boldness of their faith one thousand of those men stood up. We had not enough cards to sign. Then we had to drive them back and scare them off. We said if there was another Boxer uprising they would be in danger. And finally five hundred and thirty men that nothing could affright came over and joined the Bible classes and began to study the life of Christ, and one hundred and nineteen of them had been baptized and received into the Churches within three months of the close of that campaign.

You know what that five hundred and thirty represents? There is one of them. I took a few snapshots as I went across China. A few years ago that man was a Confucian atheist. Believing that the need of China was education, that young man resigned from the navy and started an institution in North China. He became a brilliant educationalist. My friend Robertson won his friendship and love. When this man was appointed on the great commission to study education systems and go back and work reforms in China, Robertson asked him to his house. As I sat with him, he told me how on that last night Robertson asked him if he would kneel and offer the first prayer of his life. He told me as he knelt it seemed as if a great light suddenly filled his soul. As he described it, it reminded me of the conversion of Saul of Tarsus. He arose a new creature in Christ, and all the world was new, and that night he could not sleep for joy. He said, "I had been like a man without chart and compass on a dark and perilous sea, but now I knew where I was going." The next day he went back to the city and called together his family and friends and told them why he had become a Christian. The next day back to his college, his students and the professors and trustees trailing in in their silken gowns, and sitting in that great semi-circular room, imagine this young president rising to resign his college because he can no longer bow to that tablet of Confucius. You can imagine the president of Yale or Harvard or Princeton resigning because he had suddenly become a Mormon. You can imagine the thrill of horror that went through those men when this man got up and said he could no longer bow to any one but Jesus Christ. But why? they said, and all day he stood there and opened the Scriptures and told them why. The next day at Peking he told the officials there, and one of them said to him: "Mr. Chan, to bow to that tablet is merely a matter of form; we can not let you go. Do not give up the college.

We can not spare you." He said: "Mr. Yen, you are the best friend I have on earth, but I can not do that; One has come to dwell in my heart, and I can not bow to any one but Him, so I must give up my college." And he did. Across America visiting our colleges, across Europe, around the world, and back to give his report—called back now as the Christian president of that institution, where never again will men have to bow to that Confucian tablet. I saw there the students from eighteen provinces under that great leader—the Arnold, not of Rugby, but of North China—and if you could have seen them night after night listening with wide-open ears to this leader as he earnestly witnessed for Jesus Christ and what He was to him, and what He could do for China, you would have seen the power of the single life of a leader like that.

But he is not alone. I went one day into Peking, that city of two million people, that city in which Sir Robert Hart remembered in his own lifetime seeing men who had been drowned in the main streets in the rainy season in the pools of water. Now they have paved streets there, and over these same roads we were driven in Chinese taxicabs to keep our engagements in the colleges thrown open to the public by the Government—twenty colleges thrown open for the first time to the Christian message. There where last year the emperor ascended those great steps of the high altar, now instead of the emperor praying for the people, a day of prayer is called by the National Republic of China that the people may pray for the Government and approach directly to God in heaven. Down from Pekin to another city. I had longed to visit that city. It was there that my friend and classmate back at Yale twenty years ago, Horace Pitkin, had laid down his life. He had never had a convert. Cut off in the flower of his youth. A mob had gathered at the gate to kill him. He sat that last night with his Chinese friend, a fellow worker, and sent his last message to his wife, at home sick in America. He said to tell her that God was with him at the last; that His peace was his consolation. "Tell her to send our little son Horace to Yale, where I studied, and tell my boy twenty-five years from now, when he becomes a man, to come out and take up my work for China. For China will yet believe." He had given his life. He had given his fortune, and he had never had a convert, and yet he said, "Tell my only son to come out and take up my work; they will believe my son." They showed me where the mob broke through the gate; where he fell wounded trying to defend the women; where they cut off his head and hung it as a trophy over the arch of the city gate. We had twenty-four hours of opportunity there and no more, and O, how one longed to preach and get at those men as hour after hour they listened! It seemed as if they would not go. At last I said, "How many here where you killed Pitkin and where the missionaries fell, how many of you will rise to the floor and accept Jesus Christ the Lord and Master of those whom you slew, how many will be baptized and join the Church, cost what it may, even though it should cost your lives, as it did those whom you slew?" Ninety men arose out of that audience, and some of them have already been received into the Christian Church. I have not time to go through the fourteen cities, but we will take the last one, down in Foochow, the most conservative of all those cities—the student audiences in Japan averaged eight hundred, in India one thousand, but in China they average two thousand a night all across that Republic, and when we came to that last city it was even greater. We went up to the great Guild Hall, and an hour before the meeting was announced two thousand men were packing the hall, filling every seat, and two thousand more were gathered outside in an overflow meeting, and hundreds more were kept outside by the police. We would seat two thousand in the hall and send them out the back door, and bring in two thousand more, and so go on. All that week five thousand students a day listened to the message of Jesus Christ after the one hundred years that we had waited for that opportunity. It seemed as if the leaders of that city were moved. The Parliament adjourned and asked us to come up and hold a meeting for them, which we did. The Board of Trade attended one meeting in a body. Thirteen Confucian professors of the Government college—by their invitation we visited the city, and they closed their colleges one afternoon and asked every student to go, and postponed the Government examinations so there would be nothing to interfere with the evangelistic meeting. They sat on the platform and gave us such backing as I never saw in America or in any Christian country, and at dinner raised the question of what we could do to save their young men morally, as the restraints of the old religion were losing their hold and their young men were in danger of falling into infidelity and immorality like the students of a neighboring nation. If you had told the missionaries killed that day by the angry mob that within two decades China would be a Republic under constitutional government, that in a meeting announced for women students two thousand women with unbound feet would come out to hear a lecture on the wireless telegraph and receive messages from the Chinese navy of the coast and then demand an evangelistic meeting for themselves, such as the men had, and come in larger numbers to the religious meeting than they did to the science lecture, could they have believed the prophecy? But the miracle has happened and China is open to-day. Take the next province—the same story can be told. O men, China to-day is open, province after province, capital after capital, the four hundred millions of that Republic, and what are we going to do about it? There is a challenge to us. China will turn in this decade in one of three directions: Either toward a revival of the old religions, as India did, in a reactionary movement; or she will turn towards agnosticism, infidelity, and immorality, as for a time Japan did; or she will turn towards Christianity, as Korea did. What will be the future of that great Republic? I believe it depends more than anything else upon this great

361

sister Republic across the sea. "Freely we have received, let us freely give." God hath given to us this gospel. God has given to us the means of lifting that great Republic up out of darkness into His marvelous light. Will we give them the chance?

But I close. I can not forget, as I close, the price that has been paid to open that nation. I have in my hand a picture of a tree that I journeyed far into the interior of China to see. Under that tree, back in the Boxer uprising, forty-six of our missionaries were drawn up in line to be beheaded—first the men, then the women, then the little children. First they called up one of the missionaries. His wife clung to him, but he put her gently aside, knelt down and bowed his head to have it severed from his body. Last of all there were two little girls in the line who came from a family who were friends of mine. As I visited that home a while ago the aged grandparents told me of their little grandchildren sacrificed in China. They said, "We do not begrudge them; China will yet believe." And although it was almost too sacred for any strange eye to see, they showed me the last letter written home by their daughter before she died. Her girls had been lost, her relatives gone; and she, about to die, wrote this letter home. Heroism itself. And here is what she wrote:

"My dear, dear ones: I have tried to gather courage to write you once more. How can I tell you the terrible details of these days. I would rather spare you. The dear ones at C——— Y———, including our lovely daughter, are gone. And tidings from T——— Y——— tell of an uprising there. We are now waiting our call home. I am preparing for the end very quietly and calmly. The Lord is wonderful and He will not fail me. I was very restless and excited while there was some chance of life, but God has taken away that and now I must try to meet my end calmly, because the pain will soon be over. My little baby will go with me. I think God will give her to me in heaven, and my dear mother will be so glad to see us. I can not imagine the Savior's welcome, but that will compensate for all these days of suspense. Dear loved ones, live near to God, cling less closely to earth. I would like to send a special message to each of you, but it presses me too much. I must keep calm during these hours. I do not regret coming to China, but I am sorry I have done so little."

There where forty-six laid down their lives under that tree I took another picture. Where the officers killed the missionaries the Chinese officials had a Christian meeting with Christian representatives living in the abandoned Buddhist temple, and in a meeting held there one hundred and fifty-nine men rose as inquirers for Christ—under the tree where they had been killing our people thirteen short years ago. We have gained more there in the last decade than in a century previous, and to-night China is calling to us in her unconscious need, "Come over and help us." If one man like Livingstone could stake his life against the continent, can not we place our lives against that great Republic of China? I can hear Livingstone on that last day almost, looking out at that dark continent and writing in his diary: "My Jesus, my King, my Life, my All. I again dedicate my whole self to Thee, Lord Jesus, and grant that if possible I may finish my work." Shall we not in this closing night say these words to Him as these calls have come to us from China, from Asia, from a world of need and sinning and suffering men: "My Jesus, my King, my Life, my All. I dedicate my whole self to Thee. Accept me, Lord Jesus, and grant that I may fulfill my work?"

363

IV. CLOSING WORDS.

WILLIAM F. ANDERSON.

WHEN Mr. Fisher stated that it would fall to my lot to preside this evening and that he would expect a few closing words, immediately it occurred to me that certainly there could be no way of closing such a Convention as this quite so appropriately as with some passage of God's Word. Quick as the lightning's flash this brief passage came into my mind: "I have planted; Apollos watered, but God gave the increase." What an occasion this Convention has been for the planting of the seed of the Kingdom! And what great seed has been planted during the hours of this marvelous gathering! Have you noticed it? I have heard nearly every address that has been made from this platform from the beginning of the first day until now. One note has been common to all, viz., Jesus Christ is ordained of God to be King over all the earth. However it may be elsewhere, certainly it must have been apparent to every listener that there is no slurring of the divinity of our Lord here. That however it may be elsewhere, there is no abatement of *our* faith in the belief that Jesus Christ is the Savior of the individual and the Redeemer of all mankind. If the dominant note of the Convention were summed up in one passage of Scripture, it would be this: "Jesus Christ the power of God and the wisdom of God." This Convention has written that great Scripture anew upon the banners of Methodism.

Provision has been made likewise for the watering of this seed in the report of the Committee on Policy, for these great truths are to be carried down to the entire Church. One thing is very certain—we can never be the same men that we were when we came here. If we are not better men, if we are not more efficient servants of Jesus Christ from this time forward, then we shall not be such good men as we have been. Then we shall be less efficient men. To dwell under the inspiration of the open vision of this great Convention and then to go away and not put it into actual practical application in every community is to deteriorate in the quality of our Christian experience and service.

Our Book Concern publishes a little volume entitled, "The Unrealized Logic of Religion." The title of that little volume suggests the unrealized possibilities of Methodism. If every man of us should go from this mountain top of vision to do his best for the unrealized possibilities of our branch of the Church, certainly it would count tremendously in the bringing in of the Kingdom of our Christ in all the nations of the earth.

A friend of mine, a Young Men's Christian Association railroad secretary, gave me this account of an incident at the noonday prayer-meeting of the railroad men. One of their members came in all begrimed and besooted from the engine. When he had opportunity to speak he arose and said, "I hope you will excuse me, fellows, for coming in this condition, but I just had to come. I just got in on the express from Albany. When we left Albany we were away late. I expected we would be late in coming into the Grand Central, but when I got my orders from the train dispatcher I was instructed to bring her in on time. I did not think it was possible. When I had a straight piece of road before me I pulled out the throttle and let her go, and boys, I brought her in on the minute. I was sitting there in the cab looking out of the window when to my surprise I saw the president of the road among the passengers. He came along and when he got close to the cab window he stopped and took off his hat, and reaching up, took me by the hand and said, 'A very good run, sir; a very good run.' Boys, I feel mighty good about it. I had no time to clean up. If I had waited to do that I would have been too late for the meeting, so I came as I was." Then he continued: "I want to draw a lesson from the incident. We are all making a run, and I want to pledge to you, while the inspiration is upon me, a new fealty to the ideal that in the run we are making for our Lord Jesus Christ we will do our best to make it a good run.'' The time is short. What we do we must do quickly. May there come to us the appeal in the need of the world and in the crying conditions of foreign lands, to make in the year to come and in all the years to come a good run for the Captain of our salvation, that when we shall reach the end of the journey, our Lord may say to each of us, ''Well done, thou good and faithful servant.''

It has been driven home to our hearts and consciences again and again and again during these days of high privilege that we must depend upon God for the increase. We have learned nothing about life if we have not learned that it is too much for us alone. We have learned nothing about the Christian enterprises with which we have to do if we have not learned that these problems are too big for our solution. Again and again and again each of us has been brought to the place in our experience where with God's servant of old we have cried out in agony of soul, ''Who is sufficient for these things?'' We never really find the solution of any problem until we give full play to the divine element. To practice the presence of God is to find the secret of the solution of the hardest question with which we have to deal. To have that faith that will prove God is to find the key to the open door. And this is our hope. And this is our faith as the result of this great Convention. We have stood face to face with God. We go out from this place to live the God life and to prove God's grace and to put Almighty God into our efforts for the redemption of our community and for the salvation of all the world. And with that power, even the gates of hell can not prevail against us.

PART VI.
Special Features.

Closing Prayer of Bishop Cranston.

NOW, O God, are we Thy sons, and it doth not yet appear what we shall be, but we know that when He shall appear we shall be like Him. And He has appeared unto us, every one, and our desire to be like Him is stronger to-night than ever before. We know that He has spoken by His Spirit, and we know that He has spoken by the messengers whom He has commissioned to give us the vision of a perishing world and the needs of a great country languishing in its faith because Thy sons have not been altogether true to their calling. O God, lay Thy hands upon our heads to-night, commission every one of us anew. O blessed Spirit of God, attune our hearts again to-night, and let us feel the thrill of the new life and of the reinspired purpose by which Thou art to move the world and lift it nearer to Thyself. Let it not be to us too great a thing to expect that our God shall bring us the victory; only Thou our Leader be, blessed Christ, and we still shall follow Thee.

Keep the fires burning, O Divine Spirit, keep the fires burning in our hearts; let them not for one moment languish; let not their lights fail; let not their heat be killed, but may we carry from this place to every State in this great Nation the inspirations that have come to us here. And may our Church and all our sister Churches, called of God to the same great task—the regeneration of men to the ends of the earth—prove by new works and by renewed zeal that victory is with them that believe. Give us, O God, the commanding faith, faith that will take no denial, and may we be able to speak to our people in such terms as shall communicate to them Thy will, and make them to feel that the words have been given us of God, and that back of the words there is the command of the Leader and the Spirit of the Omnipotent God. "We can do all things through Christ, who strengtheneth us."

The Lord take charge of us. Thou hast kept us in safety during these blessed days. Let every one journey home under Thy care, and may the voices which have here been inspired anew fail not in any part of the message, and as the vision grows upon us may our zeal for Christ become more and more commanding over our own actions until it shall consume us in a passion of sacrifice to accomplish the great purposes of this Convention, which are the purposes of God. Amen.

Special Features.

ALWAYS in such gatherings as this there are many highly important matters that do not fall into natural divisions. Such are the items reserved under this heading of Special Features. The Convention organization and program, the music, resolutions, committees, methods of publicity, the offering, are here gathered together as a final section of the book. There may be some things missing which many will think ought to be included. But pages fill up more rapidly than one would imagine, and before one is aware of it that last page permitted by the printer rustles noisily to its place on the desk and cries, "Be brief!" It is hoped that nothing of preeminent importance has been omitted. Where something seems to have slipped by, read it into your own copy as your memory furnishes the data.

THE CONVENTION ORGANIZATION.

THE National Convention of Methodist Men was not a mass-meeting, but a representative gathering. Admission to all sessions was by credentials only. No seats were open to the general public. Representatives were present from among the following: The Board of Bishops; General Conference Officers; Members General Missionary Committees; Members of Benevolent Boards; Educators and Secretaries; Editors; District Superintendents; Pastors; District Missionary Secretaries; Laymen, including trustees, stewards, Sunday-school superintendents, Brotherhood men, class leaders, Epworth League officers, adult Bible-class members, members of missionary committees, leaders in the local Church; Foreign Missionaries on Furlough; Home Missionaries.

The Convention was under the direction of the Laymen's Missionary Movement of the Methodist Episcopal Church, and had the co-operation of the General Conference Commission on Finance; General Conference Commission on Evangelism; Board of Foreign Missions; Board of Home Missions and Church Extension; Freedmen's Aid Society; Board of Sunday Schools; Board of Education; American Bible Society; Church Temperance Society; The Methodist Brotherhood; The Publishing Interests of the Church; The Board of Bishops; General Laymen's Association; Methodist Federation for Social Service; and Epworth League Board of Control.

But the head and directing genius of the efforts which brought together this great body of men was Fred B. Fisher, General Secretary of the Laymen's Missionary Movement of the Methodist Episcopal Church. It was his boundless faith and tireless labors which made possible this new landmark in Methodist history. In New York, he was assisted by a Convention Committee composed of S. Earl Taylor, James R. Joy, E. W. Halford, J. Edgar Leaycraft, Frank A. Horne, and Ralph Welles Keeler, while his local force at Indianapolis was generaled by Hon. Charles Warren Fairbanks and Bishop David H. Moore, Co-Chairmen of the Local Convention Committee. The following chairmen of local sub-committees had each a large force under them: J. Frank Hanly, Reception; L. C. Bentley, Place of Meeting; E. R. Hisey, Exhibits; Frank C. Jordan, Finance; H. Foster Clippinger, Publicity. C. E. Flynn was Secretary of Local General Committee; Wm. C. Higham, Jr., served as Local Executive Secretary, and H. B. Dickson as Convention Secretary.

PROGRAM NATIONAL CONVENTION OF METHODIST MEN.

TOMLINSON HALL, INDIANAPOLIS, IND., OCTOBER 28 TO 31, 1913.

TUESDAY, OCTOBER 28th.

MORNING.

J. EDGAR LEAYCRAFT PRESIDING.

Intercession, led by.....................Bishop David H. Moore.
Greeting, by...........................Joshua Stansfield.

THEME: "OUR GREAT COMMISSION."

The Central Task of the Church of Christ..Robert E. Speer.
Methodism's Mission and Message.........Bishop William Frazer McDowell.
Methodism's Achievements and Larger Op-
      portunities..........................Bishop John L. Nuelsen.
Convention Organization.

AFTERNOON.

BISHOP CRANSTON PRESIDING.

Intercession, led by.....................Bishop Robert McIntyre.

THEME: "THE CALL TO ADVANCE."

In the Circulation of the Scriptures........William I. Haven.
In Temperance Reform...................Clarence True Wilson.

SPECIAL FEATURES.

In Sunday Schools...................Edgar Blake.

In Education...................Thomas Nicholson.

In Freedmen's Aid...................P. J. Maveety.

In Home Missions and Church Extension. { Ward Platt.
{ C. M. Boswell,

In Foreign Missions...................W. F. Oldham.

EVENING.

Bishop John W. Hamilton Presiding.

Intercession, led by...................Bishop William Burt.

Theme: "The City, Nation, and World."

American Cities and the City of God......Bishop William F. Anderson.

New Americans for a New America.......Bishop Edwin H. Hughes.

An Awakened World a Challenge to Methodist Men...................Bishop Homer C. Stuntz.

WEDNESDAY, OCTOBER 29th.

MORNING.

Bishop Charles W. Smith Presiding.

Intercession, led by...................Bishop Napthali Luccock.

Theme: "The Need for a Larger Program."

The Drift of the Church...................W. B. Hollingshead.

The Size and Complexity of the Organization to be Moved...................S. Earl Taylor.

The Proposed Remedy...................J. B. Trimble.

The Leadership for the Introduction of the New Financial Plan...................John Lowe Fort.

How May Our Denomination Measure Up to the Opportunities of the Hour?........

U. G. Leazenby,	John T. Stone,
Dillon Bronson,	Alexander Bennett,
Frank C. Evans,	Thomas S. Lippy,
Robert E. Jones,	W. F. Whelan,
S. R. Smith,	D. D. Forsyth,
O. F. Hypes.	

Appointment of Committee on Denominational Policy.

MILITANT METHODISM.

AFTERNOON.
BISHOP JOSEPH F. BERRY PRESIDING.

Intercession, led by......................Bishop Frank M. Bristol.

THEME: "WHAT SOME OF THE DENOMINATIONS HAVE DONE."

The Southern Presbyterians...............C. A. Rowland.
The Disciples of Christ...................A. E. Cory.
The United Presbyterians.................J. Campbell White.

Episcopal Residential Area and Sectional Conferences.

EVENING.
BISHOP FREDERICK D. LEETE PRESIDING.

Intercession, led by......................Bishop W. P. Thirkield.

THEME: "THE SUMMONS OF THE TIME."

To Social Service........................Bishop F. J. McConnell.
To Civic Righteousness...................A. W. Leonard.
To World Conquest.......................J. Campbell White.

THURSDAY, OCTOBER 30th.
MORNING.
BISHOP THEODORE S. HENDERSON PRESIDING.

Intercession, led by......................Bishop Richard J. Cooke.

THEME: "ACTUALIZING THE PROGRAM."

The United Brethren................... { Bishop Howard,
                                        { Dr. S. S. Hough.
How Best Relate the Existing Organiza-
tions to the New Program..........Frank A. Horne,   W. F. Sheridan,
                                  H. C. Jennings,   I. Garland Penn,
                                  Harry F. Ward,   W. S. Bovard,
                                                     J. O. Randall.
One Fixed Purpose in the Life of the Church..W. E. Doughty.

AFTERNOON.
JOHN A. PATTEN PRESIDING.

Intercession, led by......................President George R. Grose.

THEME: "THE NEW DAY."

For Social Reform........................President Herbert Welch.
For the Christian Citizen.................Judge Ira E. Robinson.
For Evangelism..........................Dean L. J. Birney.

Sectional Conferences for District Superintendents, Pastors, Brotherhood Men, Sunday School Superintendents.

SPECIAL FEATURES.

EVENING.

PRESIDENT A. W. HARRIS PRESIDING.

DEVOTIONS.

THEME: "THE LAYMAN'S PLACE OF POWER."

What would You be Worth if You Lost Your Money?
George Innes.

The Witness of Laymen to the Supernatural Gospel
Fred B. Smith.

FRIDAY, OCTOBER 31st.

MORNING.

J. EDGAR LEAYCRAFT PRESIDING.

Intercession, led by.....................Bishop T. B. Neely.

THEME: "METHODISM'S LARGER OUTLOOK."

For Education.........................President W. H. Crawford.
For Christian Literature.................David G. Downey.
Adoption of Denominational Policy and Supplementary Report, Presented for the Committee by......................Bishop W. F. McDowell.
Raising of Budget to Propagate the Convention Program Throughout the Church for Two Years.

AFTERNOON.

BISHOP LUTHER B. WILSON PRESIDING.

Intercession, led by......................Bishop Luther B. Wilson.

THEME: "METHODISM'S LARGER LIFE."

The Superannuates................... { J. B. Hingeley,
                                       { Marvin Campbell.
The Deaconess Work.....................D. W. Howell.
The Church at Large....................Bishop W. O. Shepard.
A United Church a Conquering Church ..George P. Eckman.
The Ownership and Lordship of Jesus Christ...........................George Sherwood Eddy.
Closing Words, by the Chairman.........Bishop Luther B. Wilson.

373

MILITANT METHODISM.

EVENING.

Bishop William F. Anderson Presiding.

Intercession, led by . . . . President William Arnold Shanklin.

Theme: "The Larger Outlook for the Occident and the Orient."

The American Republic a World In-
fluence . . . . Bishop W. A. Quayle.

The Chinese Republic and Its Future . . . . . . George Sherwood Eddy.

Closing Message, by the Chairman . . . . Bishop William F. Anderson.

Closing Prayer, by . . . . Bishop Earl Cranston.

Final Adjournment.

NOON PRAYER AT THE SOLDIERS' AND SAILORS' MONUMENT.

One of the most impressive sights seen in Indianapolis in years was that of the march of the Convention delegates to the Soldiers' and Sailors' Monument, after the adjournment of the morning session.

Here, massed against the tribute to those who half a century ago gave themselves up for the flag of the Nation, these Methodist soldiers of the cross of Jesus Christ sang hymns of praise for blessings past and songs of hope for strength for battles yet unfought. And while the hundreds of busy passers-by stopped in their noonday rush and quiet reigned in the noisy city circle, Bishop Edwin H. Hughes led the assembly in prayer, they uniting with him in conclusion in the Lord's Prayer.

THE CONVENTION MUSIC.

The music of the Convention was one of its delightful and inspiring features. Mr. C. M. Keeler acted as precentor for the congregational singing, with the Rev. Harry B. Reddick at the piano and Mr. Paul T. Smith accompanying on the cornet. The special musical numbers were furnished by the well-known North Indiana Conference Quartette: Rev. Earl Naftzger, first tenor; Rev. Leslie J. Naftzger, second tenor; Rev. Dan H. Guild, Barytone, and Rev. Fred F. Thornburg, bass. The Claflin University Quintet: Arthur Rivers, Willie Asbury, Edmund Palmer, Ichabod Bowen, John Dangerfield, Miss Lulu Hunt, accompanist. Solos were sung by Everett R. Naftzger. Frequently the Convention broke forth in spontaneous song under the leadership of some delegate on the platform or the floor. The religious feeling found ample expression in these outbursts of fervent praise.

374

SPECIAL FEATURES.

CARRYING THE CONVENTION TO THE CHURCH.

THE spiritual earnestness dominant in the Convention brought with it the conviction that the plans and purposes which had so profoundly stirred those privileged to be present ought to be shared by the Church at large. In order that this might be made possible, S. Earl Taylor offered the Convention an opportunity to contribute an amount of money that would finance the intensive education of the Church in the New Financial Plan* for two years. This plan includes: An adequate campaign of information and education, including stewardship; an annual personal canvass of every member of the Church and congregation; subscriptions on the weekly basis to missions and benevolences, and for current expenses; the use of a uniform collecting device, such as the duplex envelope; two distinct budgets and two treasurers—one for missions and benevolences only; quarterly remittance of moneys collected for benevolences; the promotion of a spirit of systematic and definite prayer. It was brought out in the Sectional Conferences that Churches which had tried the plan and worked it intelligently had increased both income and the spiritual life of those participating in the canvass. These Churches, however, had guidance and training from those fully acquainted with the entire plan. To meet the demands for similar help from District Superintendents and Pastors, calls for larger expense than any existing budget can carry. Fifty thousand dollars per year for two years was asked for to carry on this educational campaign. Thirty-four thousand dollars per year for two years was pledged in the Convention, and the balance was underwritten by members of the Executive Committee of the Laymen's Missionary Movement of the Methodist Episcopal Church. The appeal and the response to the appeal were thoroughly devotional in spirit. Men gave themselves and their substance to the Lord freely and with gladness.

SPECIAL COMMITTEES.

THE Committee on Policy consisted of the following named persons, plus the members of the Business Committee:

Bishop Earl Cranston, Washington, D. C.

Bishop William Fraser McDowell, Chicago.

Bishop William F. Anderson, Cincinnati.

Bishop T. S. Henderson, Chattanooga.

Bishop F. J. McConnell, Denver, Colo.

J. W. McDougall, Portland, Ore.

D. D. Forsythe, Denver, Colo.

M. P. Burns, Minneapolis, Minn.

U. G. Leazenby, Crawfordsville, Ind.

J. G. Cairns, Kentucky.

John Low Fort, Baltson Spa, N. Y.

S. Earl Taylor, New York City.

C. M. Boswell, Philadelphia.

P. J. Maveety, Cincinnati.

D. G. Downey, New York City.

* Leaflets explanatory of the above may be obtained of the Laymen's Missionary Movement, 150 Fifth Avenue, New York City.

Edgar Blake, Chicago.
C. T. Wilson, Topeka, Kans.
W. S. Bovard, New York City.
W. F. Sheridan, Chicago.
J. B. Trimble, New York City.
F. B. Fisher, New York City.
E. J. Lockwood, Cedar Rapids, Iowa.
E. S. Tipple, Madison, N. J.
O. F. Wilke, Pasadena, Cal.
Luther Freeman, Columbus, Ohio.
Herbert Welch, Delaware, Ohio.
W. F. Conner, Pittsburgh, Pa.
G. W. Arnold, Atlanta, Ga.
L. J. Birney, Boston, Mass.
G. W. Brown, St. Louis, Mo.
H. B. Dickson, Philadelphia, Pa.
F. A. Horne, New York City.

C. E. Foote.
F. C. Evans, Crawfordsville, Ind.
C. E. Welch, Westfield, N. Y.
A. M. Smith, Portland, Ore.
T. S. Lippy, Seattle, Wash.
Col. E. W. Halford, New York City.
R. V. Watt, San Francisco, Cal.
W. E. Carpenter, Brazil, Ind.
F. E. Tasker, New York City.
J. T. Stone, Baltimore, Md.
L. C. Fritsche, Cincinnati.
E. E. Shipley, Cincinnati.
J. R. Joy, New York City.
John Walton, Philadelphia.
O. F. Hypes, Springfield, Ohio.
O. F. Bartholow, Mt. Vernon, N. Y.
R. E. Jones, New Orleans.

BUSINESS COMMITTEE.

Bishop L. B. Wilson, New York City.
Bishop C. W. Smith, St. Louis, Mo.
Bishop E. H. Hughes, San Francisco, Cal.
Andrew Gilles, Minneapolis, Minn.
A. W. Leonard, Seattle, Wash.
A. W. Harris, Chicago, Ill.
Thos. Nicholson, New York City.
J. W. Van Cleve, Decatur, Ill.

F. M. North, New York City.
J. E. Leaycraft, New York City.
C. M. Boswell, Philadelphia, Pa.
A. J. Coultas, Fall River, Mass.
Hanford Crawford, St. Louis, Mo.
I. G. Penn, Cincinnati, Ohio.
J. A. Patten, Chattanooga, Tenn.
Robt. A. Booth, Eugene, Ore.
F. B. Fisher, New York City.

The following Committee on Resolutions was appointed:

Bishop F. M. Bristol, Omaha.
Dillon Bronson, Boston, Mass.
H. J. Coker, Denver, Colo.
T. J. B. Robinson, Hampton, Ia.

President H. F. Rall, Denver, Colo.
W. H. Brooks, New York City.
Marvin Campbell, South Bend, Ind.
Harry C. Sampson, Pittsburgh, Pa.

S. H. Thompson, Athens, Tenn.

RESOLUTIONS AND INVITATIONS.

AGAINST THE LIQUOR TRAFFIC.

WHEREAS, The General Conference of the Methodist Episcopal Church, at its quadrennial session in 1912, declared its attitude as follows: "We stand for the speediest possible suppression of the liquor traffic. Under that divine law of absolute right, which is the source of all human law, the only proper attitude of civil government towards anything so harmful as the liquor traffic, is that of absolute prohibition; and we recommend that our people participate in every wise movement for local prohibition as a step towards State and National prohibition," and

WHEREAS, The Bishops of the Methodist Episcopal Church, in their last semi-annual meeting in St. Louis, Missouri, reaffirmed this attitude by approving the effort of the Anti-Saloon League to secure an amendment to the Constitution requiring National prohibition of the liquor traffic; and

WHEREAS, The campaign for National prohibition is to be launched at the National Anti-Saloon League Convention, to be held in Columbus, Ohio, in November, 1913; Therefore, be it

Resolved, That this Convention of Methodist Men, in full harmony with the attitude of the General Conference and the action since taken by the Bishops of our Church, do reaffirm our allegiance to this great cause, and do most heartily endorse this campaign for National prohibition of the manufacture and sale of beverage intoxicants, and urge all Methodists everywhere to immediate full co-operation in this next and final step in the solution of the liquor problem.

BIRTHDAY GREETINGS TO THE EMPEROR OF JAPAN.

WHEREAS, The 31st of October is the birthday anniversary of His Majesty, the Emperor of Japan;

Resolved, That this Convention of Methodist Men, representing a Church which has long held sentiments of respect and admiration for the imperial family and the people of Japan, would express to His Majesty their hearty felicitations on this auspicious occasion, and very sincere wishes and prayers that the blessing of the God of all nations may rest upon him in his high and noble responsibilities.

Resolved, That a copy of this resolution be sent by the President of this Convention to His Excellency Viscount Chinda, who is the Imperial Majesty's Embassador at Washington, and who is a graduate of DePauw University, and has many friends in this Convention, asking him to convey the same to His Majesty.

REPORT OF THE COMMITTEE ON RESOLUTIONS.

As Methodist Men in National Convention assembled, we would express our gratitude to Almighty God for the privileges and blessings which the members of this Convention have enjoyed.

We recognize the fact that back of these great meetings there have been the patient toil and gracious help of many workers and friends.

We would express our sense of deep indebtedness:

To the Laymen's Missionary Movement, which has brought together this memorable gathering.

MILITANT METHODISM.

To the General Committee, which has been directly responsible for its organization, and especially to Secretary Fred B. Fisher for his patient, resourceful, enthusiastic direction.

To the Local Committee for its co-operation in local plans.

To the Churches of Indianapolis for the use of their houses of worship.

To the Young Men's Christian Association for its generous hospitality and its active and valued assistance.

To the Knights of the Holy Grail and Boy Scouts for efficient service.

To the Officials of the City of Indianapolis for the use of Tomlinson Hall, and to the State authorities for the use of the Legislative Chambers.

To the Chamber of Commerce for effective aid in all local matters.

To the press of Indianapolis for the accurate, full, and informing reports which have especially marked their reporting of this Convention.

Finally, we would extend to our brother, the Honorable Charles W. Fairbanks, general chairman of the local committees of this Convention, our earnest sympathy in the bereavement which has befallen him in the death of his wife, praying that the God of all comfort may graciously sustain him in this hour of affliction.

(Signed)　FRANK M. BRISTOL, Chairman.
HARRIS FRANKLIN RALL, Secretary.
HARRY G. SAMSON,
T. J. B. ROBINSON,
HENRY J. COKER.
DILLON BRONSON,
MARVIN CAMPBELL.

AN INVITATION FOR 1915.

"The President and Directors of the Panama-Pacific Universal Exposition, to be held in San Francisco in 1915, have the honor to extend to the National Convention of Methodist Men a cordial invitation to hold its 1915 meeting in San Francisco. This city has been selected by Congress, with the approval of the President of the United States, as the official site for celebrating the uniting of the waters of the Pacific and the Atlantic through the Panama Canal, the greatest physical accomplishment achieved by man. The Exposition will not only attempt to show that which is most advanced in invention, most interesting in art, and of greatest scientific value, embracing all that is most important in the material progress of the world, but it will be the aim of the directors to make this rank in interest above all previous expositions; to bring together so much of wisdom and such a broad grasp of the world's problems, that the progress of mankind shall be advanced a quarter of a century. To assist in achieving this aim, we invite your presence in the city of San Francisco in the year 1915.

"CHARLES C. MOORE, President,
"RUDOLPH J. TAUSSIG, Secretary."

SPECIAL FEATURES.

THE CHURCH AND THE PRESS.

THE publicity of the National Convention of Methodist Men was so handled by Ralph Welles Keeler, the chairman of the committee having it in charge, that the representatives of the local newspapers, the Associated Press, and the Church editors received verbatim reports of the proceedings of each session a few minutes after adjournment. Four expert shorthand reporters were used, (two of whom, A. H. Herrick and J. C. Youker, have rendered similar service at General Conferences,) and sixteen typists. As a mark of appreciation of this unusual service, the newspaper men, through Dr. E. Robb Zaring, editor of the *Northwestern Christian Advocate*, who acted as their spokesman, presented to Dr. Keeler, at the final session, a fine leather traveling-bag.

In accepting the bag, Dr. Keeler, who is assistant editor of Sunday school publications of the Methodist Episcopal Church, said: "I have just a word of thanks to express to these men. I may say in return that I have learned, and especially here, that the daily press and the Church press are ready to spread the news of the gospel of the Kingdom when those men who represent the gospel of the Kingdom are willing to bring it to them in news form. To my mind, one of the great failures of the Methodist Episcopal Church to grasp opportunity is the neglecting to inform the world that the Church is alive. *As a Church, we have no place where a press association or a newspaper may get adequate information of the Church at large,* and the result is that we have all sorts of mix-ups in the daily press throughout the country—misrepresentations for which the press is not responsible. And I believe, from the attitude of these men who have served here from the press of this city, and the city editors of this city, that they and all other newspaper men throughout the country are anxious to print the news of which this meeting is representative. And I trust that among other things, we may consider the letting of the world know that we want the world to come to Christ, over the wire and through the pages of newspapers that are waiting for us to say something in an adequate way and in terms of every-day speech. I wish to thank these men, and I appreciate more than words can express the token they have given me now."

CONCERNING DELEGATES.

Mr. Fisher announced that there were twenty-seven hundred registered delegates, and that more than three thousand men had been in actual attendance. It would be a pleasure to reproduce here the names and addresses of all the delegates. A little reflection, however, will show that at least fifty pages of valuable space would be required for such a list. It was felt that the messages of the Convention were of such surpassing value, that the surrender of so much space would not be warranted. As between messages and a list of names, the editors decided for the former, and it is believed that the delegates themselves will approve the decision.